READING
RICOEUR

READING
RICOEUR

Edited by

DAVID M. KAPLAN

STATE UNIVERSITY
of NEW YORK PRESS

Published by State University of New York Press, Albany

For information, contact State University of New York Press, Albany, NY
www.sunypress.edu

Production by Ryan Morris
Marketing by Anne M. Valentine
This book was printed on acid-free, 50% recycled paper.

Library of Congress of Cataloging-in-Publication Data

Reading Ricoeur / edited by David M. Kaplan.
    p. cm.
  Includes bibliographical references and index.
  ISBN 978-0-7914-7525-6 (hardcover : alk. paper)
  ISBN 978-0-7914-7526-3 (pbk. : alk. paper)
  1. Ricoeur, Paul. I. Kaplan, David M.

B2430.R554R25 2008
194—dc22

2007036642

10 9 8 7 6 5 4 3 2 1

À la mémoire de Paul Ricoeur
(1913–2005)

Contents

Introduction: Reading Ricoeur

David M. Kaplan

Paul Ricoeur was many things in his life: French Protestant, pacifist, prisoner of war, professor of philosophy, author of over 500 articles and thirty books, recipient of honorary degrees from thirty universities, and winner of dozens of international awards and prizes, including the Kyoto Prize in Arts and Philosophy and the John W. Kluge Prize, sometimes known as the "Nobel Prize for humanists." The scope of Ricoeur's work is truly breathtaking. The topics he addressed himself to—in tremendous detail—over his sixty year philosophical career include: existentialism, phenomenology, philosophical anthropology, ontology, hermeneutics, biblical hermeneutics, philosophy of religion, philosophy of language, narrative theory, critical theory, philosophy of action, philosophy of history, moral philosophy, political philosophy, and philosophy of law, to name just some of the philosophical topics Ricoeur published in. He is widely recognized as among the most important philosophers of the twentieth century, moving comfortably within the worlds of French philosophy, German philosophy, Anglo-American philosophy, and the history of philosophy. He was also a socially engaged intellectual who wrote nonacademic articles about the political events of the day, such as fascism and pacifism in the 1940s, culture and colonialism in the 1960s, and memory and forgiveness in the 1990s. Ricoeur wrote on such a bewilderingly wide range of subjects that very few of us can fully understand the scope of his intellectual project.

The task of understanding Ricoeur's work is not made any easier by his philosophical style, which often leaves his readers puzzled, searching for his voice amid his massive scholarly writings. It is often difficult to find a philosophy unique to Paul Ricoeur. While clearly an original thinker, his major works take the form of lengthy studies of others. He intially appears to be more like a commentator than a creative philosopher. Whenever Ricoeur takes on a problem, he usually explains its historical development, carefully considering the positions of his interlocutors. He will then synthesize a vast range of material into a *response* to the question or problem at hand; not an *answer*, but a response. He recognizes the difficulty of genuine philosophical questions and he owns up to our limited ability to know all of the answers without giving up the attempt to address himself responsibly to the challenges questions pose.

He has described himself (only half-jokingly) as a "post-Hegelian Kantian," which means that he attempts to both mediate and not-mediate, overcome limits and accept limits. Like Hegel, Ricoeur believes we can find reason, truth, and moral right through philosophical mediation; like Kant, he believes that human experience and philosophy are riddled with aporia that have only practical responses, not theoretical solutions. He reads philosophy through the lenses of Kant and Hegel, interpreting the works of others as he creates creative responses to philosophical aporia. Ricoeur's "third term" in a debate mediates without reconciling. He sometimes refers to this method of nonsynthetic mediation as a "hermeneutic arc" drawn from one philosopher to another, that both subsumes the work of another and leaves it alone. He is undogmatic to a fault. He is the most charitable philosopher you will ever encounter.

Readers of Ricoeur have long searched for a common thread running throughout his thirty books, 500 articles, and sixty year career. It is a perfectly understandable goal. As difficult as it may be to find Ricoeur's unique philosophical voice, there is always something unmistakably Ricoeur-like in his work, even when he is faithfully explaining the thought of another. Even though he has addressed himself to (and even morphed into) every major movement in twentieth-century philosophy from the 1940s to the present, there is definitely a continuity of style and voice from book to book. On his own self-interpretation, each of his major works deals only with particular problems. For a long time he refused to see any relationship between his different books as either continuous or discontinuous, leaving that task to his interpreters.

> After having completed a work, I find myself confronting something that has escaped it, something that flies outside its orbit, becoming an obsession for me, and forming the next subject to examine.... In this way, one can say that the theme of the new book is off-center in relation to the preceding one, but with a return to subjects that had already been encountered, touched upon, or anticipated in earlier discussions. What had been a fragment becomes the new envelope, the totality."[1]

Ricoeur's readers, however, are quick to agree that the notion of human capability (*l'homme capable*) is the guiding thread that runs through Ricoeur's philosophical career, unifying his seemingly disconnected works. From his early phenomenology of the will in *Freedom and*

Nature (1950), to his investigation of psychoanalysis in *Freud and Philosophy* (1965), to his studies on the nature of self in *Oneself as Another* (1990), to his examination of memory and forgiveness in *Memory, History, Forgetting* (2004), exploring the problem of human capability has always been the focus of Ricoeur's works. To be a human being is to be capable of initiating new actions that are imputable to one as freely chosen activities. By analyzing the various ways that the verb "I can" is modified and realized in the ways that *I can speak, I can do things, I can tell a story*, and *I can be imputed* (as the author of an action), Ricoeur argues that the notion of capability forms a link between philosophical anthropology, language, and moral philosophy. It also forms a link between human action and human suffering. Our capabilities are intertwined with our vulnerabilities and the various figures of otherness that limit the will: the body, the unconscious, language, others, and so on. Ricoeur tries to show how we can conceive of a notion of the self that is neither an ultimate foundation nor a frag-mented illusion but a capable person who is able to do any number of things, the most fundamental of which are speaking, acting, suffering, recounting, and being responsible.

Unraveling the interrelated threads of the concept of capability has taken Ricoeur a lifetime. It is not difficult to see why; the concept of capability implies a web of related phenomena. It implies a notion of the will as embodied, free, and receptive. It implies an existential and material relation to the world, what Ricoeur once characterized as "the fault" (*la faute*). It implies a relation to language through which we relate to the world, initially described in terms of symbols, then texts, then narratives, then translation as successive models of the linguistic media-tion of experience. Capability implies a relation to the unconscious and other structured systems, above all language and systematically distorted communication. It implies a relation to the imagination that figures into action and language at the most fundamental condition of possible speech and action. It implies a relation to creative realms "as if" they could exist, including the realms of literature, poetry, and the divine. Capability implies a relation to the other with whom we live and without whom we would be unable even to understand ourselves. It implies moral relationships with others to whom we are accountable. Capa-bility implies the imputatibility of actions undertaken and endured, as well as the quest for recognition of ourselves, other selves, and multiple forms of alterity. It implies a relation to memory, to history, and to forgetting, the interrelated concepts that attest equally to our human capacities as to our human vulnerabilities.

In the late 1960s, around the time Ricoeur shifted his emphasis away from questions of the self and the will in the context of a descriptive philosophy toward the questions of language and action in the context of an interpretive philosophy, he offered a self-interpretation of his work as centered on the pair, speech and action, as two inseparable poles of human existence. "The question of language ... is a mode of being, a pole of existence as fundamental as action itself. A new equilibrium between saying and doing must be sought.[2] His subsequent work in the 1970s and 1980s developed this equilibrium through studies of discourse, texts, metaphors, and narratives—increasingly broad units of meanings through which we think, act, communicate, and suffer. With the publication of *Oneself as Another*, however, Ricoeur's focus on capability comes more clearly into focus. He has said as much, calling human capability "the cornerstone" of his philosophy, and that his recent work on selfhood, ethics, politics, and theology can be understood within the larger framework of his work examining it.[3] In *Memory, History, Forgetting*, Ricoeur again explains that *l'homme capable* is a "thin but continuous" thread running through his work.

> The man capable of ... speaking, acting, narrative and narrative himself, taking responsibility for his actions ... but also remembering and forgetting, making history and writing it, judging and being judged, understanding his human condition, through the painstaking work of interpretation and translation, which is a way to say something again but differently. And capable also, at the end of a long lifetime journey, of realizing, through the difficult experience of forgiving, that humans are worth more than their actions and their faults and that the climax of wisdom is the capacity to be amazed by the splendor of the simple fact of being alive as human beings ... as we are taught by those simple masters, the lilies of the fields and the birds in the sky.[4]

Domenico Jervolino calls the search for unity in Ricoeur's work a "loving struggle" between the author and his readers.[5] Readers search for unity in an author's work; authors write about what they please, leaving the question of unity to their readers. Perhaps with Ricoeur's acknowledgment of the role *l'homme capable* plays in his work, we have a framework for concluding this loving struggle. The conflict is followed by what Jervolino calls a *pax philosophica* that consists in gratitude and recognition on the part of both the author and readers. Recognition that the questions we have been struggling with are ultimately about the nature and meaning of being human; gratitude for writing, reading, and for being understood by each other. Ricoeur has given his readers so much to think about. And for that we are very grateful.

The contributors to this book express their recognition and gratitude to Paul Ricoeur in chapters written about various aspects of his work.

We are a collection of readers united only by our deep respect and appreciation for the great body of work Ricoeur left for us. We approach his work with different questions. We are of from different generations, different nationalities, and different philosophical temperaments. All of these differences become apparent in the way we read, analyze, and think with Ricoeur. It is also apparent that we had different relationships with Paul Ricoeur. For some of us, he was the author of books we read, admire, and struggle with; for others, he was our colleague; for some of us he was our professor and our teacher; for others, he was our friend, even best friend.

It is my hope that readers will recognize the how thoughtful, respectful, and caring the contributors are in their examinations of Ricoeur's work. Readers will find most of the main aspects of his various philosophical reflections covered here. I think readers will find the struggle between Ricoeur and the readers included here one that is truly loving. Each of the chapters deserves more than the brief introductions that follow.

The first chapter is by James L. Marsh, who, in "Ricoeur's Phenomenology of Freedom as an Answer to Sartre," favorably compares Ricoeur's *Freedom and Nature: The Voluntary and the Involuntary* to Sartre's *Being and Nothingness*. For Marsh, *Freedom and Nature* is one of the greatest yet most underappreciated works in the history of Continental philosophy in the twentieth century. Ricoeur's phenomenological account of the nature and limits of freedom is a dialectic of the voluntary and involuntary, activity and receptivity, freedom and necessity. Marsh contrasts Ricoeur's balanced account of a freedom that is bound by necessity to Sartre's one-sided, unbalanced, account of freedom that stresses the novel irruption of choice in the project—the fiat, the leap. For Marsh, Sartre's phenomenology of freedom lacks the subtlety and careful attention to the mediating role of the body at every level of voluntary activity: from decision, to action, to consent to the course initiated. According to Ricoeur, human life is the paradoxical unity of the voluntary and involuntary and our attempt to comprehend our paradoxical nature as both free and determined. Marsh hopes to right the historical injustice that has been done to *Freedom and Nature* by recognizing it—not *Being and Nothingness*—as the twentieth century's most important contribution to our understanding of freedom.

Bernard P. Dauenhauer, in "What Makes Us Think? Two Views," reviews the debate between Ricoeur and the neuroscientist Jean-Pierre Changeux on the nature of thought, the role of the brain in cognitive performance, and the status of neuroscientific knowledge in relation to philosophy. Both Changeux and Ricoeur reject metaphysical dualism between mind and body, but they disagree on how precisely to characterize the interactions between bodily processes and thinking. Changeux believes that the brain and its activities are sufficient to account for all thinking; Ricoeur maintains that the brain is a necessary condition for thought, but not sufficient for it. Changeux and Ricoeur also disagree on the even larger issue of what thinking could accomplish. Changeux holds that the supreme achievement of the human brain is the search for truth, culminating in the organized scientific inquiry; Ricoeur maintains that third-person explanations of causal events in the brain are different from first-person reports about one's experience. Furthermore, whereas scientific explanations are falsified on the basis of empirical evidence, one's lived experience can never be proven, but only attested to. Dauenhauer clarifies the positions of Changeux and Ricoeur and analyzes two central issues in the debate: the nature of memory and the relationship of scientific practice to its social-cultural milieu. Dauenhauer both pinpoints the differences between lived experience and scientific explanation and also highlights ways to integrate scientific activity into the world of experience.

David E. Klemm, in "Philosophy and Kerygma: Ricoeur as Reader of the Bible," analyzes Ricoeur's philosophical anthropology. The thread that unifies Ricoeur's wide-ranging, diverse interests—from *Fallible Man* to *Oneself as Another*—is the concept of human capability. Klemm examines Ricoeur's philosophy of human capability in relation to the limits of human thought, clarifying what the limits are, how they are constituted, and how they can be known. Starting with Ricoeur's early philosophical anthropology, Klemm explains how we are both capable yet fallible, finite yet infinite, subjective yet objective—opposites mediated only by the transcendental imagination, in the Kantian sense. Next he shows how Ricoeur extends our understanding of the limits of our being human through creative and imaginative uses of language that produce new ways to see and be in the world. He explains how Ricoeur adopts Kant's limit ideas of self, world, and God, but pushes those limits and offers the possibility of imaginative, creative ways of understanding the full depth of meaning of self, world, and God. Klemm concludes with a reflection on how linguistic innovation at the theological level reveals the extraordinary meaning-function of the name "God"—the limit of all limits of understanding and the full extent of our linguistic capacities.

Richard Kearney, in "On the Hermeneutics of Evil," examines the concept of evil, an abiding concern of Ricoeur's philosophy. From his early work *The Symbolism of Evil* published in 1960 to his more recent 1985 chapter, "Evil: A Challenge to Philosophy and Theology," Ricoeur has given a great deal of attention to the challenge evil presents to human capability and human understanding. In the first part of his study, Kearny shows how Ricoeur addresses the problem of evil in light of his early philosophical anthropology (in which fallibility creates the possibility for evil) and phenomenology of symbolism (the myths and other indirect means by which we comprehend the reality of evil). In the second part, Kearny shows how Ricoeur, in his 1985 chapter, broadens and expands both the concept of evil and our responses to evil in light of a more fully developed hermeneutic philosophy. In this work, Ricoeur is even more attentive to the various ways that the enigma of evil challenges us and calls us to responsibility. Narratives and testimony play a key role in understanding and responding to evil. In the final part, Kearny explores Ricoeur's threefold hermeneutic model of the experience of evil in memory and history, which involves, (1) practical understanding and action, (2) acknowledgment of suffering and working through it, and (3) pardon and forgiveness.

William Schweiker, in "Paul Ricoeur and the Prospects of a New Humanism," examines the connections in Ricoeur's work on human capability (our "effort to be") and his version of humanism. Schweiker endeavors to show precisely how Ricoeur's humanism reflects his basic philosophical orientation to articulate the effort to be and how, in turn, the human effort to be determines the outlines of a humanism Ricoeur believed necessary for the present age. Schweiker finds a theological humanism implicit yet undeveloped in Ricoeur's work by contrasting Greek rational humanism and biblical fideist humanism—what Ricoeur once called the possibility of a "third man." Schweiker presses beyond Ricoeur to develop a distinctively Christian humanism. In contrast to Nietzsche's "human, all too human," and Levinas's "human, otherwise than human," Schweiker's formula is "human, truly human" in which our human capacities are developed in relation to distinctively Christian sources. It is a distinctive form of humanism rooted in an affirmation of human capability to act responsibly with and for others, chastened by our fragility and fallibility, and thankful for the gift of life as revealed through the Gospel. Schweiker shows how we can follow Ricoeur and take a detour through Christian texts in order to develop a theological humanism that is distinct yet conversant with other kinds of humanism—perhaps the very realization of Ricoeur's third man.

Merold Westphal, in "Ricoeur's Hermeneutic Phenomenology of Religion," proposes five theses that constitute Ricoeur's version of phenomenology. Westphal then examines Ricoeur's reflections of biblical texts to develop a substantive phenomenology of religion in light of these theses. The first three theses place Ricoeur alongside of Heidegger and Gadamer within the hermeneutic tradition: (1) understanding is a matter of interpretation rather than intuition, (2) interpretation takes place within the hermeneutic circle, and (3) interpretation takes philosophical reflection on detours through prephilosophical texts. The fourth thesis, that the hermeneutics of recovery needs to be supplemented by the hermeneutics of suspicion, tests the limits of hermeneutic phenomenology and calls into question assumptions about the self as a transparent center of experience. The fifth thesis, a hermeneutic phenomenology involves a movement beyond intentionality, further displaces the ego as the center of meaning by opening it up to others (both human and divine) who always precede us and call us to respond and to be responsible. This inversion of intentionality—toward, rather than from, me—is necessary in order to let that which is beyond me show itself to me. Westphal finds a substantive phenomenology of religion in Ricoeur's meditation of the ideals of justice and love. Westphal argues that, for Ricoeur, justice and love are dialectically related, yet never reconciled and always in tension.

André LaCocque, in "Love Proceeds by Poetic Amplification," pays tribute to his friend by discussing Ricoeur's distinction between justice and love, the latter understood in the sense of the Hebrew word ḥesed and which translates as love, goodness, compassion, generosity, and graciousness. In the first part of the chapter, LaCocque develops Ricoeur's thesis that justice proceeds by conceptual reduction, love proceeds by poetic amplification. LaCocque reflects on each of the three pairs of contrasting terms: justice and love, conceptual and poetic, reduction and amplification. He finds that in each pair, the second term is broader and encompasses the first. Justice and its well-reasoned orientation toward equality and reciprocity are never enough. The aim of a righteous life is to surpass justice toward ḥesed, a creative act of loving compassion. In the second part of the chapter, through a reading of the story of Ruth and her journey back from Moab to Israel, LaCocque finds an example of the poetic amplification of understanding the law. When Ruth breaks the law of marriage for the sake of remaining loyal to her family, she is rewarded by the law of redemption, a form of justice richer and greater than mere compensation or retribution. The story of Ruth is an example of how the poetic amplification aims not only to establish justice but also to redeem and restore humanity.

Pol Vandevelde, in "The Challenge of the 'such as is was': Ricoeur's Theory of Narratives," shows how Ricoeur's theory of narrative is designed to account for not only how we experience things, but also to show how narratives are already part of the very nature of action, time, and selfhood. Narratives are thus not mere descriptions of life, but are part of the ontological constitution of life. The phenomenological aspect of a narrative is the meaning content (or noema) of what is recounted; the hermeneutic aspect of a narrative is the interpretive mediation of experience. Vandevelde focuses on the phenomenological character of narratives to clarify Ricoeur's strong claim that narratives tell us what really takes place because action and experience have a prenarrative quality. When a narrative recounts things or people "such as they were" it makes a claim to accurately depict what happened. Vandevelde carefully distinguishes between the activity of narrative understanding and the product of narrative understanding in a way that Ricoeur does not. He also clarifies Ricoeur's threefold conception of *mimesis* in *Time and Narrative*, reworking Ricoeur's confused distinction between narrative prefiguration and narrative configuration. Vandevelde argues that there is a grammar of justification embedded in narratives, transforming Ricoeur's claim that narratives depict the world "as if" it were true to the stronger claim that narrative depict the world "such as it was."

Patrick L. Bourgeois, in "Ricoeur and Lyotard in Postmodern Dialogue: Symbol and the Sublime," places two interpretations of Kant's *Critique of Judgment* at the heart of the debate between philosophical modernism and postmodernism. According to Bourgeois, Lyotard gives Kant's notion of the sublime such a central position that it collapses philosophy into literature. By contrast, Ricoeur extends Kant's notion of the sublime into a narrative function as a third kind of reflective judgment. While Lyotard expands the role of the sublime in Kant's aesthetics and explodes any rule orientation by means of Kant's notion of invention, Ricoeur extends the role of the sublime and the symbolic function and keeps a rule orientation in making this new type of function determinative. Ricoeur thus goes far beyond Kant by developing novel applications of the productive imagination, but without going as far as Lyotard in jeopardizing the role of reason. Bourgeois argues that Ricoeur's expansion on Kantian limit and imagination broadens the context of thinking and philosophy. He shows how Ricoeur has followed Kant concerning the boundary of theoretical knowledge, the limits of thinking and speculation, and has expanded on these through the use of symbol and semantic innovation yet he does not fall prey to the tendency of postmodernism to substitute literature and poetry for philosophy. Bourgeois' Ricoeur is an attractive alternative to Lyotard and postmodern deconstruction.

Olivier Abel, in "Paul Ricoeur's Hermeneutics: From Critique to Poetics," examines how Ricoeur orients hermeneutics toward a critical hermeneutics and reorients it toward a poetic hermeneutics. Abel explains how hermeneutics for Ricoeur overcomes the aporia of phenomenology—owning up to an intrinsic ineliminable ambiguity of experience—in a double orientation. One orientation is toward a critical hermeneutics and involves a search for the limits of experience; another orientation is toward the poetic and takes the form of a search for new, creative interpretations of the experience. Abel explains that different types of hermeneutics can be brought together under what he calls the "principle of the implicit question": the meaning of a text is a function of the implicit question it is meant to answer. Critical hermeneutics responds to this principle by pointing in two directions: one toward the distance between our context and the text; the other toward the belonging of interpreter to what is questioned. This play of distance and belonging constitutes a critical hermeneutic. Abel then explains how a poetic hermeneutics results when interpretation is geared toward unfolding meanings "in front of" the text, opening the possibility for creative interpretations of the world. The same creative, narrative interpretations figure into the self and moral deliberation. Abel thus creates a topology of hermeneutics that divides into four orientations: critical, ontological, poetic, and ethical.

David M. Kaplan, in "Ricoeur's Critical Theory," examines Ricoeur's contributions to the Western Marxist tradition of ideology critique. Philosophy for Ricoeur is critical in the Kantian sense of identifying the limits of understanding as well as in the Marxist sense of uncovering false consciousness and the material conditions of thought and action. Kaplan highlights this latter sense of critique, focusing on four themes in Ricoeur's work that are particularly relevant to a critical social theory in the Western Marxist tradition: (1) The hermeneutics of suspicion, where Ricoeur distinguishes his version of critical hermeneutics from the philosophical hermeneutics of Gadamer, and which forms an internal connection between interpretive experience and critical consciousness. (2) The mediation of the Habermas–Gadamer debates, where Ricoeur integrates Habermas's theories of universal pragmatics and discourse ethics into hermeneutics and moral philosophy. (3) The theory of ideology and utopia, where Ricoeur forges a link between creative, narrative discourses with the critique of ideology. (4) The fragility of political language, where Ricoeur offers a modest, limited critique of political legitimacy that affirms democratic political and economic institutions yet is keen to avoid the hubris often associated with Enlightenment political philosophy. Kaplan endeavors to bring Ricoeur in the conversation on critical theory and to encourage readers of Ricoeur to pay more attention to the critical dimension of his work.

David M. Rasmussen, in "Justice and Interpretation," reflects on issues regarding public reason, global justice, and political differences. The dilemma of justice on a global scale is that any attempt to both affirm the legitimacy and validity of individual claims to rights might conflict with the claims originating from the distinctiveness of other political cultures. Rasmussen turns to Ricoeur's reflections on political philosophy and his interpretation of Rawls in *Oneself as Another* and *The Just* to develop a model of public reason designed to steer this delicate path. Rasmussen explains how Rawls's position has evolved from a pure proceduralism and deontological theory of rights to a political constructivism that involves judgment and interpretation. Rawls's own development reflects Ricoeur's central criticism of him, that public reason requires an interpretive framework not a purely constructivist one. Rasmussen shows how Ricoeur's framework proposed in *Oneself as Another* of an asymmetrical model between self and other can be used not only for individual self-understanding in politics but also for constructing a global framework. The key is the notion of a narrative identity that is capable of constructing a notion of selfhood that accounts for both self-identity and cultural identity while preserving the differences between the self and other. Rasmussen argues that Ricoeur's notion of selfhood allows us to reconstruct Rawlsian notions of reasonability and public reason that preserve the uniqueness of political culture to a global conception of human rights.

Domenico Jervolino, in "Rethinking Ricoeur: The Unity of His Work and the Paradigm of Translation," discusses the relationship between the notion of *l'homme capable*, the thin but continuous common thread that organizes Ricoeur's work, and the model of translation as Ricoeur's final version on the linguistic mediation of experience. Jervolino reads Ricoeur's last works as an effort to understand human capability in relation to metaphysics and to morals through the (reflexive) medium of language. The problem of converting the universal and transcendental into something contextual and practical is the problem of translation. The labor of translation is never ending; it is always possible to re-say something because perfect translation is impossible. Instead, the capacity to translate reveals a new form of vulnerability that reminds us of our limitations in understanding and communicating with others. Translation is the paradigm of our relation to the other—an asymmetrical yet mutual relation between self and other, including other cultures, religions, and historical ages. Jervolino relates Ricoeur's model of translation to his notion of recognition developed in his final book, *The Course of Recognition*: both attempt to respect the other while preserving the alterity of the other.

Charles Reagan, in "Binding and Loosing: Promising and Forgiving; Amnesty and Amnesia," gives a reading of Ricoeur's *Memory, History, Forgetting* to make sense of the way that people and groups bind and unbind themselves to each other. Reagan begins with an account of promising and its relation to narrative identity in *Oneself as Another*, where Ricoeur shows how promising establishes the kind of permanence in time appropriate to selfhood. Promising binds us to do something or to be someone into the future. Forgiving, however, unbinds us from something done in the past. Reagan develops the notion of forgiveness by tracing Ricoeur's detour through remembering and forgetting. Ricoeur's main points are that we have no other resource to the past than memory and false memories can only be corrected by true memories, just as false testimony can be corrected only by true testimony. Forgetting, of course, poses a challenge and a threat to memory and history. Ricoeur discusses ordinary forgetting, pathological forgetting, manipulated forgetting, and commanded forgetting, or amnesty. Forgiveness is different. It is asymmetrical; only another can forgive, and forgiveness is unconditional, directed toward the unforgivable (the *fault*, from *Fallible Man*). Ricoeur struggles to bridge the gap between the unforgivable fault and the impossible forgiveness. The dialectic of promising (which establishes identity and predictability into the future) and forgiving (which is asymmetrical and restores what is irreversible) constitutes the difficult relationship of binding and loosing.

In his epilogue, Reagan recounts his final visit with Paul Ricoeur in Paris at the end of February 2005, and describes the funeral in Chatenay-Malabry in May 2005.

NOTES

1. Paul Ricoeur, *Critique and Conviction* (New York: Columbia University Press, 1998), p. 81.
2. Paul Ricoeur, Foreword to Don Ihde, *Hermeneutic Phenomenology: The Philosophy of Paul Ricoeur* (Evanston: Northwestern University Press, 1970), p. xiv.
3. Paul Ricoeur, "Ethics and Human Capability," in *Paul Ricoeur and Contemporary Moral Thought,* ed. John Wall, William Schweiker, and W. David Hall (New York: Routledge, 2002), p. 285.
4. Paul Ricoeur, *Memory, History, Forgetting*, trans. Kathleen Blamey and David Pellauer (Chicago: University of Chicago Press, 2004), pp. 505–506.
5. Domenico Jervolino, chapter 13, "Rethinking Ricoeur: The Unity of His Work and the Paradigm of Translation."

Ricoeur's Phenomenology of Freedom as an Answer to Sartre

1

James L. Marsh

It has always seemed to me, after many years of reading and learning from Paul Ricoeur and incorporating his insights into my own work, that his *Freedom and Nature: The Voluntary and the Involuntary* is one of the great, underappreciated works in the body of his own work and in the history of Continental philosophy in the twentieth century. This is not to say that I do not have my own favorites from among his work after *Freedom and Nature*, such as *Freud and Philosophy*, *Interpretation Theory: Discourse and the Surplus of Meaning*, and *Oneself as Another*. Nonetheless, it has always seemed to me that *Freedom and Nature* is at least on a par with those works and perhaps even more fundamental and more important.

My reasons for saying this are, first, the positively valuable and true account that Ricoeur has given of freedom. No one text in the history of philosophy can claim to answer all questions and resolve all problems. But there are some that come close or seem to come close to doing so, as I think *Freedom and Nature* does in relation to a whole set of questions concerning freedom arising from thinkers like Nietzsche, Kierkegaard, and Sartre and the challenge they raise for more rationalistic accounts of freedom in thinkers such as Aquinas, Kant, and Hegel.

My second reason for this claim is that, as I was trying to do philosophy in my own voice, Ricoeur was an invaluable influence and source of direction. He was a model for me, what a philosopher should be. My third reason is that *Freedom and Nature* may be said to supply a phenomenological basis, which is at once descriptively sound and dialectically comprehensive in its unity of opposites such as voluntary and involuntary, continuity and discontinuity in the process of making a choice, subjectivity and objectivity, and necessity and freedom, for all of Ricoeur's later work. Ricoeur's procedure here is one of arguing for a paradoxical unity of these sets of opposites, and this unity is the basis of his criticizing other thinkers who illegitimately stress, eliminate, or minimize one or more of these aspects.

Sartre is one of these thinkers. It is clear that he is one of the major, and maybe the most important, voices in *Freedom and Nature*, from whom Ricoeur both learns and criticizes. What he learns is Sartre, that like both Kierkegaard and Nietzsche, stresses the novel irruption of choice in the project, the fiat, the leap. What Ricoeur criticizes is Sartre's general tendency to overemphasize these aspects in relation to the receptive, motivated, deliberate charter of freedom. Both of these sets of aspects must be accounted for and integrated in an adequate account of freedom.

What I propose to do in this chapter, therefore, is to read Ricoeur's account of freedom as an answer to Sartre. The emphasis will be on Ricoeur in that I use Sartre's questions and difficulties to point to Ricoeur's answer concerning the nature, limits, and kinds of freedom. While the account of Sartre is less detailed than that of Ricoeur, I hope to suggest this account as a plausible hypothesis: that Ricoeur in a fundamental and comprehensive way answers Sartre in terms of the questions, difficulties, and forms of one-sidedness that emerge in *Being and Nothingness*. The structure of my chapter follows the general outline of Ricoeur's book as that moves from an account of choice, action in the world, and consent to necessity. In my project, the two main texts will be Sartre's *Being and Nothingness* and Ricoeur's *Freedom and Nature*. When necessary, however, I will have recourse to other texts as well.

CHOICE AND THE PROJECT

In *Existentialism and Human Emotions*, Sartre argues that existence proceeds essence in the sense that I choose myself and the kind of person I will be. I have the freedom to create my own essence. It is not written in the heavens that I should be reasonable or unreasonable, heterosexual or homosexual, Catholic or Protestant, peaceful or violent. Because it is not so written, none of these options is objectively preferable to the other.

Sartre illustrates this point by considering a young man who came to him for advice during the Second World War. The young man's father was on bad terms with his mother and inclined to be a collaborator, his older brother had been killed in the German offensive of 1940, and the young man wished to avenge him. The young man's mother lived alone with him, and her son was her only consolation. So what should the boy do: leave for England and join the Free French against the Germans or stay with his mother and help her carry on?[1]

Sartre argues that no so-called system of ethics or values can be of any help here because it is too vague, and one can contradict another.

An ethics of heroism and devotion to one's country is in this instance in tension with an ethics of sympathy and compassion for one's mother, and I am equally righteous in choosing one or the other. If I go to somebody else for advice, for example a priest, my own prior commitment to one course of action makes me prefer one priest over another. If the young man chooses a priest who is resisting or collaborating, he is already deciding on the kind of advice he is going to receive. "I can neither seek within myself the true condition which will impel me to act, nor apply to a system of ethics for concepts which will permit me to act."[2]

This striking example suggests certain consequences to Sartre. First, there is no reciprocity between objective motive (or reason) and subjective choice. Freedom determines which motive or set of motives will count. But here a bothersome question emerges about the difference between a reason and a rationalization, between a choice based authentically on genuine sifting and sorting and clarifying and distinguishing true reasons from false, and a choice that simply bases itself on an alibi or rationalization for what it wanted to do anyway—meanwhile disguising to itself or others its true reasons. Second, freedom does not seem receptive in any way to motivation. A problematic, either-or disjunction between active and passive seems to emerge here, an implication that is confirmed by *Being and Nothingness*.[3]

Third, because existence precedes essence, consciousness seems to be pure upsurge, nothingness, negation of any positive being or trait, of what is in itself. But is Sartre correct in such a move? Is all positivity and positive structure to be removed from consciousness? This move seems to be contradicting Sartre's own description of consciousness as totally lucid and transparent, temporal, projecting value and possibility, present to the world through embodiment, and a natural desire to be God. Sartre's account of freedom on the level of choice seems to leave us with a set of paradoxes, anomalies, and contradictions, which go against what a patient, phenomenological account of experience would suggest.

Enter Paul Ricoeur. In his initial chapter on an eidetics of choice, he argues for the reciprocity of the voluntary and involuntary. "The initial situation revealed by description is the reciprocity between the voluntary and involuntary."[4] His account of freedom occurs in three progressively more concrete stages. To say "I will," means that first I decide, second that I move my body, and third that I consent. The body becomes the correlate of freedom on all three levels, first as a basic source of motives, second as an organ of willing, and third as the basis of character, the unconscious, and life as basic forms of the necessary.[5]

All three parts of *Freedom and Nature* are divided into a tripartite structure: first a static eidetics, second an account of the body in relation to freedom, and third a discussion of the process of deciding, moving, and consenting. The basic, eidetic law of choice is "I decide because...."; the process of making a choice is one of choosing a project with three different aspects: a possible action depending on me, imputation of myself as the author of the project, and finally a motivating of the project by reasons. "A decision signifies, that is, designates in general, a future act which depends on my and which is within in my power."[6]

Already we see an essence in freedom in the formula "I choose because ..." and in the definition of the project. Moreover, we see that for Ricoeur freedom is not only active upsurge and thrust. That is certainly an aspect of freedom, and thus Sartre has it partially right, but freedom is also receptive listening and attentiveness to motives and values. Here Ricoeur draws an analogy between choice and the activity of perceiving. Just as perception turns toward the world and the human other in a welcoming way, so also freedom turns toward the world and the human other in a welcoming way, which is the other side of the generosity that irradiates and embraces the received being. One consequence of a union of activity and receptivity is that "being obedient to" and "being faithful to" are not necessarily impositions on freedom or violations of it. Such a consequence does follow if one conceives freedom as totally active, independent, and sovereign, but such a freedom for Ricoeur is an alienated, one-sided freedom.[7]

The body, the basic involuntary at this stage of decision is not the only source of motives, but is the basic, fundamental source. All other motives and values are elaborated in relation to it. When I give preference to other values, for example, when I fast to protest injustice, I consciously subordinate or sacrifice a bodily value for a moral value. All other values assume a serious or dramatic significance in relation to the values that enter history through the body.[8]

The eidetic relationship between voluntary and involuntary clarifies the interaction between will and body in choosing a project. My hunger, my sexual desire, my thirst, my love of art, and my desire for justice all refer to my willing as possible motives. The circular relation between motive and project demands that I recognize my body as a body-for-my willing and my willing as a project-based-on-my-body. Thus, the involuntary is for the will, and the will is by reason of the body.[9]

When we move from pure eidetics to reflection on the history of a decision, the body appears as a source of possible motives for a project. "Where should I go for a vacation: New York City or Stratford, Ontario, in Canada?" In making this decision, I have to consider possible motives of ease, efficiency, financial cost, my interest in theater, and a need for relaxation and quiet and slowing down. Which motive should I prefer and which reject, which highlight and which ignore, which give attention to and which neglect? The body is a question or the fundamental source of questions to which the final decision is the answer. On a practical as well as a theoretical level, I am a question for myself.[10]

The history of the decision is one of a process in which I move from an original question and confusion through a period of sifting, clarification, and evaluation to a moment of clarity and unity. "I choose to go to Canada because ..." A crucial factor in this process is attention, which has both passive and active aspects; I pay attention to this motive rather than that in the sense of being open to its meaning and value. On the other hand, I actively conduct the debate rather then sinking into the apathy of indecision or the security of what "they" do. "Decision advances and lives as process from hesitation to choice."[11]

As a result of a process and history, decision is both discontinuous and continuous. It is discontinuous in the sense that it is an upsurge, a fiat, an active breaking off the debate with myself that brings into being something new, my decision to go to Canada. Decision is continuous in that it is the ripe fruit of the process of discernment and choice, and the decision is not intelligible without this process. Sartre, from Ricoeur's point of view, emphasizes the discontinuous fiat and ignores or minimizes the continuity, but a full, comprehensive phenomenologically and dialectically adequate account requires that we relate both aspects, continuity and discontinuity, receptive and active, termination of attention and irruption of project.[12]

To drive home this point, Ricoeur tries two different readings of choice, one stressing its continuity and the other its discontinuity, and shows how each reading comes to a point where it breaks down and requires its opposite. A reading of choice in terms of continuity sees it as the last judgment in a series of judgments, but misses the fact that no last judgment is necessary in relation to a previous set of judgments. Even in making a mathematical or logical argument, I could break off my attention at the last instance, or ask, like a contemporary postmodernist, "So what's so great about consistency?" or "What's wrong with contradiction?" Authentic freedom, a good will toward the process of the argument and what it implies, is required for mathematical or logical or philosophical ratiocination; such good will is even more obviously requisite for normal decisions that deal with the more or less probable, and not the necessary. If I am not open to where rational reflection leads, then a rationally or logically necessary conclusion means nothing to me and can be freely avoided, contradicted, or ignored.[13]

The other reading, that of discontinuity, draws its plausibility from examples that are peculiarly modern and receive emphasis in modern philosophy and literature, such as life crises in choosing a vocation or a marriage partner or a course of action, Sartre's example, in which my whole life seems up for grabs. But Ricoeur suggests that adequacy and variety are necessary in our choice of examples; there are other instances of choice that are more ordinary such as my deciding to get a drink of water or going outside to smoke a cigarette if I am in a New York restaurant in which smoking has been forbidden. The dramatic examples make plausible a nation of decision in which the sovereign will reigns supreme, and I invent my existence from day to day. "As the contemporary formula puts it, existence precedes essence."[14]

In this reading of choice, decision seems to determine fully its reasons and to be a creation of values. "Voluntarism carries with it this temptation to annul attention to values as inauthentic, to submerge evaluation in decision, the receptivity of freedom in its activity and, finally, the involuntary in the voluntary."[15] This temptation finds a descriptive basis in the analysis of the pretext or "bad reason" to which voluntarism seeks to reduce motive. And Ricoeur does admit that the ordering of or our reasons is often only a little comedy that we put on for others and in which reasons function as rationalizations. Yet "this comedy is secretly denounced by a truer idea of motivation which stands in judgment over; it a pretext is a false reason, a sham motive. A pretext is bad faith in the strict sense, and it is still good faith which qualifies it as bad faith. Yet what is good faith if not the very idea of a choice which appeals truthfully to the conviction of its own motives and bases itself on his conviction. Every pretext gives itself out as an authentic motive."[16]

Sartre's very distinction between good faith and bad faith, therefore, is in tension with his voluntarism and implies the idea of a receptive will. So also does his indeterminism imply the opposite of determination in different senses: the indetermination of indecision at the beginning of the process of making a decision gives way to the determination of choice, the indetermination of a free attention versus the determinate character of a motive, the indetermination of multiplicity and determination of unity. Ricoeur's phenomenology is descriptively and dialectically adequate in the sense that freedom in the world is a unity of opposites: receptive and active, motive and leap, positive and negative, continuity and discontinuity, essence and existence, determination and indetermination. His account of freedom, not only on this level but on all three levels, is a veritable playground of opposites, a bacchanalian revel of opposites emerging, clashing, and being integrated at least in a partial way. Ricoeur's phenomenology is a version of *Vernunft*, or reason, in Hegel's sense: reason as reconciling opposites after they have emerged from the either-or impasse of understanding.

Sartre's account, by way of contrast, is one of *Verstehen*: freedom and his philosophy of freedom at war in an either-or conflict of opposites. Sartre insightfully recognizes the moment of upsurge or fiat, but leaves out or minimizes or explains away the opposite moment of continuity, of attention to values, and the ultimately involuntary content of motive. The role of attention in coming to a decision is missed, and his examples, as we have seen, are partial and selective and favor a reading of choice in situations in which my own life is up for grabs. There is a tension in his approach between a phenomenology trying to be faithful to the evidence and an existentialist will to an absolute, which leads to the various either-or dichotomies already described. Consequently, a tension or contradiction emerges between an account of freedom stressing the upsurge of the fiat, and his desire to make a distinction between good and bad faith, and this distinction in turn is in tension with his tendency to reduce motives to pretexts, reasons to rationalizations.[17] This contrast between Ricoeur's dialectical both-and phenomenology and Sartre's undialectical, either-or phenomenology continues as we move to more concrete level tasks of moving and action and consent to necessity.

MOVING AND ACTION

Let us start this section with a provocative example, one of the many in *Being and Nothingness* that provokes thought and that thus are one of the book's strengths. I am on a hike with friends, and after several hours I become so fatigued that I drop by the side of the road and say that I cannot go on. Some of my friends resist this decision by me and see it as an imposition on them. They live or exist their fatigue differently, says Sartre, and the fact that they do indicates that it is not fatigue that motivates my decision, but my freely chosen project that constitutes the fatigue and makes it what it is. Consequently, I do not encounter limits as such in a receptive way. "Thus our freedom itself creates the obstacles from which it suffers."[18]

It is not that freedom does not encounter obstacles, but that the meaning that these have come entirely from freedom. For a person who lives his body in a different way, an obstacle and even fatigue would not be a reason for sitting down but a reason for going on. I enjoy the struggle, the challenge, and the zest in overcoming myself and scaling the mountain. But, we might ask in reply, does not the obstacle appear as an obstacle and is not fatigue still experienced as fatigue to both climbers, one who sits down and the one who goes on? Once again we suspect an arbitrary preference for and emphasis on the active, voluntary side of the self over against its receptive, involuntary aspect.[19]

Ricoeur's approach at this second stage or level of freedom is to combine these two aspects. The body as lived, as mine, as that which I am rather than that which I have, is and can be said to be an expression of my freedom. But this expression never takes place without an accompanying involuntary dimension. There is, first, the level of preformed skills, the spontaneous ability to reach out my hand and grasp an object or to turn my head to follow somebody walking or to turn my eyes away when I see something unpleasant. All perceptual learning takes place on the basis of this spontaneous unlearned wisdom of the body; it functions as an a priori that not only precedes my freedom and my perceptual exploration of the world, but as a condition for such freedom and exploration. And such an involuntary is at the basis of all projects, whether to go on in experiencing fatigue or to give up and sit down. Preformed skills are not formed by freedom but are the condition of the possibility for having any project at all.[20]

A second kind of involuntary involved in the process of incarnating projects in the world is emotion. Emotion releases preformed skills into becoming active in movement. In emotion there is no hiatus between thought and movement, but rather the passage from thought to movement is carried out on the level of the involuntary, this side of effort. The involuntary aspect of emotion is intelligible only in relation to a willing that it agitates and which in turn moves only if it is moved. When I see a long-lost friend, my joy incites me to move to her and embrace her passionately. Emotion, whether on the level of admiration or scorn, love or hate, desire or repulsion, joy or sorrow, enlivens our lives. My life in the world is no dry exercise of churning out projects that are merely willed by, me, but my joyous, desiring, wondering engagement with the world.[21]

In his discussion of emotion, Ricoeur critically considers Sartre's account in *Existentialism and Human Emotions*. For Sartre, emotion is a ruse of consciousness. One example that Sartre uses is that of a patient of P. Janet, who throws himself into a nervous breakdown in order not to go through an overly difficult confession. Another example is that of an enraged person for whom rage appears as a least costly solution to a practically insoluble problem. Emotion is freely adopted by consciousness in order to avoid a superior conduct that is more difficult. For Ricoeur, this account misses the circular relationship between involuntary and voluntary, emotion and will. It is not that Ricoeur denies that people can act this way, that they can use emotion as a ruse. But this is a derived, secondary complication of emotion, on the level of passion, that presupposes the more fundamental relationship previously described. Emotion always has the possibility of turning into passion because it is a nascent disorder that poses a question for freedom. But emotion does not necessarily take this form, and its more basic function is a desire to overcome, not flee, obstacles in some kind of alibi or self-deception. When I see my beloved in the distance, I spontaneously run and leap over any obstacles to get to her.[22]

"More fundamentally, this interpretation tends to eliminate the initiative of the body stressed by our circular interpretation in favor of the sole spontaneity of consciousness."[23] The body is more than an organ of consciousness that degrades itself to the level of magic. Sartre is not innocent of the fact that emotion is undergone, but how can he say that even in the birth of physiological disturbance the body follows the intention of consciousness? Moreover, Sartre's idealism is manifest in his ignoring and insufficiently distinguishing multiple aspects of the involuntary—motives, resistances, irremediable situations—to which willing responds by choice, effort, or consent, in favor of treating the body simply as an organ for freedom. He is insufficiently attentive, as a phenomenologist should be, to differences between voluntary and involuntary, among preformed skills, emotion, and habit, between fundamental emotions like joy and derived or deranged forms. Ricoeur seems to be the truer friend of difference here, as well as giving a more comprehensive, synthetic account.[24]

The third aspect of the lived involuntary as it relates to action and effort is habit. Habit as something learned is a prolongation of preformed skills. I may have some natural musical talent, but I develop and realize it through forming habits in long, tedious hours of practice. I may have a natural athleticism like Michael Jordan, but I only become Michael Jordan through many hours on the court. And habit, it seems, is not just corporeal, but can also become intellectual, volitional, and moral. Through long years of education, I become adept at philosophy or science, and I acquire knowledge that becomes habitual and that I can apply in the process of thinking about a question in the present and acquiring new knowledge. Everything new that I learn becomes part of a habitual, lived, subjective context of knowledge that can be brought to bear on new problems and new situations. Consequently, there is all the difference in the world between a novice in philosophy, however talented she may be, and one who is expert and accomplished and has paid his dues.[25]

As is always the case in living out or thinking about different relationships of the voluntary to the involuntary, there is always the danger of falling into an extreme that leaves out or minimizes one pole. One danger with habit is that we begin relying on it too much and thus fall into an automatism. I cease to be open to the different and new in my life and simply opt for the customary and familiar. "The old ways, Matilda, are the best ways." There is always "the temptation to resign my freedom under the inauthentic form of custom, of the 'they,' of the 'only natural,' of the already seen and already done."[26] Consequently the talk of freedom is one of constant self-recovery from such extremes. "The organic unity of nature and willing to which the naturalization of the will testifies turns constantly to the ethical duality of spontaneity and effort. I am one only in a constantly repeated conquest of the renascent scission."[27]

Toward the end of his discussion of moving and effort, Ricoeur reflects on the work of Maine de Baran, and his insights here also constitute an implied critique of Sartre. Here the concern is with de Baran's claim that without effort I can know nothing. Ricoeur concedes that knowledge is a kind of action and attention is a kind of effort. I see by looking, I hear by listening, and I smell by inhaling. But this kind of attentive perceiving is different from effort in the narrow sense, in which I try to realize a project by acting in the world. It is true that I do learn something about the world when I try to drive a car and crash it into a curb, but the pair action-passion is not reducible to or equivalent to the pair perception-object. Perception presents the object to me in a full presence in a way not reducible to moving-effort and is indeed a precondition for moving and effort. I could not try to drive the car unless I first perceived it in a driveway.

Such a line of reflection leads Ricoeur to say that the key to the problem of truth does not lie in a consideration of the will. "A philosophy of the will has no right to become a voluntarism and to exercise an imperialism over all the sectors of philosophical reflection."[28] At the same time, de Baran validly admits and alerts us to the unity of effort coming from the will and present in acts of the Cogito and thus frees us from the temptation of embracing a sensualism, in which the self becomes a bundle of impressions.[29]

It seems to me that Sartre can be criticized for a similar or analogous voluntarism on all three levels, decision, effort, and consent. On the level of decision, we see this tendency present in the reducing of reason to rationalization, motive to pretext. On the level of moving and effort, we have seen it in making obstacles and emotions derivable from freedom conceived as effort flowing from choice. To perceive the rock as obstacle is not to produce it as obstacle freely. When I turn my attention to the rock, perception functions relatively autonomously in relation to freedom. I choose to perceive, to turn this way or that, but what I perceive is not up to me. There is an involuntary aspect to perception, both in the object perceived and in the subject perceiving, that Sartre does not recognize. We will see this same tendency manifest in our next section on consent, in which freedom produces through its fundamental project the various necessities it encounters.

In contrast to Ricoeur, Sartre insufficiently distinguishes and relates not only the voluntary and involuntary on all three levels, but also these three levels themselves. They are jumbled together indiscriminately and mixed up. Moreover, there is little or no recognition of the irreducibility to freedom of the involuntary of effort in all three of its aspects of preformed skills, emotion, and habit; the different forms such as emotion, magic, and passion that can occur, and the distinction between emotion as basic and passion as derived.

NECESSITY AND CONSENT

Even though decision, action, and freedom's relationship to necessity are discussed together, issues concerning necessity and consent arise most saliently and obviously in "Being and Doing: Freedom," from Part Four of *Being and Nothingness*, "Having, Doing, and Being." Here Sartre says that two solutions and only two are possible in the question that arises concerning freedom's relationship to necessity: "either man is totally determined (which is inadmissible, especially because a determined consciousness—i.e. a consciousness externally motivated—becomes itself pure exteriority and ceases to be consciousness), or else man is totally free."[30] Sartre thus pursues on this level the same strategy as on the levels of decision and action, what Sartre calls the facticity of freedom, an inexact synonym for necessity in Ricoeur's sense, is the given that freedom has to be and which it illuminates by its project. What follows are several discussions of instances such as freedom's relation to place, its body, its past, human others, and the ultimate other, death.[31]

Common sense, of course, would object that much of my life seems to be limited by and even victimized by determinisms of various kinds. I am not able to escape the limit of having been born in a certain class, family, sex, and nationality. But, Sartre says, such objections have never troubled the partisans of freedom, who recognized that the will is infinite, and that the coefficient of adversity in things that seems to resist, limit, or confine me is not an argument against freedom, for it is through freedom that the coefficient of adversity arises. A particular snag that manifests a profound resistance if I wish to displace it will be a valuable aid if I wish to climb it to see the surrounding countryside. Even if, after such an observation, there remains an unthinkable residuum that belongs to the in-itself and which ensures that one crag will be more favorable for climbing than another, it is still thanks to the residuum that freedom arises as freedom. For projects to be realizable, for there to be a distinction between a possible end from realization of this end, the in-itself is necessity. With regard to my past, I cannot by my freedom make it to be the case that certain events did or did not happen. Nonetheless, by my freedom I decide the meaning of my past. I can decide whether the time I spend in prison after a theft was fruitful or unfruitful, whether my marriage is to be discontinued or continued, or whether a trip is educational or not.[32]

Bothersome questions arise, however, similar to those we have asked earlier. Is there a sufficient distinction here between different forms of freedom such as decision, effort, and consent to necessity? Is there an illegitimate equation of consciousness with freedom such that any meaning recognized is itself chosen. Is there enough justice done to the involuntary pole of necessity such as this arises in my character, unconscious, and life. If my life undergoes change, similar to that which Beethoven endured in being blind, I have to choose a stance toward that change. But the loss of sight is undergone by me in such a way as to force me to change. I cannot go on as before, even if, like Beethoven, I choose to remain a composer.

In considering the necessary as a final aspect of the involuntary in relation to freedom, we reach the most concrete stage's of our inquiry. Our trajectory has moved from decision through effort to consent. In consent, freedom becomes most concrete in taking necessity into itself. This is an act of freedom that operates in the present. "Yes, let it be." "Fiat." "I accept this." Unlike decision and effort that will and carry out a project to be realized in the future, consent takes place in the present. "Let it be." Unlike decision, in which a project is chosen as dependent on me, consent says "yes" to what does not depend on me and which exists necessarily. Also, in moving from character to unconscious to life in our reflection, we move from what is most intimate to freedom, personal style or character, to what escapes freedom most and operates most independently of it. And yet even life is related to freedom not as what it chooses in projects, but as the condition of all projects and moving.[33]

But why should I consent rather than revolt? Ricoeur's limited incomplete answer is that freedom integrates itself with its opposite in the form of personal character of style, in the form of a "matter" of the unconscious that freedom has to integrate with its own life, and biological life that functions as a condition sine qua non of freedom as being in the world. As freedom relates to opposites and becomes fully freedom on the levels of decision and movement, so also here. As tied to a particular kind of character, freedom is an infinite finite. As linked to and nourished by the indefinite matter of the unconscious, freedom is a unity of definite form and indefinite matter. As projected in the world, in myself and for myself I am the union of freedom and life. I am alive as organic in order to exist as free.[34]

In negotiating such consent, freedom is tempted, as on the first two levels, by the magic of extremes that minimize or negate the reciprocity between involuntary and voluntary. There is the possibility of being seduced by a one-sided objectivism and determinism of character, unconscious, or life. I can be so tempted by the role and importance of the unconscious, for example, that I can be led to think that my freedom is merely illusory. However, "consciousness can announce itself as a dupe only before an undeceived consciousness,"[35] which is not merely illusory and which pronounces on the truth of the illusion. Such a determinism is inherently self-refuting. I win back from the temptation of such determinism that . . . "it is I who think, give meaning, weigh my motives, wish, and move my body."[36]

The opposite extreme is one-sided negation. Negation in the form of refusal is motivated by the rejection of necessity as the limitation of character, the formlessness of the unconscious, and contingency of life. Freedom in confronting this triple negation can also move into a triple negation of refusal, manifesting itself as a wish for totality in the face of limitation of character, total transparence of consciousness in the face of the unconscious, and a self-positing in relation to the contingency of life. Such self-positing, Ricoeur suggests, falls to the ground as merely idealistic in relation to a concrete condition that is simply refused. Like it or not, my real body as particular is the basis of character, unconscious, and life. Freedom as one-sidedly posited comes off as a disappointed idealism, which can only regard the world as absurd. To put the matter in Sartrian terms, freedom is a frustrated desire to be the unity of in-itself and for-itself, and is always going to be disappointed and regard both itself and the world as absurd. Freedom functioning as consent, however, functions in the light of a transcendence to which phenomenology can only allude us and leads to a contemplative wonder, affirmation, and hope in the whole. The ideal trajectory, then, is from doubt about the self and its relationship to the world to affirmation of the self to the second Copernican revolution grounding an affirmation of transcendence. Sartre, from Ricoeur's point of view, remains caught in the second moment and even articulates an inadequate version of that. Indeed, for Ricoeur, one of the implications of Sartre's inadequacy is the lack of openness to transcendence.[37]

Ricoeur thus indicates in this work a sense of philosophical authenticity that resists the magic of extremes, either pure objectivism or pure subjectivism, pure determinism or pure indeterminism, pure passivity or pure activity. In responding to Sartre's either-or of total freedom or total determinism, Ricoeur argues for a third alternative, the unity of voluntary and involuntary. In this stance, he reminds us of Kierkegaard's account of the authentic self in *Sickness into Death* as a unity of finite and infinite, temporal and eternal, necessity and possibility. Sartrian freedom in its one-sided stressing of the ideal, infinite, and possibility falls into its own kind of despair, by Kierkegaard's criteria, despair at willing to be oneself and one-sidedly ignoring or minimizing finitude, necessity, and actuality.[38]

At the end of our study and reflecting on the encounter between Sartre and Ricoeur at this third level, the most basic difference between the two thinkers seems to be that between Sartre's identification of consciousness and freedom and Ricoeur's sense of the human being as a unity of voluntary and involuntary. Freedom runs all the way down into the depths of the human being for Sartre, whereas for Ricoeur it is the relationship between voluntary and involuntary that runs all the way down. Other differences that we have articulated flow from this basic difference, which we see most clearly only at the end of our study. Why choose Ricoeur over Sartre? First, all the way through this study, I have indicated the phenomenological one-sidedness or incompleteness of Sartre's account, its lack of nuance and subtlety and differentiation in relation to Ricoeur. Ricoeur's account is more verifiable phenomenologically than Sartre's.

Second, Sartre's one-sidedness leads him to various kinds of logical and performative contradiction that Ricoeur avoids. The reduction of reasons to pretexts or rationalizations, for example, leaves us with no reason for preferring Sartre's account to other accounts. If his own phenomenology of freedom is merely his own arbitrarily chosen stance, then there is no reason to see it as true or truer in relation to other competing positions. If, on the other hand, Sartre's intention is to defend his own account as true, and that surely is his intention, then the reasons for preferring his positions are not merely pretexts. Sartre's performance as philosopher contradicts his explicit doctrine of freedom.

Let's test this conclusion a bit and in so doing give Sartre a chance to talk back to us. Sartre might say that I and Ricoeur ignore experiences of radical rupture in which I change my fundamental project. Ricoeur's answer to that objection is that any rejection of a past self involves the choosing of another past. "However radical a conversion is imagined to be, it annihilates a dead past only to discover and stir up behind it a living past which the 'crisis' has liberated."[39] Here Ricoeur quotes Camus: "In every act of rebellion, man experiences not only a feeling of revulsion at the infringement of his rights, but also a complete and spontaneous adhesion to a certain part of himself."[40] For this reason, Ricoeur says, we can no longer say that value is a mere lack as Sartre says it is, but it is the active positing of the existence of another as correlative of mine, and the other and I myself as having existence value. "Let us not say therefore that value is lack, but that scandalous situations lack value, fall short of value."[41]

CONCLUSION

What I have done here is to lay out Ricoeur's account of freedom as a response to Sartre. I have intended this exposition as a plausible hypothesis, not as a full demonstration of the superiority of Ricoeur's answer. That would take at least a book, or maybe two or three books. The question, "Have I been fair to Sartre?" admits of two answers, one of which is illegitimate. I have certainly been unfair to Sartre if the reader expects equal time given to Sartre and a fuller demonstration. But that answer is unfair to me, because that is not what I have tried to do.

Within the limits of what I have tried to do, I have been fair to Sartre. I recognize that *Being and Nothingness* is a great book, one of the classics of twentieth-century phenomenology, and the source of many true insights, challenging questions, and provocative descriptions of experience (e.g., the Look). Also if one takes Hegel seriously that one should not simply reject understanding in his sense for reason, but sublate it within reason, then Sartre's *Being and Nothingness* with its sharp, either-or antitheses, questions, and descriptions must not be rejected simply but lifted up into a more dialectically and phenomenologically adequate account of freedom. His account of the leap needs to be related to an account of motivation, and his account of the negative to an account of the positive. As Ricoeur says, "Refusal is thus the militant soul of the transcendence of the will. Nolition is volition."[42]

On the other hand, picking up on my remarks at the beginning of this chapter, the greater historical injustice has been done to *Freedom and Nature* rather than to *Being and Nothingness*, and this chapter attempts to redress, to some extent, that imbalance. The greatness and fruitfulness of this early work by Ricoeur need to be more recognized. And here I wish to make one final comment concerning the implications of my argument. If both texts are foundational in relation to later efforts by both thinkers, as I think they are, and if there is something to be said in favor of the truth of my hypothesis, then we might expect unhappy philosophical consequences in Sartre's accounts of the Other in *Being and Nothingness*, of the fused group in his *Critique of Dialectical Reason*, difficulties, well known, in his working out of an ethic, and his account of the relationship between freedom and God. A hypothesis for future research, therefore, is to link some of the later accounts with the inadequate phenomenology of *Being and Nothingness*, showing how difficulties and inadequacies as well as positive insights and steps forward are linked to the earlier account, either as resting on it too much or as going beyond it.[43]

If, on the other hand, Ricoeur's phenomenology of freedom is more successful than Sartre's, then we might expect *Freedom and Nature* to be the basis of the balance and nuance in that later work, for example, his reflection on the relationship between Gadamer and Habermas, in which Ricoeur argues for linking a Gadamerian hermeneutics of respect with a Habermasian hermeneutics or suspicion as two aspects of hermeneutics; his *Interpretation Theory: Discourse and the Surplus of Meaning*, in which he argues for a notion of discourse that is both descriptive and explanatory; and his ethics, in which he argues for a blending of Kantian deontology and Aristotelian teleology, right and good, duty and happiness.[44]

The founding roles played by their phenomenologies in later works suggests a point about the importance and limitations of descriptive, eidetic phenomenology. It is important as an almost indispensable base and foundation in a mediated, qualified sense. If one does not ground fundamental concepts arising out of experience with careful, nuanced description and eidetic analysis of that experience, then use of those concepts will make the later work more or less flawed and problematic. If one does get those concepts right or mostly right, and I think Ricoeur does, then that can have a positive, beneficial effect on the later work. On the other hand, both Sartre and Ricoeur do not confine themselves to descriptive, eidetic phenomenology. Sartre moves to a synthesis between phenomenology and Marxism in his later work, and Ricoeur moves to a hermeneutics oriented both to understanding and explanation and an ethic and theory of justice that takes him beyond strict descriptive phenomenology. Learning and taking our cue from both of these thinkers, we are tempted to say, or at least to hypothesize, that descriptive, eidetic phenomenology, while necessary, is not sufficient for a fully comprehensive philosophy. There is more in heaven and earth than can be dreamed of in a strictly descriptive, eidetic phenomenology.

NOTES

1. Jean-Paul Sartre, *Existentialism and Human Emotions*, trans. Bernard Frechtmann and Hazel Barnes (New York: Philosophical Library, 1957), pp. 24–27.
2. Ibid., p. 27.
3. See my criticisms of Sartre on this point in my *Post-Cartesian Meditations* (New York: Fordham University Press, 1988), pp. 96–99. Jean-Paul Sartre, *Being and Nothingness*, trans. Hazel Barnes (New York: Philosophical Library, 1956), pp. xlv–lxvii.
4. Paul Ricoeur, *Freedom and Nature: The Voluntary and the Involuntary*, trans. Erazim V. Kohak (Evanston: Northwestern University Press, 1966), pp. 4.
5. Ibid., pp. 7–8.
6. Ibid., pp. 66–67, quotation from p. 43.
7. Ibid., pp. 80–83.
8. Ibid., p. 85.
9. Ibid., pp. 85–86.
10. Ibid., p. 143.
11. Ibid., pp. 151–56, quotation from p. 149.
12. Ibid., pp. 163–65.
13. Ibid., pp. 168–71.
14. Ibid., pp. 175.
15. Ibid.
16. Ibid., pp. 175–76.
17. Hegel, *The Logic of Hegel*, trans. William Wallace (New York: Oxford University Press, 1904), pp. 143–55. For a full discussion of the distinction between good and bad faith, see Sartre, *Being and Nothingness*, pp. 47–70.
18. Sartre, *Being and Nothingness*, pp. 53–54.
19. Ibid., p. 489.
20. Ricoeur, *Freedom and Nature*, pp. 231–50.
21. Ibid., pp. 250–80.
22. Ibid., pp. 273–74.
23. Ibid., pp. 274.
24. Ibid., pp. 274–78.
25. Ibid., pp. 280–82, 292–96.
26. Ibid., pp. 301.
27. Ibid., pp. 297.
28. Ibid., pp. 336.

29. Ibid., pp. 331–37.
30. Ibid., Sartre, *Being and Nothingness*, p. 442.
31. Ibid., p. 489.
32. Ibid., pp. 481–82.
33. Ricoeur, *Freedom and Nature*, pp. 341–47.
34. Ibid., p. 347. Ricoeur's answer, by his own admission, is philosophically limited because only a religious perspective sketched by me a little bit later in my text can fully answer the question, "Why consent?"
35. Ibid., p. 404.
36. Ibid., pp. 403.
37. Ibid., pp. 463–64.
38. Ibid., pp. 463–66.
39. Paul Ricoeur, *History and Truth*, trans. Charles Kelbley (Evanston: Northwestern University Press, 1965), p. 332.
40. Ibid., p. 323.
41. Ibid.
42. Ibid., p. 312.
43. See my critical discussions of Sartre on the human other in *Post-Cartesian Mediations*, pp. 144–48; on the fused group in *Critique, Action, and Liberation* (Albany: SUNY Press, 1994), pp. 87–93; and on his atheism in "Freedom, Receptivity, and God," *The International Journal for the Philosophy of Religion*, VI (Winter 1975): 219–35.
44. See my discussion and use of Ricoeur's account of Gadamer and Habermas in *Post-Cartesian Meditations*, pp. 169–77; of discourse in *Post-Cartesian Meditations*, pp. 116–18, and of his ethics in "Ricoeur's Resolution of the Communication Ethics Controversy," *Ricoeur as Another*, ed. Richard Cohen and James L. Marsh (Albany: SUNY Press, 2002), pp. 223–34.

What Makes Us Think? 2
Two Views

Bernard P. Dauenhauer

We know that we think. But what makes us think? Are the structure and functions of the brain sufficient for us to do so? If not, what else is required? Exchanges between Paul Ricoeur and the distinguished French neuroscientist Jean-Pierre Changeux shed significant light on a cluster of issues that this basic question raises.[1]

In this chapter I will first set forth two of the main issues they address. One of these deals with the brain's function in all cognitive performances. The second concerns the status of neuroscientific knowledge vis-à-vis any other sort of knowledge. Finally I will offer reasons of my own for preferring Ricoeur's positions.

CONTEXT

To set the context for the Changeux-Ricoeur exchanges, let me recall two passages from Descartes' Sixth Meditation. First: "I had some reason for holding that the body I called 'my body' by a special title did really belong to me more than any other body did. I could never separate myself entirely from it, as I could from other bodies. All the appetites and emotions that I had, I felt in the body and on its account. I felt pain, and the titillations of pleasure, in parts of *this* body, not other, external bodies."[2] And second: "Now there is no more explicit lesson of nature that I have a body. . . . Nature also teaches by sensations of pain, hunger, thirst, etc. that I am not present in my body merely as a pilot is present in a ship; I am most tightly bound to it, as it were mixed up with it, so that I and it form a unit."[3]

For Descartes, the "I," the mind, is the "thinking thing," a substance different in kind from substances that are bodies. But, he says, the I and its body form a "kind of unit." What kind of unit? These two substances cannot interact. How could they form a unit? How could this unit think and still be bodily?

Both Changeux and Ricoeur agree that a human being is a unified thinking thing. For them, as for Descartes, the term "thinking" includes doubting, understanding, asserting, denying, selecting, rejecting, sensing, imagining, and, I should add, remembering.[4] Furthermore, Changeux and Ricoeur, unlike Descartes, both agree that thinking is a bodily activity. They both reject metaphysical dualism. Their disagreement is about how one should understand the multifaceted bodily process that we call thinking, in the broad Cartesian sense.

Neither Changeux nor Ricoeur would agree that our bodies have a part that is in any way analogous to a pilot in a ship. But do our bodies have a specific part that accounts for all the ship's movements, for all thinking? Briefly put, Changeux holds that there is such a part—namely, the brain. The brain and its activity, in his view, are sufficient to account for all thinking. And the science of the brain can, at least in principle, fully account for all the brain's activity and what that activity yields. Ricoeur, on the other hand, holds that the brain and its activity, as Changeux describes them, at most form the substrate necessary for thinking, but are not sufficient for it. For Ricoeur, I think because of my bodily makeup, which of course includes the brain. But the brain alone is insufficient for thinking. Furthermore, no particular science can fully account for the entirety of thought.

THE BRAIN AND COGNITIVE PERFORMANCES

Consider now Changeux's discussion of what makes us think. His basic question is: "Can the anatomical organization and physiological states of the brain be shown to be causally related to the mind's higher cognitive functions and, in particular, to the acquisition of knowledge and the testing of its truth or falsehood?"[5] His aim is to show that the answer to this question is yes and that the brain's structure and functions are sufficient to account for all cognitive phenomena.

Changeux proposes a model of the brain according to which it is an autonomous system that is spontaneously active prior to and independent of any interaction with its environment.[6] Rather than being simply the recipient of impressions from external stimuli, the brain constantly transmits energy to the external world. Indeed, this "spontaneous electrical activity appears early in the development of the embryonic nervous system."[7]

In the course of its spontaneous activity, the brain constantly produces what Changeux calls prerepresentations that it then projects, through the senses, onto the external world. Depending on the signal that the brain receives back from the world, the prerepresentation is either stabilized or not. Those that are confirmed by the world are stabilized in the brain as verified. A negative response, though, sends the brain back to the drawing board. Through this process of trial and error, "causal relations internal to the brain are ... established between external objects and mental objects."[8]

In the course of its life, the individual will progressively "exploit innate endogenous memories or else memories from prior experiences. Learning and rules of behavior are internalized by education."[9] An individual will thus incorporate in its brain a sketch of its personal history. This sketch will come to include its family's social and cultural history and ultimately the history of its wider society.

At every stage of this process, memory traces are stored in the brain. A person utilizes these traces again and again to construct knowledge both about the external world and about himself or herself. In every case, Changeux says, "this will be a matter of *reconstruction*. Every evocation or memories is a reconstruction on the basis of *physical traces* stored in the brain in latent form.... But the *efficacy* of such knowledge in his future behavior and mental operations, and in the reasoning for which they furnish the primary material, serves to bring out the criterion of truth, of objectivity. Validation will be obtained through personal experience, but also through the scientific community and the accumulated knowledge that it possesses. An increase of knowledge follows. No other human activity is characterized by such cumulative progress."[10] In short, spontaneous brain activity is at the core of both knowledge claims and the testing of their truth or falsity.[11]

As Changeux himself points out, several important theses are implicated in his position. Among them are (a) an essential feature of matter is its capacity for organization;[12] (b) prerepresentations are at the root of the brain's ability to make sense of the world and are the sources of imaginative activity;[13] and (c) all prerepresentations, representations, and mental objects are themselves physical objects.

The human brain is, of course, the outcome of an evolutionary process. According to Changeux, prior to the appearance of Homo sapiens, the brain states of ancestors of human beings reached an initial agreement with the environment in which they lived. Those species whose genetic makeup enabled them to form sufficiently accurate representations of their environment to ensure their reproduction survived.

All human beings have in common a specific set of genes. This set is fixed in our chromosomes, particularly at the level of regulatory sequences. This genetic capacity, or envelope, circumscribes the brain's ability to form and communicate conscious representations of the world as well as to test their accuracy.[14] Nevertheless, for Changeux, the brain and its abilities are not exclusively the outcome of its genetic inheritance. On his hypothesis, there are connections among neurons that get established in stages through a process of selection that proceeds by way of trial and error. Changeux calls this process epigenesis. This hypothesis, he claims, "gives us fresh insight into the mechanisms of memory, the retrieval of stored information, and the acquisition, testing, and transmission of new knowledge—in a word, into the appearance of culture, which, in the case of humans, developed in an exceedingly brief period of time."[15] Thus, our genetically underdetermined capabilities get specified and stabilized through the process of epigenesis.

In support of his hypothesis, Changeux points to several features of the process of learning a language. First, in the course of learning its first language and the phonemes proper to it, a child's genetically established capacity to distinguish from one another a notably wide range of phonemes shrinks. Second, the babbling of young children gradually gets differentiated according to the linguistic environments they inhabit. Third, both learning a second language and hearing it after about age twelve are different, as MRIs confirm, from learning or hearing one's first language. And finally, learning to read and write leaves deep epigenetic traces in the brain that last into adulthood. Changeux also reports, as another example of epigenesis, that in some cases of early blindness, brain imaging shows that after a year of intense training in Braille, the visual areas of the brain of these subjects can receive and process tactile information.[16]

Because of the connections between the genetic and the epigenetic processes in the development of each human brain, there is great diversity and variability both between brains and within any particular brain. In the course of this development, begun in the early stages of the embryo's existence and continuing until puberty, each of us not only acquires some particular skills but also loses the capacity to develop some other ones. Thus, "the individual character of each person is … a unique synthesis of one's genetic endowment, circumstances of birth and upbringing, and subjective experiences of the social and cultural environment in which one has grown up."[17] Furthermore, the developmental process of the individual person has "made possible the development of a cultural memory that is not directly subject to the intrinsic limitations of the brain, and so can be transmitted at the level of the social group."[18]

Ricoeur, for his part, does not challenge any of the scientific evidence that Changeux adduces to support his position. Though he grants that the brain is *necessary* to account for all cognitive performances, Ricoeur rejects the claim that it is *sufficient* to do so. Hence, for Ricoeur, the task of the neurosciences is not to determine what makes us think, but rather to examine "what makes it possible for me to think, namely the neural structure without which I could not think. That is not nothing, but neither is it everything."[19]

Ricoeur's explicit challenge to Changeux springs from his careful analysis of the multiple kinds of remembering and their relationships to forgetting.[20] Consider, he says, the actual experience we have of trying to remember some object or event and then succeeding in doing so. Do we not have the paradoxical sense, especially in cases of long-term memory, that not only is the absent thing now present but that it also belongs to a more or less distant past? Furthermore, does not this paradoxical sense of the presence now of something both absent and temporally distant also include the sense of our having undergone something, the sense of our passivity in initially experiencing it?[21]

This complex sense of having successfully recalled to presence something now absent that occurred in the past is what distinguishes remembering from imagining. As Ricoeur puts it, what distinguishes the act of remembering from other mental functions is "the relation of the representation to time and, at the heart of this relation ... the dialectic of presence, absence, and distance."[22] Indeed, it is the matter of distance that poses the problem of the reliability of memories not only in our ordinary lives but especially for historians. This problem does not arise for imaginings. "Recognizing a memory 'for a memory' sums up the entire enigma."[23]

Ricoeur charges that Changeux fails to account for the full complexity of the phenomenon of memory. Relying as he does exclusively on the reactivation of cortical traces to explain memories, Changeux fails to show why our memories are of things not only absent but also past.

All cortical traces are "inscriptions" fully present in the brain. When activated they bring memories to actual presence. But nothing about the cortical trace can represent the distance or pastness of remembered things. To account through cortical traces alone not only for the absence but also for the distance of the remembered thing, one would have to claim that they are not only present traces but also signs that point to the distance of what they represent. But how could a cortical trace, the inscription or imprint of the remembered thing, at the same time be a sign pointing beyond the remembered thing to the past "shock of the thing"? How could it be a sign of the impact that the now distant remembered thing once made on us rather than the representation of the thing that the brain has constructed?[24] For Ricoeur, this question is unanswerable.

Ricoeur himself proposes to overcome Changeux's problem by positing a second kind of trace, namely, a psychic trace. Recalling the metaphor of the wax imprint that Plato and Aristotle used to explain how memories are retrievable as memories, Ricoeur hypothesizes that just as cortical traces correspond to images that are imprinted so do psychic traces correspond to the impression or affection that striking events make upon us and survive in such a way that they are recallable.[25]

We know about cortical traces only through science. We have no lived experience of their presence in the brain or of their activation. Science has to teach us everything we know about them. Psychic traces, on the other hand, do not appear to be accessible to scientific investigation. We come to posit them only "retrospectively." That is, we postulate them to make sense of specific life experiences that we have. And, we must admit, psychic traces presuppose the brain and its cortical traces.[26]

The crucial experiences that warrant the positing of psychic traces are those of recognition. In the moment of recognition, I take the present image to be the image of the same thing that in the past affected me with some degree of intensity. Thus, I may say: "It's really you, Sam. After all these years and all the changes we have both undergone, I recognize you, the one who saved my child's life." Along with the image of the thing or event in question, a feeling previously forgotten but not obliterated is reactivated.

In the cases of recognition relevant here, the recognizer experiences some hesitation or doubt. This gives recognition a dramatic character, a character not explicable exclusively in terms of cortical traces and their activation. Psychic traces account for the element of drama. By reason of them I experience the pleasure, or pain, "of recalling what I once saw, heard, felt, learned, acquired."[27]

Ricoeur's analysis thus requires that we admit an element of passivity or receptivity in at least some of our experiences of remembering. This gives one reason to reject Changeux's claim that the brain, as spontaneously active, is sufficient to account not only for our ability to think, in the full Cartesian sense of thinking, but also both actual thinking and what we think about.

For Changeux, one will recall, the brain is spontaneously active and, in the course of its functioning, constructs and reconstructs knowledge both about the external world and about itself. It proceeds by way of trial and error on a path of exploration that it initiates and maintains. For Ricoeur, by contrast, we are born into what Husserl has called a lifeworld. This is the elementary world in which "human beings orient themselves, choose signals that are meaningful for them, and anticipate events with a view to making it a relatively practicable world, which is to say a habitable world."[28] Our primitive relationship to the lifeworld is one that is prior to the "refined" distinction between doing and undergoing or suffering. It is much like the being-in-the-world that Heidegger calls Care.[29]

On this view, I experience myself as a unitary body that is both my opening onto the world and the avenue by which the world affects me. I both act into and receive from the world. In my body, acting and receiving are inseparable. To act is to modify the world somehow and to receive is to be modified and stimulated to respond.

Furthermore, I experience myself as inhabiting a world with other human beings who have the same sort of capabilities as I do. Indeed it is with and through them that I come to know just what my capabilities and vulnerabilities amount to. And it is also with and through them that

I constitute and revise my sense of my own identity. For example, it is from others that I learn what it was to have been a baby and what it is to age and eventually die.

Changeux's claim that "everything takes place in the brain,"[30] Ricoeur argues, leads him to misunderstand the intentionality of consciousness. Properly understood, consciousness "is not a box in which there are objects.... The great advance of phenomenology was to reject the containing/contained relationship that made the psyche a place. Thus I do not at all accept the conception of 'mind'.... I simply say that I am outside myself when I see, which is to say that seeing consists of being confronted by something that is not myself, and therefore participating in an external world.... Consciousness is not a closed place about which I might wonder how something enters it from outside, because it is, now and always, outside of itself."[31] Or, from another perspective, consciousness is "the disposition to act, the attention to life, by which the relation of our body to action is expressed."[32]

The intentionality of consciousness not only disallows any claim that would posit any radical cleavage between the realm of the internal and the realm of the external. It also shows us that the world confronts us as an already meaningful world. It is not a world that lies vacant, available for our spontaneous construction and reconstruction of meaning. Consciousness "applies to" or "is applied to" a lifeworld that is already meaningful. This relationship of meaning between consciousness and its lifeworld is a fundamental, irreducible structure of our being-in-the-world.

Likewise, my consciousness is always, from the outset, in communication with other persons. There is no genuine problem of solipsism. "Intersubjective understanding is a part of understanding in general. Thus we are in the world in the plural, and mutually understand that we understand the world together."[33]

In short, Changeux is wrong to hold that the brain is sufficient to account for thinking. As the analysis of memory illustrates, however necessary brain functions are for cognitive performances, they are not sufficient.

THINKING'S ACHIEVEMENTS

During their exchanges concerning what makes us think, Changeux and Ricoeur also discuss the even larger issue of what thinking could accomplish. Here again their views diverge. As I indicated earlier, Changeux holds that in the course of the individual person's development as a thinking being, he or she epigenetically acquires the achievements of other thinkers, predecessors and contemporaries, that are preserved in what he calls a cultural memory.

Changeux acknowledges that the mechanism by which this socio-epigenetic evolution takes place remains poorly understood. Nonetheless, he takes it that the supreme achievement of human intelligence is its search for truth, that is, its ability to extract, store, and evaluate knowledge, to communicate it, and to discuss it with other people. Considered in terms of the lengthy evolution of Homo sapiens, this search for truth has culminated, in a remarkably short time span, in the organized scientific inquiry we know today. This kind of inquiry, which replaces mythic thought, is the supreme achievement of the human brain.

Admittedly, the neural mechanisms at work in the scientist's brain that control evaluations and rewards are still far from well understood.[34] But, Changeux argues, at least this much can be said. The evolutionary process that has led to scientific knowledge culminates in a pattern of inquiry that aims at objectivity and universality. This kind of inquiry combines the "efforts of a great many researchers who constitute what is rightly called the scientific community."[35]

For Changeux, scientific knowledge properly so called is ultimately the outcome of a dual process of detachment. This kind of knowledge is not only detached from sensory perception. It is also detached from the imaginary world of "myths and the social structures in which they are embedded."[36] Thus, there is need for an "authentic science of mythic thought ... so that the operation of irrational belief may be compared with the rational search for truth that descended from it."[37] That is, scientific thought ultimately has to account not only for its own occurrence but also for the occurrence of non-scientific thought, thought that lacks objectivity and universality.

Furthermore, scientific knowledge and the freedom of thought that it requires, belong to a more comprehensive struggle for "equality and fraternity among human beings."[38] Ultimately, our frame of reference will "*deliberately* evolve from the highly emotional, selfish, and ethnocentric ways of thinking that so far have been dominant in human history to a universalist conception of humankind."[39]

In sum: "The main architectural principles if the human brain are common to all the various representatives of the [human] species. Men and women are not simply rational beings. They are also social beings. They possess singular traits that are the hallmarks of *humanitas*: innate capacities, not only for reasoning and creativity, but also for attributing knowledge and desires to others and for feeling the'moral' emotions of sympathy and aversion to violence. They also possess an instinct for learning, together with a set of epigenetic dispositions favoring the storage and retrieval of individual memories within a social, or cultural, context. Though naturally inclined to seek personal rewards, they respond no less favorably to shared rewards at the social level. Moral norms can therefore be seen as distinctive expressions of a general disposition to ethical behavior."[40] Hence, all knowledge claims and all justifications for conduct are defensible just insofar as they are compatible with the principles and achievements of genuine scientific inquiry, inquiry that systematically resists encroachment by individual or cultural bias.

Ricoeur, for his part, rejects Changeux's claim that scientific knowledge stands at the apex of thought and that science is the ultimate arbiter of the significance and worth of any and all knowledge claims. Granted that the twofold detachment described by Changeux—detachment from (1) sensory perception, and (2) the "imaginary world" of myths and the social structures that embody them, for example, religious beliefs and practices—is necessary for scientific knowledge, it does not follow that it is necessary or perhaps even possible for all knowledge to be demonstrably compatible with scientific knowledge.

As Descartes did in the Sixth Meditation, Ricoeur points out that there is a significant difference between my experience of my own body and that of any body, including my own, that is an object for scientific study. In and through the involvement I always have with the world and other people, I experience my body, my lived body as the zero-point of my orientation in the space and time of the world. By contrast, an objectivated body, mine or anyone's, has no uniquely assignable place or time, no particular, specified here or now. As bodily, I encounter you, another lived body with your own distinctive orientation. So too do I encounter other specific, identifiable lived bodies as well as the myriad particular animals, plants, and inanimate things that I perceive or imagine or remember. The objectified body may be one of a multiplicity of objectified bodies, but all such bodies can be substituted for one another. Not so with lived bodies. They cannot be substituted for one another. It is always a particular body that suffers some actual occurrence of hunger or disease or that enjoys actual delights or health. The objectivated body as such is simply the site of such possible experiences.

Furthermore, whereas there can be an objective study of the set of capabilities and vulnerabilities that are taken to be constitutive of a human being, in my lived body I directly experience them as they are instantiated in me. For example, it is one thing for a person to study the factors that in general determine what is required to learn a foreign language. It is another for that person to experience directly the pains and pleasures of actually learning a particular second language. So too for all the basic capabilities such as the abilities to speak, make or do, tell stories, and make imputations and their corresponding vulnerabilities that Ricoeur has identified as being constitutive of human existence.[41]

There is a distinctive kind of evidence for my experience of my own particular capabilities and vulnerabilities and of those of other people with whom I am reasonably well acquainted. Ricoeur calls this kind of evidence "attestation" as distinct from empirical evidence. The term "attestation" means "the sort of assurance or confidence that each person has of existing in the mode of selfhood [i.e., as a unique agent]. In saying assurance, I do not say certitude. In saying confidence, I do not say verification. I repeat: assurance is, if one wishes, a belief; but it is a non-doxic belief, if one means by doxic belief that which is expressed by the "I believe that. . . .' I would prefer to speak of credence, as opposed to belief-opinion. The grammar of credence would be expressed in terms of 'believing something' or 'believing in something or someone.' The witness believes what he or she says and one believes in the witness's word [even if one doubts the accuracy of what the witness says]. Assurance is linked with confidence in the sense in which one's word is believable or not."[42]

The differences between my lived body, and my experience of the particular capabilities and vulnerabilities that I have by virtue of it, and that same body as an object for study are reflected in the differences between the discourses in which I talk about them. The discourse that goes with lived bodies is a discourse that cannot avoid the use of indexicals, such as, I, you, he, she, here, now. Discourse about objectivated bodies, scientific or otherwise, by contrast, in principle excludes the use of indexicals.

In Ricoeur's view, there is no evident way to reduce either of these discourses to the other or to subsume without remainder both of them into some third discourse. "Either I speak of neurons and so forth, and I confine myself to a certain language, or else I talk about thoughts, actions, and feelings, and I tie them to my body, with which I am in a relation of possession, of belonging."[43]

To recognize the irreducibility of these two discourses does not commit one to adopt some sort of metaphysical dualism. The dualism in question is, rather, a semantic dualism. Ricoeur accounts for the possibility of this semantic dualism, and indeed of semantic pluralism, by way of the Aristotelian notion that every intellectual discipline has its own subject matter that is treated from a distinctive point of view. For example a human being can be studied anatomically, psychologically, genetically, and so on. Each of these ways of studying human beings specifies the ultimate referent of the discipline in question and is recognized as such by the discipline's practitioners. The ultimate referent of a discipline is therefore defined in the course of defining the discipline itself. Developing a new discipline requires specifying a new ultimate referent for it.

Two consequences follow from noticing that each discipline has its own proper ultimate referent. First, and obviously, every discipline is limited. There is no empirical discipline that has the world as a totality and all the aspects thereof as its ultimate referent.

Second, and of more immediate relevance here, it is entirely illegitimate to transform a dualism of referents into a dualism of substances.[44] Thus, even though mental experience implies bodiliness in a sense that is not reducible to that of the objective body that the sciences study, it does not follow that the term "mental" is equivalent to the term "immaterial." In Ricoeur's words: "To the body-as-object is semantically opposed the lived body, one's own body, my body (whence I speak), your body (you, to whom I am speaking), his or her body (those about whom I recount the story). There is but one body that is mine, whereas all the body objects are before me."[45]

Given the fact of semantic dualism, there is no reason, Changeux notwithstanding, to unequivocally privilege scientific knowledge of any sort over what one can call first-person knowledge. The discourses in question simply do not have the same ultimate referent. In fact, there is reason to hold that scientific knowledge has roots in lived experience that it never entirely extricates itself from.

According to Ricoeur, we expand our knowledge by objectifying the relations among things and meanings that make up lived experience.[46] Though the process of objectivation is admittedly not fully transparent, this much can be said. Objectivation requires a double detachment from lived experience. Like Changeux's process, Ricoeur's objectivation detaches the things a person experiences from the person who experiences them. But unlike Changeux's process, Ricoeur's other detachment is not from "mythic thought" but is instead the detachment of some object from the lifeworld and the placement of it within a system of similarly detached objects. Consider John's kissing his beloved as seen by me, his friend, and by an anthropologist studying human ways of expressing affection. Through objectivation, the scientist or anyone can learn what the anthropologist learns. But the kiss, for John as well as for me and for his rival, will have its own meanings whether an anthropologist or anyone studies it objectively.

Each science, as I have said, has its own ultimate referent reached by a process of objectivation. But none of these processes eliminates the object's tie to the lifeworld whence it was detached. All objectivations are subject to what Ricoeur calls the "inverse operation of compensation," namely, "ascription, which consists in attributing an act or a mental state to someone. Human understanding, or mutual comprehension is possible precisely because objects of meaning can circulate from subject to subject."[47] That is, it is always some specific person who makes or learns a scientific object. Similarly, it is always someone specific who takes on a role or has a role imposed on him or her. Every objectivation is ascribable and thus is always related to someone's lifeworld from which it is detached.

Hence, Ricoeur's double conclusion. On the one hand, to gain a fuller understanding of ourselves we always need to detach the contents of our lived experience, of what we perceive, imagine, and remember, and submit them to one or more kinds of objective explanations, among which are scientific explanations. "And among the objects of science ... there is the brain."[48] But, on the other hand, to understand ourselves we also always need to reincorporate scientific practice and its results into our lived experience of the capabilities and vulnerabilities that are constitutive of us as persons, as selves. At bottom, it is this latter task that Changeux has failed to take into account and has thus led him to exaggerated claims for the unqualified supremacy of scientific thought over all other kinds of thought.

ASSESSMENT

Ricoeur's analysis of the phenomenon of memory, especially of long-term memory, serves as an effective counterexample to Changeux's claim that the brain's structure and functions are sufficient to account for all cognitive performances. As Ricoeur emphasizes, cortical traces alone cannot explain how the things and events we remember are remembered as being not merely absent but also as belonging to a bygone past. Cortical traces as such are simply present in the brain. Nothing about them points to the pastness of what we remember. Accordingly, it is hard to see how Changeux could explain, solely through cortical traces, the differences between our rememberings and our imaginings.

To supplement cortical traces, Ricoeur postulates the existence of psychic traces to account for rememberings. Unlike cortical traces, there is no empirical evidence for psychic traces. Nevertheless, we can attest that we have experienced the impact of at least some past things as something we have undergone, as something that has impinged upon us though completely unbidden and not infrequently as a surprise. These impacts, Ricoeur hypothesizes, leave psychic traces. Even though no empirical evidence verifies the existence of psychic traces, our attestation to our having undergone these striking experiences does supply important evidence for them.

It is, however, by no means clear that Ricoeur's postulate solves Changeux's problem. We not infrequently have different feelings on different occasions of remembering one and the same thing or event.[49] For example, I could remember last week with pleasure Sam's courteous behavior when he returned the credit card I had lost. But after I learn that he illicitly used the card before returning it, when I again remember the event I feel quite different about his "courteous" behavior. This example shows that there is no one-to-one correspondence between the content of a particular memory recorded in the cortical trace and the feeling that I have on some occasion of recalling the content, a feeling that supposedly activated a psychic trace. Context obviously matters. But the postulated psychic trace does not explain just how context fits in.

One can also question whether Ricoeur does not use the term "trace" equivocally. Besides speaking of cortical traces and psychic traces, Ricoeur also speaks of cultural traces, for example, a statue of Lincoln, a biography of Lincoln, an annual celebration of Lincoln's birth. Cultural traces are all somehow "localized" in the world, but not exclusively in any particular person's body. Every psychic trace is registered in some particular person's body, but there is no empirical way to determine just where it is in the body. Cortical traces are always localized in the brain and there is empirical evidence to show that this is the case. These different sorts of localizations make one leery about accepting that they all have any property common to them as traces other than their referring to something that is now past.

Though I have no alternative to propose in place of Ricoeur's psychic traces, these traces do not seem to be the supplement to cortical traces that Ricoeur's analysis of memory needs. Nonetheless, Ricoeur's conclusion that cortical traces alone cannot fully account for all memories is well founded. Thus, his analysis of memory stands as an effective counterexample to Changeux's contention that the brain suffices to account fully for all cognitive performances.

Ricoeur's alternative to Changeux's conception of the connection between scientific knowledge and lived experience is, on the other hand, compelling. In place of Changeux's elevation of the achievements of science to a position of such self-sufficient independence that it can, at least in principle, account fully for all thinking other than scientific thinking, Ricoeur emphasizes the inescapable rootedness of science in lived experience.

As Ricoeur points out, the things and meanings I experience in my lived body are by no means transparent. They are open to and invite analysis and explanations of various sorts. An obviously important and sound way in which people have responded to the opacity of lived experience is through the development of the sciences. Through the complex activity of objectifying the relations among things and meanings that make up lived experience, scientists have greatly expanded knowledge not only of our selves but also of the world we inhabit.[50] This scientific knowledge has objectivity and universality as its necessary properties.

Nevertheless, one should not lose sight of the fact that scientific findings are the outcome of a set of practices that some people (scientists) have deliberately developed. One becomes a scientist by deliberately adopting an appropriate role and cultivating appropriate habits of thinking and acting. But the choice to become a scientist takes place and is sustained in a lifeworld that one has not chosen. The choice is always a response to that lifeworld. No scientist talks solely in terms of his or her science. The very practice of science cannot be conducted in complete isolation from the lifeworld. The selection of members of a research team and their conversations, arrangements for the dissemination of scientific results, the securing of funding for scientific projects all require the use of the first-person discourse that is the characteristic discourse of lifeworld communication. Without the use of lifeworld communication scientific work would grind to a halt. In short, scientists inhabit a lifeworld they neither choose nor can choose to exit except through death.

Furthermore, for all its objectivity and universality, every science has a history. So too is there a history of scientific activity as a whole, as well as of what makes scientific thought scientific. These are histories not only of achievements but also of mistakes and dead ends. Admittedly, these histories can, at least in principle, be told wholly in some third-person discourse. But at least implicit in any telling is room for imputing the achievements, or mistakes, to specific scientists. Whenever there are these imputations, there is a tie back to the lifeworld into which we are born, in which some of us decide to be scientists and others do not, and in which all of us die.

In sum, Ricoeur is correct to insist that science always retains roots in the lifeworld, that science cannot give an exhaustive account of lifeworld experience, and that science, for all its grandeur, remains just one of the several domains of genuine thought, for example, the domains of fictional literature or of religion, that lifeworld experience can give rise to.

Of course, there is nothing infallible about what we deal with in first-person discourse. We all have been and are ignorant or mistaken or prejudiced about many matters. Scientific discoveries have dispelled any number of notions of these sorts and will continue to do so. Nonetheless, because we all come first to experience ourselves and one another as bodily, mortal, and possessors of the same basic abilities and vulnerabilities within the bounds of our lifeworld, scientific activity will always have lifeworld roots that it presupposes, that continuously underpin its very possibility, and that indeed continuously nourish it.[51]

NOTES

1. See Jean-Pierre Changeux and Paul Ricoeur, *What Makes Us Think?*, trans. M. B. DeBevoise (Princeton and Oxford: Princeton University Press, 2000), hereafter WMUT. Changeux further develops his position in *The Physiology of Truth: Neurosciences and Human Knowledge*, trans. M. B. Debevoise (Cambridge: Belknap Press, 2004), hereafter PT. Ricoeur has also returned to this topic in *Memory, History, Forgetting*, trans. Kathleen Blamey and David Pellauer (Chicago and London: University of Chicago Press, 2004), hereafter MHF.

2. Descartes, *Philosophical Writings*, trans. and ed. Elizabeth Anscombe and Peter Geach (Indianapolis: Liberal Arts, 1971), pp. 112–13, hereafter PW.
3. PW, p. 117.
4. PW, p. 70.
5. PT, p. 5.
6. WMUT, p. 112.
7. PT, p. 25.
8. WMUT, p. 116.
9. Ibid., p. 116.
10. Ibid., p. 116. See also PT, pp. 32–36.
11. PT, pp. 9, 26, 39–40.
12. PT, p. 8.
13. PT, p. 60.
14. PT, p. 176–78.
15. PT, p. 185.
16. PT, p. 206–207.
17. PT, p. 208.
18. PT, p. 208–209.
19. MHF, p. 426.
20. MHF, p. 412–43.
21. WMUT, p. 150 and MHF, p. 426.
22. MHF, p. 426.
23. MHF, p. 436. See also MHF, p. 414.
24. MHF, pp. 416, 425–26, 439–40, and WMUT, pp. 149–50.
25. MHF, pp. 414–15.
26. MHF, p. 417.
27. Ibid., p. 417. For a fine fictional depiction of memories that psychic traces would help to account for, see Charles Todd, *A Fearsome Doubt* (New York: Bantam Books, 2000), esp. pp. 3–20.
28. WMUT, p. 117.
29. Martin Heidegger, *Being and Time*, trans. John Macquarrie and Edward Robinson (New York and Evanston: Harper & Row, 1962), pp. 235 ff.
30. WMUT, pp. 118–19.
31. WMUT, pp. 119–20. In a similar vein, John Searle has remarked that consciousness is a "unified field" in which particular experiences appear as modifications. See Searle, "Consciousness: What We Still Don't Know," *New York Review of Books*, LII, 1 (January 13, 2005): 37.
32. MHF, p. 434.
33. WMUT, p. 122.
34. PT, p. 244.
35. PT, p. 252.
36. PT, p. 234.
37. PT, p. 235.
38. PT, p. 237.
39. PT, p. 262. My emphasis.
40. PT, p. 262.
41. For a fuller account of these constitutive capabilities and vulnerabilities, see Ricoeur, *Oneself as Another*, trans. Kathleen Blamey (Chicago and London: University of Chicago Press, 1992); Ricoeur, "Le Destinaire de la Religion: L'Homme Capable," Archivio di filosofia, 61, 1 (1996): 19–34; and Ricoeur, "Autonomie et Vulneribilite," in his *Le Juste* 2 (Paris: Editions Esprit, 2001), pp. 85–105.
42. Ricoeur, "L'Attestation: entre phenomenology et ontology," in Paul

Ricoeur: *Les Metamorphoses de la Raison Hermeneutique*, ed. Jean Griesch and Richard Kearney (Paris: Cerf, 1991), pp. 381–82. The distinction between verification and attestation is crucial for Ricoeur's position. Unless attestation provides a valid kind of evidence different from the evidence gained by empirical verification, Ricoeur would have no solid basis for insisting, with Kant, that persons are irreducibly different from all other kinds of entities.

43. MHF, p. 420. Thomas Nagel has a different, but compatible, account of the irreducibility of these two discourses. See his *Equality and Partiality* (New York and Oxford: Oxford University Press, 1991), pp. 10–20.
44. MHF, p. 419.
45. Ibid., p. 419.
46. WMUT, p. 125.
47. WMUT, pp. 127–28.
48. WMUT, p. 129.
49. I owe this point to my colleague, Beth Preston.
50. WMUT, 125.
51. I owe thanks to Beth Preston and Joseph Walsh for their critiques of an earlier version of this chapter.

Philosophy and Kerygma: 3
Ricoeur as Reader of the Bible

David E. Klemm

> In the end, I do not know what man is. My confession to myself is
> that man is instituted by the word, that is, by a language, which is
> less spoken *by* man than spoken *to* man.... Is not the Good News
> the instigation of the *possibility* of man by a creative word?
> —Paul Ricoeur, "The Language of Faith"

For Paul Ricoeur, the central questions of philosophy are "What is
human being?" and "What does it mean to be human?" His entire
philosophical corpus is an extended, systematic rumination on these
questions. In this chapter, I propose to reflect on Ricoeur as a reader of
the Bible within the larger context of his philosophical anthropology.
Therefore my chapter contributes in larger measure to an understanding
of the place of Ricoeur's biblical interpretation within his philosophical
project than it does to the material content of his biblical exegesis.
Nonetheless, I think that an understanding of Ricoeur's approach to the
Bible can assist his readers in grasping the import of his specific readings
of biblical texts. Let me explain this point further.

The focal problematic and starting point of Ricoeur's philosophical
anthropology is the problem of *human capability*; the theme of his work
is "I can"—a conjunction of the first-person pronoun with the modal
verb of possibility.[1] This starting point has enabled Ricoeur to inquire
into the meaning of human being in all of its complexity and diversity by
combining the modal verb with other infinitive verbs: "I can think," "I
can speak," "I can act," "I can tell stories," "I can assume responsibility."
In each of these cases, the "I" is agent of activity as origin point of all
willing. At the same time, the "I" is the judge of activity through its
capacity to reflect critically on the structure of human activities, to
discern the standards of judgment that are immanent in them, and to
apply the standards to its own performances.

Ricoeur's philosophy stands in the great tradition of Cartesian–Fichtean reflective philosophy—but with a difference. In common with this tradition, Ricoeur acknowledges that the starting point and foundation for all reflection is the positing of the being of the "I" in thinking: when I think, I am. In contrast to his predecessors, however, for Ricoeur the self-evident truth that I am a thinking being cannot constitute a first principle from which to deduce a substantive ontology. According to Ricoeur, the truth of the *cogito* is "as abstract and empty as it is invincible."[2] For self-awareness to have content and therefore genuine meaning, the self must appropriate the expressions of its desire to be and effort to exist in the symbols, narratives, actions, and institutions that objectify it. Because for Ricoeur the symbolized self always precedes the "I think," we live deeper than we think. Thinking is always attempting to catch up to itself by recovering the meaning of the self in its acts of existing, and the meaning of the self that posits its being in thinking is finite (but not yet fallen) freedom. For Ricoeur, the thinking "I" freely appropriates itself as freedom by deciphering its own expressions in the linguistic world around it. Because thinking is always appropriating a prior depth, and because appropriation signifies that the initial situation from which reflection proceeds is "forgetfulness," the practice of reflection is in principle a moral task leading from alienation to freedom. For this reason, thinking qua thinking for Ricoeur has the formal identity of a moral striving.[3] Philosophy for Ricoeur is philosophy of the will.

What about the Bible? Does it have anything to contribute to the philosopher's quest to understand human being? How does the "I" of biblical witness relate to the self-active and self-judging "I" of reflective philosophy in Ricoeur? Let me first point out a possible misunderstanding of Ricoeur's approach to the Bible—namely, the view that Ricoeur is a Christian philosopher who draws his motivation from biblical witness and whose biblical hermeneutics presume the stance of faith. We know that Paul Ricoeur's paternal grandparents raised him in a devout, Protestant environment. Reading the Bible and attending church services were extremely important in his youth, and he remains a member of the Christian community.[4] This fact leads some people to suspect a religious motivation in Ricoeur's continuing interest in biblical texts and themes, such as the problems of evil, suffering, and redemption. The question is asked whether or not Ricoeur, as a listener to the Word, should be understood to be a Christian philosopher in the sense that I just mentioned.

If to be a Christian philosopher means to draw warrants for philosophical argumentation from biblical sources or theological speculations, then Ricoeur is not a Christian philosopher. Ricoeur rigorously separates his work as a philosopher from his participation in the religious tradition of French Protestantism. Although Ricoeur does not deny the possibility of religious motivation for raising certain philosophical questions, he insists on the clear distinction between motivation and argumentation. He claims that his philosophical work makes no argumentative appeal to the Bible, even in its ethical dimensions.[5] Ricoeur arduously holds to the autonomy of philosophy and its independence from commitments of religious faith. His philosophical works, including his readings of biblical texts, are wholly accessible to anyone who cares to think seriously. There is no privileged entrance point for the Christian believer in Ricoeur's biblical hermeneutics. What, then, is distinctive about Ricoeur as a reader of the Bible? I should like to point out two fundamental yet distinctive aspects of his approach to the Bible.

The first aspect is Ricoeur's approach to the *semantic autonomy* of biblical texts. The notion of the autonomous text is a direct application from Ricoeur's philosophical hermeneutics. Of course Ricoeur's notion of the text applies to the reading of any text—not just to biblical texts. Nonetheless, this distinctive general feature of Ricoeur's hermeneutics deserves central consideration in characterizing Ricoeur's approach to biblical texts. I will develop the notion of the autonomous text here, in order to return to it later in the chapter.

Ricoeur is a major contributor to the current movement in literary-hermeneutical approaches to the Bible, with a focus on its religious dimension. He is an indefatigable reader of biblical exegesis, who largely eschews interpretations of biblical texts written by theologians. Theology, says Ricoeur, is a composite form of speculative discourse in which philosophical thinking is inextricably intermixed with biblical thinking. Ricoeur admits that theology has a legitimate place within the totality of thinking, but he himself does not engage in it. Rather, Ricoeur makes the conscious decision to engage in both biblical exegesis and philosophical reflection without blurring the two.[6] An enduring question for Ricoeur interpretation is how does he conceive the relationship between these two disciplines?

With regard to biblical exegesis, Ricoeur respects the historical-critical method for the precision of its scientific approach in separating distinct strata of textual composition within their *Sitze im Leben*. However, historical-critical methods play only a preliminary role in Ricoeur's reading of the Bible, for they fail to respect the autonomy of written texts. Historical criticism binds textual meaning too tightly to the original author's intention and the interests of his or her historical community. Ricoeur claims that "to know who wrote what at what time is completely useless in understanding the text" because the meaning of a text can grow and change considerably beyond the intention of its author.[7] Similarly, Ricoeur rejects the approach of "canonical" criticism, which does not work with the original layer of textual authorship but rather with the authoritative redaction of texts that play a founding role in a particular community of faith. Canonical readings also fail to recognize the semantic autonomy of texts by closing the canon and ignoring the ongoing life of the text. Ricoeur expands his reading of the Bible beyond both the historical-critical moment and the canonical-critical moment by attending more completely to the *Wirkungsgeschichte* or *Nachgeschichte* of these sacred texts. This expansion follows from Ricoeur's applying his concept of the autonomous text to biblical writings. What, then, is the notion of autonomous text?

According to Ricoeur, a text is a form of discourse with a specific difference. Like any discourse, a text displays the fundamental structure of noun-verb combinations that form sentences, by means of which a speaker can say something about something. Moreover, because sentences say something about something through the medium of linguistic signs, all discourse displays the duality between *langue* and *parole*—code and message—that justifies both semiotic and semantic approaches to discourse within philosophical hermeneutics.[8] Furthermore, all discourse is actualized as an *event* in time, but understood as a *meaning* that endures in the propositional content of the sentence.[9] As such, meaning is *subjective* as what the speaker intends to say (the utterer's meaning) and *objective* as what the conjunction of noun and verb in a sentence yields (the utterance meaning). Finally, the meaning of discourse divides into *sense* (*Sinn* as the "what" of meaning) and *reference* (*Bedeutung* as the "about what" of meaning). All of these features are ingredient in both spoken and written discourse, but in spoken discourse the opposing elements tend to combine into an inseparable unity.

Textual discourse distinguishes itself from spoken discourse in ways that make writing the complete actualization of what is still virtual and implicit in living speech, namely, the detachment of meaning from event, the exteriorization of objective from subjective elements of discourse.[10] In a dialogue, the two speakers can clarify their meanings in a face-to-face situation, and they share a common world of reference. In reading a text, the author is no longer a dialogue partner. The reader responds directly to the text. Consequently, the distinguishing characteristic of text is its "semantic autonomy," which marks the collapse of the central dialogical conditions that interlocutors shared in a face-to-face conversation. For example, in reading a text, the subjectivity of the text itself replaces the subjectivity of the speaker. Since there is no speaking subject to give gestures and phonic clues as to how the respondent ought to understand the event of meaning, the text itself occupies the position of subject over against the reader. Furthermore, the world projected by the text replaces the world of ostensive reference shared between speakers.

In reading a text, there is no shared horizon of dialogue, so the text requires that the reader work out the kind of world that the text does present.[11] The loss of immediacy in conversational engagement is, however, a gain in both the reader's productive imagination to construe meaning from textual signs and the capacity of the text itself to renew and multiply its meanings in different interpretative situations. Writers of texts exploit the feature of semantic autonomy in order to facilitate a tradition of ever-evolving interpretations.

Through his notion of the semantic autonomy of the text, Ricoeur expands his reading of the Bible beyond both historical criticism and canonical criticism in two dimensions. He focuses on the traditions of interpretation that are incorporated into the biblical texts through intertextual references. In addition, he attends to the reception of biblical texts within a series of communities of reading and interpretation that the original authors of the text could not have anticipated.[12] Biblical texts are neither merely written artifacts of historical criticism nor merely parts of an authoritatively determined canon. In addition and most important, they live within dynamic trajectories of meaning that are propelled through their interaction with the memories and imaginations of living communities. "The text exists, in the final analysis, thanks to the community, for the use of the community, with a view to giving shape to the community."[13]

A second unique element in Ricoeur's approach to the Bible is his notion of *biblical thinking*, which he takes to be a form of thinking distinct from philosophical thinking. Biblical thought is one of the "modes of thought other than those based on Greek, Cartesian, Kantian, Hegelian, etc. philosophy." The world of discourse closest to biblical thinking is "the metaphorical language of poetry," in that it is "not scientifically descriptive or explanatory, one that is not even apologetic, argumentative, or dogmatic."[14] How are the modes of philosophical and biblical thinking different?

Ricoeur initially contrasts their respective "attitudes" in reading texts. The philosophical attitude of reading is dominated by *critique*. This is true even of the Platonic perspective in which the world of ideas precedes the act of reflection and is recalled in and through that act. "Critique" here means the attitude that dislodges the immediate givenness of whatever appears to the mind or senses. The thinker in the critical attitude dislodges givenness of being by questioning the standing connections between the signs, sense, and reference of assertions. What is more, according to Ricoeur, the critical attitude is always tied to powers of reflection that are under my control as a reader. In the critical attitude, the "I" of self-critical reflective thinking is both the origin point of thinking and the judge of thinking.

By contrast, the attitude of reading appropriate to biblical modes of discourse is dominated by *conviction*. "Conviction" is a religious attitude in the sense that "it is the moment of adhering to a word reputed to have come from farther and from higher than myself, and this occurs in a kerygmatic reading within a profession of faith."[15] The religious attitude arises on the basis of a Word that precedes my thinking, sustains itself by means of the dynamic trajectory of writing, and determines itself within the limits of a history of interpretation attentive to the effects of the text on a community. Biblically speaking, the Word is the Word of God—the founding and final Word that is held to be encoded in biblical texts and available within the hermeneutical circle between the proclaimed Word and the communities sustained by the traditions of reading and interpreting it. Moreover, biblical thinking respects the "difference in altitude" between the authoritative Word and the one who responds with conviction. In biblical thinking there is a conscious and accepted asymmetry marking the difference in relationship between master (the Word) and disciple. In philosophical thinking, by contrast, a symmetry exists in principle between one critical thinker and the other. In biblical thinking, the "I" freely submits to the higher authority of the Word, understanding that the Word is Word only in the free act of interpretation.

Nonetheless, Ricoeur insists that one need not be a believer, a religious reader, in order to comprehend biblical thinking. By means of imagination and empathy the philosopher can enter into the circle of biblical discourse to place herself within the life trajectory of the receiving historical community in the mode of "as if." In this way, biblical texts address a potentially universal audience, even as their religious life sustains itself within the communities of belief.

The task for the remainder of this chapter is to connect the ideas of biblical thinking and semantic autonomy for the sake of indicating how Ricoeur reads the Bible. I propose to begin this task within the broad framework of Ricoeur's philosophical problematic: the problem of human capability as a cornerstone of philosophical anthropology. I thus intend to consider biblical thinking as a particular human capacity in relation to others. My thesis is that for Ricoeur the biblical text is the linguistic embodiment of a higher agency than the "I" of critical reflection—namely, God as divine agency. Biblical thinking is thinking that responds to and is empowered by the Word of God. Biblical thinking is a human capability that overturns and exceeds natural human capability. To show that this position is by no means a throwback to precritical Christian consciousness, I will build up my case by beginning with philosophical thinking and proceeding to biblical thinking, with narrative thinking as an intermediary step. I claim that Ricoeur's philosophy taken as a whole makes an enormous contribution to the problem of conceiving how biblical thinking is possible as divinely empowered thinking.

PHILOSOPHICAL THINKING

In this section, I focus broadly on the human capacities to think and to act, all of which occur through the medium of language. I begin with *Fallible Man*, where Ricoeur constructs an abstract model of human being as thinking being, that is, as a being whose very act of existing brings about mediations between a finite element and an infinite element. One mark of finite human thinking is that the subject must bring about mediations between disproportionate elements at three levels—namely, the theoretical, practical, and affective levels.[16] At the level of theoretical synthesis, the "I" constitutes objects of knowing by mediating between finite *seeing* (perceiving) and the infinite capacity of *saying* (signifying or determining the meaning of perceived things) through the *transcendental imagination*, which projects an image as intermediary between particular percept and universal concept. More exactly, the "I" synthesizes singular representations arising from bodily receptivity with general representations arising from conceptual determination in language according to a rule or principle of synthesis.[17]

At the level of practical synthesis, the "I" projects images of the person that I could become by synthesizing the fixed qualities of selfhood with a vision of how that self could achieve happiness. Here thinking mediates between the finite conditions of personal *character* and the infinite intention of *happiness* (a good life), according to the principle of the moral law and guided by the feeling of *respect* for the person. Here the projected synthesis is an intended course of action. The practical synthesis is weaker than the theoretical synthesis because of the split in the agent between willing an action out of respect and actually performing it. One can will a moral act and still not do it; one cannot signify a perceived object without seeing it.[18]

The weakness discernible in the split will become more serious at the level of affective synthesis. At the affective level, we find the inner conflict of the heart. Feeling for Ricoeur combines an intention and an affection. One's feeling of something at the same time both constitutes an evaluation of qualities felt in the thing, person, or world (e.g., as good or bad, pleasant or unpleasant) and it manifests the way in which the self finds itself inwardly affected (e.g., as attracted or repelled). Whereas knowing designates the duality of subject and object, feeling manifests a prereflective or hyperreflective sense of what it means to inhere in and belong to the totality of being—"something more profound than all

polarity and duality."[19] Feeling is the motivational source for all theoretical and practical determinations, and in it the mediating self is torn
between the finite sensible desire (*epithumia*) for *pleasure* and the infinte
rational desire (*eros*) for spiritual beatitude by means of the *spirit* (Plato's
thumos). The mediating heart of feeling remains a field of conflict
between the vital feelings for particular pleasures (e.g., having, power,
and worth) and the spiritual feelings of openness to the totality of being
(e.g., joy, anxiety, and hope). In principle, the purity of heart that can
will one thing is less easy to achieve than either truth in thinking or right-
ness in doing.

Taken as a whole, human being is a structure of fallibility in having
to mediate between discontinuous and conflicting aspects of itself and
the world. Fallibility names the whole movement of *infinite originating
affirmation* (the infinite term of thinking, willing, and feeling) through an
existential difference (the finite term of each) by *human mediation*.[20] To
put his analysis in different but consistent terms, Ricoeur conceives of the
self as a structural unity composed of the following elements:

1. A principle of *universal subjectivity* (the "I" as source of intellectual
   functions of conceptual determination).
2. A principle of *particular personality* (the physical and psychic body of
   "this one here" as source of sensible functions of perceptual receptivity).
3. A principle of *individualized subjectivity* (the individualized unity
   in difference of the universal "I" and particular person—the embodied
   self).

With each step of Ricoeur's analysis of the self—from the theoretical to
the practical to the affective—however, the fragile mediations brought
about by thinking become more tentative and fraught with risk. At its
core the self is conflict—a sensed noncoincidence of the self with itself
that is reflected on objects of knowing, sensed as the task of becoming a
person in doing, and experienced as the alternation between misery and
love in feeling.[21]

Fallible Man should be considered a work of dialectic in the sense of
a thinking about thinking. Dialectic here constitutes the *identity* of philosophical thinking as *critique*. The reason is that in their thinking
activities humans are constantly bringing about mediations, which can
themselves be mediated. To think therefore means to question the
meaning and truth of these mediations—and to put into question one's
own being as thinking.[22]

Ricoeur's dialectical reflections also establish the *limits* of critical
thinking both vertically and horizontally, as it were. Vertically Ricoeur
establishes both a lower limit and an upper limit to thinking. At the
lower limit, thinking arises out of an original *arche*, and at the upper

limit thinking proceeds toward a final end or *telos*.[23] He calls the modes of discourse referring to these limits "originary affirmation" and "eschatological hope" to indicate the nonconceptual nature of thinking at both the lower and upper limits. Abstractly considered, both affirmation and hope are forms of *conviction* that signify the end of mediation and hence a negation of thinking. On reaching these limits, critical thinking ceases to be possible because mediation collapses into immediacy. Ricoeur does not offer dialectical formulas by which to denote the postulated content of the limit concepts. However, it seems to me dialectically appropriate to designate the lower limit as the *ground of unity prior to any difference* between opposites of saying and seeing, and the like, and the upper limit as the *fully determinate unity of opposites.*

Ricoeur also establishes horizontal limits of thinking in his analysis of theoretical, practical, and affective syntheses. If one takes either side of the mediating activity in abstraction from its reciprocal other, one reaches a limit to thinking. For example, viewed from the standpoint of the theoretical synthesis, *seeing* with no admixture of *saying* (or, conversely, saying with no admixture of seeing) each constitutes a limit. Viewed practically, *character* without happiness, or *happiness* without character, also each constitutes a limit. Similarly, at the affective level, purely sensible feelings of *pleasure* without spiritual feelings of *beatitude*, or purely spiritual feelings without sensible ones, each constitutes a limit. The principle of active synthesis is that neither element in a pair of opposites can appear without the other element.

This brief summary of philosophical thinking shows that human being is a finite process of mediating within limits and between disproportionate levels of being. Insofar as thinking qua thinking always brings about mediations at the theoretical, practical, and affective levels, the "I" is always acting in time and it is always liable to make mistakes in its mediations. Fallibility is the structural possibility for error inscribed at the heart of human being. Even more, fallibility is a potency for evil, a power to fail, which becomes fault when it is concretely actualized.[24] Pure reflection cannot follow the leap from fallibility to the actual content of fallenness, however, because reflection cannot derive the actuality of evil from its possibility. Freedom, not necessity, accounts for the fall; and freedom binds and impairs itself thereby. As a result, acknowledgment of fault is a decisive moment in the history of philosophical thinking, whether collectively or individually considered, with the following implications for the moral identity of thinking.

First, the avowal of evil is a crucial material cause or occasion of *hermeneutics*, which is evoked in order to decipher the symbolic languages in which the anguished conscience confesses the content of actual fault. According to Ricoeur, after the fall, freedom is opaque to itself. Fallen freedom is an enigma, and its expressions in language require decoding. After the fall into evil, hermeneutics is the necessary reflective discipline for understanding, interpreting, and reappropriating the desire to be and effort to exist. In *The Symbolism of Evil*, Ricoeur begins his long hermeneutical detour in order to understand expressions of astonishment at evil experienced successively as the stain of an infecting agent, as awareness of a broken relationship, and as my personal responsibility. The cycle of symbols and myths of evil push out and objectify the multileveled "experience of being oneself but alienated from oneself."[25] Ricoeur says, "the consciousness of self seems to constitute itself at its lowest level by means of symbolism and to work out an abstract language only subsequently, by means of a spontaneous hermeneutics of its primary symbols."[26] Hermeneutics thus arises in response to confessions of evil: someone agonizes—appalled at what he has done. Someone else interprets the meaning of the avowal of evil. Yet another person interprets the meaning of the interpretation. Someone else again questions the principles, concepts, and rules under which interpretations can be justified. Philosophical hermeneutics arises in incremental steps leading from the fall. Ricoeur's multiple studies in the hermeneutics of texts—studies such as *Interpretation Theory*, *The Rule of Metaphor*, and *Time and Narrative*—are thus of a piece with the primary language of confession. Hermeneutics reflects on expressions of human moral striving.

Second, the avowal of evil, along with the hermeneutical debate arising from it, is at the same time the birthplace of the *ethical vision of the world*, by which Ricoeur means "our continual effort to understand freedom and evil by each other."[27] In other words, on the one hand, freedom is the finite ground of evil's appearance in the world; on the other hand, the avowal of evil is the condition of consciousness of finite freedom. This guiding theme of Ricoeur's thought is extremely powerful, and he constantly returns to it with the notion of the bound will that claims its freedom by admitting its personal responsibility for evil.[28] It is important to understand that consciousness of fault as my own also sets in motion a temporal dynamism to the guilty conscience. In remorseful contemplation of the past, the guilty conscience recollects itself in repentance; yet in hopeful anticipation of the future, the penitent projects the possibility of regeneration, reconciliation, and redemption in eschatological fulfillment. Within these limits, humanity is "the Joy of Yes in the sadness of the finite."[29]

NARRATIVE THINKING

At this point I want to give a brief account of narrative thinking in order to construct a bridge between philosophical thinking and religious or biblical thinking. It is my contention that, for Ricoeur, biblical thinking responds to confessions of fallenness within the ethical vision of the world by providing the divine grace needed to transform one's life in conformance with the Word. To show how this is possible requires a detour through narrative thinking. The direct link between philosophical thinking and biblical thinking is Ricoeur's notion of the threefold mimesis of action in plot. A brief review of narrative mimesis will supplement our account of thinking—especially the temporal dimension of thinking. The reflection on time and narrative will in turn lead to biblical thinking, because narrative mimesis provides a formal, temporal framework for hearing the Word of God as a word whose timing does not originate with the idea of the transcendental ego but rather with the idea of God. I turn now to the question of time—and narrative.

At this level of philosophical thinking, the subject of thinking constitutes itself as finite temporal thinking. Time determines all thinking. What then is time? Ricoeur begins *Time and Narrative* by recognizing the aporia in ancient thinking about time. On one side, following Aristotle, reflection construes time as a series of "now" points—that is, as objectively given and measured chronological or cosmic time. On the other side, following Augustine, reflection comprehends time as a "present" moment, in which past, present, and future are grasped together in and for the subject—that is, as a nonchronological or psychological time. No speculative resolution of the aporia is possible. In the modern period, Kant brought into theoretical focus both sides of the aporia without suggesting a poetic-practical solution.

According to Kant's doctrine, time has its source in the transcendental ego as the pure form of intuition. In other words, time is not a property of things in themselves as they appear to the senses. Time is the pure form through which we intuit appearing things.[30] As such, time does not appear; it is a condition of all appearances. Thinking occurs in time as generated a priori by the transcendental ego in its self-constituting nature. Kant's notion of time is not, however, purely a psychological one. Ricoeur points out that the Kantian doctrine of time as a pure form of intuition is neither merely objective nor merely subjective. On one hand, the transcendental determination of time establishes the objectivity of the objective (the axioms of nature, such as the perdurance of substance and the necessity of causal laws). On the other hand, the transcendental determination of time establishes the subjectivity of the subject insofar as it constitutes as well the form of inner sense or self-apperception. In Ricoeur's reading of Kant, time is in this way both subjective and objective precisely in its origin in the transcendental ego. Thinking as mediating generates time—the timing of thinking in reciprocal correlation with the timing of natural being. According to Ricoeur, the task for thinking about time is to understand human being embraces both psychological and cosmological dimensions of time.

In *Time and Narrative*, Ricoeur argues that narrative is the privileged place for understanding the meaning of human being in light of the twofold meaning of time. The thesis of *Time and Narrative* is that "time becomes human time to the extent that it is organized after the manner of a narrative; narrative, in turn, is meaningful to the extent that it portrays the features of temporal existence."[31] How so? What does this double claim mean? Consider the first part of the statement: "Time becomes human time to the extent that it is organized after the manner of a narrative." Ricoeur here means that narrative activity responds to the aporia of time with a poetic solution to the speculative paradox, thus saving human time from meaninglessness. The key to the poetic solution lies in the plot, or, better, emplotment, as the structural principle of narrative.

According to Ricoeur, storytelling poetically solves the theoretical aporia between cosmic time and psychological time because when I tell my story both the chronological (objective) and nonchronological (subjective) dimensions of time come into play at once and together. The temporal character of human existence comes to light when the prefigured elements of time-consciousness attain configuration in the action sentences of narrative, with their presupposed existence of agents, motives, goals, cooperative interactions with other agents, and outcomes leading to changes in fortune toward happiness or unhappiness.[32] The basic elements of narrative thinking are *episodes*, or particular narrated events. Of course, narrative thinking does not merely collect episodes; such a collection would not be a story. Narrative thinking synthesizes a manifold of episodes into an intelligible whole or "thought" through the *plot* as a structural principle of order. Emplotment of episodes is a synthesis of the heterogeneous, a submitting of discordant events to a principle of temporal order or concordance. A story is followable when a reader understands how and why the successive episodes lead to its conclusion. The followability of narrative thus bridges the theoretical aporia between cosmic time and lived time, rendering the fragile mixture that Ricoeur calls "human time" as "narrated time."

Consider now the second claim that narrative is meaningful to the extent that it portrays the temporal features of existence. According to Ricoeur, narrative texts, whether historical or fictional, specifically refer to the temporal character of human experience for the sake of refiguring it. Historical narratives aim to recount the lived time of past events against cosmic time and owe a specific obligation to the memory of the dead, an obligation that makes history accountable to the documentary archives. Fictional narratives, by contrast, are freed from the documentary trace of the past to invent imaginative variations on the theme of the fault separating the two perspectives on time: personal lived time and apersonal cosmic time. Fictional works in particular have the capacity to present a fundamental fictive experience of time and thereby to become "tales about time."

Tales about time have, according to Ricoeur, a "reflexive temporal structure" that plays with a universal feature of all narrating, namely, that the act of storytelling divides into two moments: the narrative both recounts events within the structure of the plot and the narrative reflects on what happens.[33] Grasped temporally, these two moments are the narrated time (the chronological time of the narrated episodes inscribed and frequently dated within the story) and the time of narrating (the nonchronological time of the narrator's direct address to the reader).[34] Narratives become tales about time by placing the two moments into dialectical play with each other, so that the story both narrates (times) events and comments on its timing of narrative events. The controlled play between narrated time and the time of narrating refers the reader to an implied fundamental fictive experience with time, without its being considered directly as a theme.[35]

The fictive experience of time enables the literary work to escape its own structural closure and directs the reader into the mode of being proposed by the work against the background of open possibility. Fictional exploration of possible being through imaginative variations on the temporalization of time has, according to Ricoeur, the experiential value of eternity when human time opens to and is infused with the eternal.[36] In the act of reading, the world of the text and the fictive experience of time at stake in it intersect with the world of the reader and his or her temporalizing of time. Self-critical appropriation of a mode of timing inscribed in the text can be both revelatory and transforming: a matter of refiguring the self in the temporal meaning of its being. Narrative refiguring of the self results in what Ricoeur calls a "narrative identity," or "that sort of identity to which a human being has access thanks to the mediation of the narrative function."[37]

BIBLICAL THINKING

In this final section, I want to assemble the pieces from the analyses of philosophical and narrative thinking in order to interpret what Ricoeur means by biblical thinking. In my account I will necessarily go well beyond what Ricoeur himself explicitly says about biblical thinking to render an interpretation that is entirely consistent with statements Ricoeur does make about biblical thinking, with his actual exegetical practices, and with his philosophical program as a whole. It is necessary to go beyond Ricoeur by means of Ricoeur because of his reluctance to engage at all in theological thinking. If, however, thinking about biblical thinking is in the nature of the case a form of theological thinking, which I believe it is, then theological thinking is unavoidable, even for Ricoeur.

Let me begin by characterizing biblical thinking in relation to both philosophical thinking and the semantic autonomy of texts—especially in relation to the narrative function of texts.

Biblical thinking, for Ricoeur, is responsive thinking; it is thinking that responds to the Word of God in texts. By this statement I mean to say that biblical thinking begins with biblical texts in their semantic autonomy. For Ricoeur, these biblical texts represent the concrete existence, the linguistic embodiment of the idea of God. In other words, "the God-referent" of biblical texts appears (exists) in and through the texts themselves such that the "I" can respond to the God-referent of biblical texts precisely in the concrete act of understanding and interpreting the texts themselves. The God of biblical texts is there in the texts themselves, precisely in their textuality. The "I" who listens to or reads these texts can respond to the God-referent of biblical texts by interpreting them properly. To interpret the biblical texts properly means to approach them as texts by means of the hermeneutics that Ricoeur so painstakingly spells out in his entire philosophical corpus. If one approaches these texts properly, the "I" of biblical reading or listening can recognize the divine agency present in these texts and can learn to respond to that agency. To respond to divine agency linguistically embodied in biblical texts means to rethink (German *nachdenken*) on one's own and for oneself, together with one's community within its historical trajectory, what it means to be human before God. It does so by rethinking the testimonies of biblical authors as expressed in biblical texts and comprehending what is expressed in them. What is more, this rethinking of biblical testimony can transform the theoretical, practical, and affective dimensions of human being in the image of God. In summary, biblical thinking is a responsive thinking that is made possible by the existence of God in biblical texts and that empowers the transformation of human being. Such is Ricoeur's conviction. I will elucidate this statement in three steps.

The Idea of God

If, for Ricoeur, biblical texts in their semantic autonomy constitute the linguistic embodiment (the existence) of the idea of God, the first question to answer is, How should one think the idea of "God"? Let me propose an answer. We recall from Ricoeur's *Fallible Man* that human being is a structural unity composed of the following elements: (1) a principle of universal subjectivity (the "I" as source of intellectual functions of conceptual determination), (2) a principle of particular personality ("this one here" as source of sensible functions of perceptual receptivity), and (3) a principle of individualized subjectivity (the individualized unity in difference of the universal "I" and particular person). Although Ricoeur does not like to talk about the being of God, refusing as he does to do philosophical theology, nonetheless it is entirely consistent to say for Ricoeur that divine being can analogously be construed as a structural unity composed of three elements:

1. A principle of *universal essence* (the abstract idea of "God" as absolute *arche* and *telos* of all thinking and being).
2. A principle of *particular embodiment* or existence (the biblical text in both its particular textuality and its historical reception within a community of interpreters).
3. A principle of *absolute individuality* (the living unity in difference of essence and existence—the abstract idea of "God" concretely embodied in the biblical text).

I understand that Ricoeur himself would reject my proposal to think the idea of God as absolute individuality that is both subject and object for itself. Nonetheless, I contend that Ricoeur himself provides the warrant for this theological idea in his philosophical anthropology. Only this idea of God can account for the infinity and eternity of God along with the concrete appearance of God. If so, then the next question to ask is: How is it possible to think the concrete appearance of God in the biblical texts?

The Idea of God Embodied in Biblical Texts

My claim is that Ricoeur enables us to think the linguistic embodiment of God in a text by analogy to the embodiment of universal finite subjectivity in a human body. The warrant for so thinking is that, according to Ricoeur's notion of semantic autonomy, a text has both an intention (meaning) that exceeds authorial intention in principle and an integral structure that remains the same over time. For example, a narrative text, has the minimal temporal structure of a beginning, middle, and end. The structure is the organizing principle of all concrete details within the text. For example, in a narrative text, every episode contributes to the plot. The combination of intention and structure within the materiality of the text makes a text an analogue to a human being. In reading a text, we can have a dialogue with another voice than our own. In this vein, we recall that, thanks to their semantic autonomy, texts can manifest a subjectivity quite separate from that of their authors and thereby assume a voice of their own. Moreover, through their semantic autonomy texts can project a world of possible being for the reader or listener to enter, understand, and possibly to appropriate as his or her own. The intention of the text, its subjectivity, and the world it projects are available only through the text itself precisely in its textuality (its coherent unity of parts and whole). The text in this sense is the linguistic embodiment, hence the voice, of its *human* intention. Is it possible to think analogously of biblical texts as the linguistic embodiment of a *divine* intention?

To answer this question, I want to call to mind distinctions that Ricoeur makes among kinds of texts. *Descriptive texts* use the conceptual syntheses of ordinary and literal discourse to project images of an actual world of sense perception. Descriptive texts refer to real persons, places, and things within the actual world. They engage the capacity of the self as reader to reflect the real world, its structure and contents. *Literary or poetic texts* overturn the reference of descriptive texts to an actual world and manifest in its place a possible world as a redescription of the actual world. They do so through the metaphorical process at the level of text: the "is not" of the literal meaning evokes an "is like" of figurative meaning, which projects a network of meaningful connections—a "world of the text"—as horizon for a possible "mode of being." In other words, through the metaphorical process the poetic text is a model for the imagination that has the capacity to redescribe reality in the mode of possibility through semantic innovation. Narrative texts are forms of literary-poetic texts, and they can manifest the metaphorical process whereby they activate the imaginative capacity of their readers to understand their lives differently. What about biblical or religious texts?[38]

Biblical texts are poetic texts with a difference. Ricoeur writes, "It is the naming of God by the biblical texts that specifies the religious at the interior of the poetic."[39] Ricoeur devotes considerable time analyzing the different subgenres of biblical language. The Hebrew Bible contains subgenres of narrative, law, hymn, and wisdom. The New Testament contains subgenres of narrative, proclamations, parables, and proverbial formulas. Whereas narrative is the dominant subgenre, the mixture of subgenres enables them to work together in concert to refer beyond the horizon circumscribed by any one of the subgenres to the open horizon that embraces them all. "The God-referent is at once the coordinator of these varied discourses and the index of their incompleteness, the point at which something escapes them."[40] As a result, whereas poetic texts intend new modes of being, these religious texts intend the infinite source and goal of any possible mode of being because they possess a reference to God within them.

Certain features of the narrative structure additionally fortify this reference to God at the heart of the ensemble of biblical texts. Biblical narrative spans the totality of time prior to human recollection and beyond human anticipation. The grand narrative runs from creation to final judgment and thus provides the cosmic temporal framework within which the imagination can stretch to the limits of thinking as *arche* and *telos*. In *Time and Narrative*, Ricoeur recalls Augustine's experience of time as illustrated in the memorization of a psalm. The self in its present attention distends itself (*distentio animi*) between memory and expectation. At the beginning of a recitation, the self distends itself forward over the entire psalm in anticipation. As the recitation proceeds, the self distends itself backward in memory over the portion that has been recited and forward over the part yet to be recited. At the completion of the psalm, everything has passed into memory. The point is we experience past and future as distentions of the present so that time past and time anticipated are both modifications of present time. The soul's capacity to distend itself in this way makes it possible to experience time as a flowing reality that moves from a beginning toward a conclusion.[41] Now, in Augustine's thinking, God's mind is to the whole of the grand narrative of history what the human mind is to the whole of the recited psalm. The totality of historical time is only possible with reference to the mind of God. Insofar as the Bible in its narrative structure begins with accounts of creation and anticipates final judgment, the Bible refers its readers beyond the finite timing of the "I" and finite time of the "world" to the eternal timing of the divine mind.

Another feature of biblical narrative points to the idea of God (beyond the ideas of the self or world) as its source as reference. It is that biblical narrative combines both historical and fictional dimensions of narrativity. In its historical dimension, the Bible uses calendar time (e.g., "forty years") and iterations of the sequence of generations to make the biblical texts themselves a document or trace of the past. The Bible functions as a documentary monument to historical events that once happened and are now only remembered. The Bible itself constitutes a trace or vestige of times past. In this sense, the Bible contains a powerful reference to the "world" in its historical reality. But the fictional dimension of biblical narrative overturns the worldly reference in favor of the central God reference. The presence of literary-poetic elements alongside historical elements in biblical narrative opens the worldly reference to the kingdom of the possible. The name God—rather than the world or the "I"—dominates the biblical texts. God—rather than the world or the "I"—speaks through the Bible. The Bible for Ricoeur is the Word of God precisely in its textuality.

Thoughtful Responding to the Idea of God in Biblical Texts

The next question is: How can reading biblical texts transform human thinking and being? Again, I maintain that Ricoeur's philosophy makes it possible for us to comprehend how biblical texts have intentionality of their own. This intentionality is a "qualitative transformation of reflexive consciousness."[42] According to Ricoeur, the reference to God at the center of biblical texts can invert the normal interpretative relationship in reading. Instead of interpreting the mode of being projected in the world of the text, the reader finds his or her interpretative imagination at once expanded and overturned. The God-referent interprets the reader's existence and is revelatory of it.[43] How do biblical texts perform this inversion? Let me consider first the possibilities of fundamental transformation that are ingredients in the metaphorical process.

Ricoeur's theory of metaphor focuses on the mediating function of imagination beyond the threshold of the productive capacities of cognitive understanding. But what is most germane for my purpose is the extension of the metaphorical mediation to the level of attunement and feeling.[44] This extension bears directly on the religious possibility of a change of heart through hearing or reading the word. Let me explain.

Feeling is for Ricoeur integral to the act of schematizing the metaphoric meaning. When the imagination forms an image of the new figural congruence from a literal incongruence, the emergent meaning is not only visualized but is also *felt*. The hearer or reader is thereby assimilated to the meaning precisely as she or he performs the predicative assimilation. Ricoeur says, "We feel like what we see like" in metaphor, which in part means that the icon structures a mood.[45] What is more, feeling plays an important role in the imaginative projection of a new mode of being within the metaphorically formed world of the text. Just as the imagination suspends the first-order referential world when reading poetic texts, so imagination reverberates on feeling in order to affect an *epoche* of bodily emotions directed to literal objects. With the clearance of first-order feelings, a deeper attunement to being as such can come to the fore. The poetic experience thereby can "insert us within the world in a nonobjectifying fashion."[46] In the act of appropriating the specifically metaphorical level of meaning—in which the "I" claims the emergent meaning as its own and is restructured affectively accordingly—the real possibility for a positive change of heart appears. Let's see how this possibility plays out at the level of religious texts.

According to Ricoeur, biblical texts religiously modify poetic texts by the presence of "limit-expressions." Limit-expressions function to transgress or overturn the normal course of metaphorical process and to intensify its effect so that forms of poetic language "converge upon an extreme point, which becomes their point of encounter with the infinite."[47] In his analyses of various New Testament texts, Ricoeur shows how the expression "Kingdom of God" functions as a limit expression together with tropes of extravagance in the parables, techniques of overturning in the eschatological sayings, and instances of paradox in and hyperbole in proverbial formulae. Through the use of limit expressions, the interpretive intention *breaks out* of the closure of the narrative and the God referent *breaks into* the act of interpretation. Let's focus more closely on the New Testament, which Ricoeur repeatedly cites as a paradigmatic religious text.

In the New Testament, Jesus as Christ is the teller of the parables, sayings, and formulas, which open up the God-reference in these texts. Jesus as Christ is also, however, the hero and hence subject of the inclusive New Testament passion narrative in which the parables, sayings, and formulas appear. Consequently, these texts individually and collectively refer the reader or hearer precisely to the new being of Jesus as Christ as revelatory of the being of God. The name "Christ" humanizes the infinitely self-negating Name of God; the name "Christ" signifies the advent of a Wholly Other God from beyond the limits of human thinking. At the same time that the "Christ" of the gospels manifests what it means for God to be God, "Christ" reveals the transformed human being of the individual and collective readers or hearers. The name "Christ" discloses what it finally means to be human in unity with God. What is the content of this disclosure?

Ricoeur tells us that within the community of biblical readers, limit-expressions point to and actualize *limit-experiences*. Within the Christian context, these limit-experiences are encounters with the Christ figure of the Gospels.[48] Ricoeur himself does not say much more than that to determine what he means by the term "limit-experience." However, I should like to propose an interpretation of what Ricoeur must mean by this term based on his dialectical thinking from *Fallible Man* and elsewhere. In strict conceptual terms, limit experiences are impossible experiences; they cannot be conceived because they arise outside the limits of thought. But, religiously speaking, limit-experiences are necessary experiences; they give actual content and power to the meanings of biblical texts. At this point I propose to ask: Where and how does the reading of biblical texts take on power? The answer lies at the limits of thinking.

Recall the distinction between vertical and horizontal limits in Ricoeur's analysis of thinking. Vertically, Ricoeur establishes both a lower limit and an upper limit of thinking. The lower limit is the original ground or source of unity prior to difference; it signifies the *goodness of creation* prior to the separation of being and thinking. The upper limit is the final end of fully determinate unity; it signifies *the highest good* for moral striving—the restored unity between willing according to the moral law and justly deserved happiness. A limit-experience would therefore be the experience of a moral conversion, a change of heart that would heal the split will and make possible the willing of the highest good. For the sake of discussion, call this mode of being with Ricoeur "fallibility without fault" or the mode of timing all one's activities through the good will of moral regeneration or the mode of being of "openness to the good." Biblical texts take on power when the reader is empowered in the core of his or her motivations both to recognize the goodness of being and to strive toward the highest good.

Ricoeur's analysis of horizontal limits of thinking can also provide content to the notion of limit-experiences. Recall the horizontal limits Ricoeur establishes in his analysis of theoretical, practical, and affective syntheses. Theoretically, the limits are saying and seeing (thinking and perceiving); practically, they are character and happiness (or who I am and who I should be); and affectively, they are spiritual feelings and sensible feelings (or intellectual beatitude and bodily pleasure). A limit-experience would therefore be an experience that transcends the conflict between these disproportionate terms without effacing the differences between them. In the domain of theoretical experience, the limit-experience would be an intuition of perfect correspondence between perceiving and thinking—that is, an experience of *truth itself* as presupposed in all thinking that intends to become knowing. In the moral striving characteristic of practical experience, the limit-experience would be a perfect unity of character and happiness. A limit-experience in the practical domain therefore would overcome the conflict between my actual circumstances in life and the ones I would choose for myself. It would be an experience of *justice* as presupposed in all moral judgments. In affective experience, the limit-experience would be the perfect unity between feelings of bodily pleasure and feelings of spiritual beatitude. A limit-experience in the affective domain would overcome the tear or conflict between bodily and spiritual feelings. It would be an experience of *meaningfulness* presupposed in life itself. This dialectical thought experiment allows us to imagine the qualities of limit-experiences.

All of these imagined limit-experiences, I would argue, are descriptions of eternity in time that do not negate human temporality. In other words, all of them share the quality of revealing the perfection of being that underlies even the defects of fallible and fallen being in time. Specifically, I mean by that statement that limit-experiences reveal the depth in eternity of human being as being in time. That feature is clearly spelled out by Heidegger in *Being and Time*, and Ricoeur refers to it frequently: *Dasein*'s being is Care (*Sorge*), and the temporal meaning of Care is being toward death (*Sein zum Tode*). For *Dasein*, being in time authentically is to anticipate the end, the completion of one's life, and the completion of human life is death. Such is the highpoint of philosophical thinking about being in time.

By contrast, however, biblical thinking about being in time responds to a limit-experience of eternity in time—an experience arising from beyond time and beyond death. It would be an experience of eternity breaking into time without negating time. It would be an experience of human life freed from the being toward death, because such a graced life would be timed in eternity. It would be an experience of human life free of the burden of care, for it would be grounded not in the anxiety of life in time but in the joy of life in eternity. Its fundamental mood would not be anxiety, but rather joy.

What kind of transformation is it to be affected by limit-experiences while reading the Bible? Clearly, the encounter with God as linguistically embodied in biblical texts cannot and does not alter the fundamental structure of fallible man. Nor can it overturn or undo the fact of human fallenness. Humans who respond properly to the Word of God in biblical texts do not thereby shed their humanness. Far from it. On the contrary, biblical thinking as a responding to God's presence in biblical texts transforms human being by enabling human thinking to accept its humanity and say "Yes" to its fallibility and even fallenness as gifts from God. For responsive biblical thinking, divine being is not elsewhere in some metaphysical domain; it is here now as a present Word speaking to humans in the midst of our suffering and wrongdoing. The identity of human thinking remains that of critique, with all of its exposure to negativity and lack of knowledge. But biblical thinking as responsive thinking affirms critique from the standpoint of a lived conviction that fragile mediations occur on the basis of and by the power of God's absolute mediation, which is truth, justice, and joy.

Placed in terms of New Testament discourse, biblical thinking is testimony: a testimony to God's act in Christ. Testimony divides into both the historically narrated testimony of actual biblical texts and the present act of testifying by the reader of biblical texts in response to narrated testimony. Biblical testimony is testimony from a transformed sense of time. Biblical testimony recalls the past as the trace of God's living presence; it anticipates the future in hope of God's advent; it accepts time in the present as donated by God in grace. It is the lived attestation, that despite fallibility and fault, ultimate reality is truly figured in the biblical symbols of faith, hope, and love.

In conclusion, I want to say a few words about the relationship between philosophical thinking and biblical thinking in Ricoeur. Ricoeur, the philosopher, does not place biblical thinking in relation to philosophical thinking according to the formula of relating answers to questions, along the lines of Paul Tillich's method of correlation. Biblical thinking does not provide symbolic answers to existential questions. Such a method would run contrary to Ricoeur's decision to forswear theology. It would make philosophy into a prolegomenon to theology. Nor does biblical thinking overturn or contradict philosophical thinking by providing trustworthy revelation of divine truths that exceed the human capacity to think and must be accepted as self-interpreting, along the lines of Karl Barth's theology. Such a method implicitly denies the very nature of thinking as mediating. For Ricoeur, all meanings, including meanings in biblical texts, are mediated by human thinking. Ricoeur's approach is distinctive and unique. For Ricoeur, biblical thinking as responsive thinking reflects human philosophical and narrative thinking as touched by and grounded in divine eternity. Biblical thinking does not thereby escape the fallibility and fallenness of philosophical thinking. Biblical thinking does disclose—for those with eyes to see and ears to hear—that fallible and fallen human thinking is always and already the image of God.

NOTES

1. Paul Ricoeur, from his oral response to a set of papers delivered at a conference on Paul Ricoeur and Contemporary Moral Thought entitled "Ethics and Meaning in Public Life," at the Divinity School, the University of Chicago, October 21–22, 1999.
2. *Freud and Philosophy: An Essay on Interpretation*, trans. Denis Savage (New Haven and London: Yale University Press, 1970), p. 43.
3. See the important pages in "The Hermeneutics of Symbols: II," in *The Conflict of Interpretations: Essays in Hermeneutics*, ed. by Don Ihde (Evanston: Northwestern University Press, 1974), pp. 326–330. Henceforth I refer to this work as CI. The quoted term "forgetfulness" is on p. 328.
4. Charles E. Reagan, *Paul Ricoeur: His Life and His Work* (Chicago and London: University of Chicago Press, 1996), pp. 4, 125.
5. Reagan, *Paul Ricoeur*, p. 120.
6. André LaCocque and Paul Ricoeur, *Thinking Biblically: Exegetical and Hermeneutical Studies*, trans. David Pellauer (Chicago and London: University of Chicago Press, 1998), p. xv.
7. Reagan, *Paul Ricoeur*, p. 121.
8. Paul Ricoeur, *Interpretation Theory* (Fort Worth: Texas Christian University Press, 1977), p. 3.
9. *Interpretation Theory*, p. 12.
10. *Interpretation Theory*, pp. 25–26.
11. Ricoeur, Qu'est-ce qu'un Texte? Expliquer et Comprendre," in *Hermeneutik und Dialektik: Aufsätze II*, ed. Rudiger Bubner, Konrad Cramer, and Reiner Wiehl (Tübingen: J. C. B. Mohr, 1970), pp. 184–85.
12. *Thinking Biblically*, p. xii.
13. *Thinking Biblically*, p. xiii. See also p. xvi: "It is in interpreting the Scriptures in question that the community in question interprets itself. A kind of mutual election takes place here between those texts taken as foundational and the community we have deliberately called a community of reading and interpretation."
14. *Thinking Biblically*, p. xvi.
15. Paul Ricoeur, *Critique and Conviction: Conversations with Francois Azouvi and Marc de Launay*, trans. Kathleen Blamey (New York: Columbia University Press, 1998), p. 144.
16. *Fallible Man: Philosophy of the Will* (volume II, part 2), trans. Charles Kelbley (Chicago: Henry Regnery, 1965). Henceforth I refer to this work as FM.
17. FM, pp. 26–71.

18. FM, pp. 72–121.
19. FM, p. 129.
20. FM. p. 207.
21. FM, pp. 122–202.
22. FM, p. 6.
23. See, for example, "A Philosophical Interpretation of Freud" in CI, pp. 173–76.
24. FM, p. 223.
25. SE, p. 8.
26. SE, p. 9.
27. FM, p. xxiii
28. In *Oneself as Another*, Books 7–9, Ricoeur develops an "ethics" out of the ethical vision of the world. He claims that the ethical intention is "aiming at the 'good life' with and for others, in just institutions." See Paul Ricoeur, *Oneself as Another*, trans. Kathleen Blamey (Chicago and London: University of Chicago Press, 1992), p. 172.
29. FM, p. 221.
30. For Ricoeur's discussion of Kant on time as pure form of intuition, see Paul Ricoeur, *Time and Narrative*, volume III (Chicago and London: University of Chicago Press, 1988), pp. 44–59.
31. Paul Ricoeur, *Time and Narrative*, volume 1, trans. Kathleen McLaughlin (Chicago and London: University of Chicago Press, 1992), p. 3.
32. See Ricoeur's discussion of the threefold mimesis in *Time and Narrative*, volume 1, pp. 52–87.
33. *Time and Narrative*, volume 3, pp. 100, 61.
34. *Time and Narrative*, volume 3, p. 68.
35. *Time and Narrative*, pp. 80–81.
36. Paul Ricoeur, "Narrated Time," in *On Narrative*, ed. W. J. T. Mitchell (Chicago: University of Chicago Press, 1981),
37. Paul Ricoeur, "Narrative Identity," in *On Paul Ricoeur: Narrative and Interpretation*, ed. David Wood (London: Routledge, 1991).
38. Ricoeur does not draw a distinction between religious and biblical texts. For him religious texts are biblical texts.
39. "Naming God," *Union Seminary Quarterly Review* 34/4 (1979): 219
40. "Philosophy and Religious Language," *Journal of Religion* 54 (1974): 83.
41. *Time and Narrative*, volume 1, pp. 16–32.
42. *Symbolism of Evil*, p. 356.
43. "Philosophische und theologische Hermeneutik," *Evangelische Theologie* (Munich: Sonderheft, 1974), p. 40.
44. "The Metaphorical Process as Cognition, Imagination, and Feeling," *Critical Theory* 5/1 (1978).
45. Ibid., p. 156.
46. Ibid., p. 157.
47. Paul Ricoeur, *Essays on Biblical Hermeneutics*, edited with an introduction by Lewis S. Mudge (Philadelphia: Fortress Press, 1980), p. 109.
48. Paul Ricoeur, *Figuring the Sacred: Religion, Narrative, and Imagination*, trans. David Pellauer (Minneapolis: Fortress Press, 1995), pp. 61–81, 95, 234.

On the Hermeneutics of Evil 4

Richard Kearney

SYMBOLS OF EVIL

The publication of *The Symbolism of Evil* marked Ricoeur's transition from a phenomenology of will to a hermeneutics of symbol. It signaled a departure from descriptive phenomenology, as a reflection on intentional modes of consciousness, in favor of the hermeneutic conviction that meaning is never simply the intuitive possession of a subject but is always mediated through signs and symbols of intersubjective existence. When confronted with evil, we are reminded that there are meanings and experiences that defy the transparency of consciousness and contravene our will. The refractory character of evil, as something endured or suffered, prompts a philosophy of reflection to think again about the perennial problems of human fallibility, fault, and finitude that by their very nature challenge the transparency of a purely immanent volition. Consequently the attempt to grasp the complexity of evil involves, at the outset, an interpretation of the myths and symbols of culture that mediate the experiences of evil, boundary experiences that cannot be immediately grasped by the rational faculties of the mind.

Ricoeur's main aim in *The Symbolism of Evil* is to show how we can move from the category of *fallibility* to that of *fallenness*. How do we move from (a) the possibility of evil to (b) the actualization and avowal of evil. Common to both is the ontological condition of the human being as *fault*—in the double sense of a fault line or fracture within the self that in turn allows for the reality of disproportion and dislocation in our moral acts, usually expressed in the soul being at variance with the passions. But this noncoincidence between self and self does not mean that we are *intrinsically* evil; only that this potential exists within each one of us—and, as such, may be activated or not according to our free choice. One of the central arguments running through Ricoeur's first hermeneutic work—the second part of the second volume of Ricoeur's

Philosophy of Will (the first part was entitled *Fallible Man*)—is that the Adamic and biblical notions of evil represent a significant moral progress relative to previous cosmological and tragic accounts of evil as an external and ineluctable force in the universe. Against such deterministic accounts, Ricoeur is determined to show how the emerging *anthropological* account of sin and guilt places the responsibility for evil more and more squarely on the shoulders of human agency. Where archaic notions of "defilement" saw evil as a contaminating force added to the soul from outside, the more ethical notion of "guilt" attributes evil to our own misuse of freedom. In short, where defilement sees evil as originating in an Other, guilt recognizes it as originating in the self. The guilty self is one that recognizes its own "servile will." Instead of blaming or scapegoating others, it takes responsibility for itself as a "bad choice that binds itself."[1] Moral conscience thus emerges as the internalizing of punishment and the acknowledging of wrong as one's own fault.

In *The Symbolism of Evil*, Ricoeur engages in a rigorous interpretation of the seminal myths of evil in Western culture. These include (1) the myth of cosmic creation; (2) the myth of tragic blindness; (3) the myth of the Fall; and (4) the myth of the exiled soul. The heroes who dramatize these mythic narratives include Prometheus, Oedipus, Adam, and Orpheus. Adam represents for Ricoeur the most explicitly anthropological account in that it separates evil from good unlike the stories of Prometheus (where the external divine figure of Zeus bears most responsibility for his misfortune) or Oedipus (where the monstrous sphinx and other agencies of cosmic destiny dictate his suffering and wrongdoing, e.g., parricide and incest). With the myth of Adam, we read of someone who brings evil into the world by his own decisions and actions. But while Ricoeur clearly privileges the Adamic myth, he does not dismiss the potential truth-content of the other narratives. On the contrary, he suggests that a comparative cross-interpretation between the various myths reveals more and more of each one in a way that would not be possible if we took them purely in isolation.

Suspending the conventional definition of myth as a "false *explanation* by means of fables," Ricoeur attempts to recover myth's genuinely *exploratory* function. Once we accept that myth cannot provide us with a scientific account of the actual origin of evil, we can begin properly to appreciate its disclosing role as a *symbolizing* power. Ricoeur defines a symbol as a double intentionality, wherein one meaning is transgressed or transcended by another. As such, symbols of evil are works of language (signification) that provoke thought (interpretation). If we want to think evil, we must therefore begin with mythico-symbolic expressions such as the *stain*, the *fall, missing the mark, being imprisoned* or *wandering from the path*, all of which tell us something about the experience of the human being in the grips of evil.

Symbols of evil (like all symbols) have a literal meaning and a secondary analogical meaning. Thus, to take Ricoeur's famous example from *Symbolism of Evil*, the primitive image of somebody being "defiled" refers both to its *literal* function as a sign of physical uncleanliness and to its *symbolic* allusion to man's impure or deviant relationship to the sacred. The literal meaning of a stain points beyond itself to the existential condition of contamination, which is *like* a stain. Clearly, we are not talking about an empirical stain on the soul, but rather a blighting of one's inner existence analogous to the act of staining something white. What cannot be said directly—because it exceeds the limits of rational cogitation—is thus said indirectly or obliquely. As Ricoeur puts it: "Contrary to the perfectly transparent technical signs, which say only what they want to say in positing that which they signify, symbolic signs are opaque, because the first, literal, obvious meaning itself points analogically to a second meaning which is not given otherwise than in it."[2] It is because there is no *direct* discourse for the confession of evil that symbolism becomes the privileged means of expression. In other words, the experience of evil is always conveyed by means of expressions (defilement, rebellion, straying from the road, bondage, and so on) borrowed from the field of everyday physical existence—expressions that refer *indirectly* to another kind of experience, namely, our experience of the sacred.

But the symbolization of evil does not condemn us to irrationalism. On the contrary, says Ricoeur, it calls us to deeper and more complex modes of interpretation. "The symbol," as he puts it, "gives rise to thought" (*le symbole donne à penser*). Ricoeur describes the basic rationale of *The Symbolism of Evil* as follows: "The servile condition of the evil will seemed to elude an essential analysis of phenomena. So the only practicable route was that of a detour via the symbols wherein the avowal of the fault was inscribed during the great cultures of which ours is the heir: the primary symbols of stain, guilt and sin; the secondary symbols of myths of tragic blindness, of the fall of the soul, of wandering or decline; the tertiary symbols and rationalizations of the servile will or of original sin. *The Symbolism of Evil* thus marked the turning of Husserlian phenomenology, already extended to the problematic of fallibility, towards a hermeneutics of symbols. "By 'symbols' I understood ... all expressions of double meaning, wherein a primary meaning refers beyond itself to a second meaning which is never given directly."[3]

What is original about Ricoeur's approach is his attempt to 're-enact in sympathetic imagination' the foundational myths whereby Western culture sought to communicate its first experiences of good and evil. Myths are understood by Ricoeur as symbolic stories—or, to be more precise, as "species of symbols developed in the form of narration and articulated in a time and a space that cannot be coordinated with the time and space of history and geography."[4] This hermeneutic act of revisiting the cosmic narratives of evil demands that Ricoeur abandon Husserl's phenomenological dream of a "philosophy without presuppositions." Indeed, it presupposes that which descriptive phenomenology often tended to ignore—*language*. The hermeneutics of symbols must begin from a full language, insists Ricoeur, from the recognition that before reflection and intuition *there are already symbols:* "It is by beginning with a symbolism already there," Ricoeur observes, "that we give ourselves something to think about."[5] The symbolism of evil is one of the most powerful, and disturbing, provocations to such thought.

FROM MYTH TO RESPONSIBILITY

In his 1985 essay, "Evil, a Challenge to Philosophy and Theology," Ricoeur returns to several of the issues raised in *The Symbolism of Evil* and offers a more developed hermeneutic critique of the different discursive responses to evil: these include, along with myth—lament and blame, wisdom, and theodicy.[6]

The first discursive response—*lament* and *blame* (witnessed in the Hebrew Bible, for example)—differentiates between evil as suffering and evil as wrongdoing. Lament refers to an evil that befalls us from outside. By contrast, blame refers to evil that arises from within us and for which we are responsible. Or, to put it another way, if lament sees us as victims, blame makes culprits of us.[7] Ricoeur observes that, in fact, these two categories are almost always intertwined. We can feel guilty for committing an evil act while simultaneously experiencing seduction, or invasion, by an overwhelming force outside of us. But for the moment, we'll let the distinction stand.

The next discursive genre—*myth*—allows for the incorporation of evil into "great narratives of origin" (Mircea Eliade). These genealogical narratives, as Ricoeur had already argued in *The Symbolism of Evil,* seek to explain the origin of evil in terms of the genesis of the cosmos (cosmogony). They offer a "plot" that configures the monstrosity of evil, explaining the source of the obscene and thereby taking some of the shock out of it. Such mythic spectacles make the foreign curiously familiar, the unbearable bearable, the outrageous accessible.[8] In mythological legends, considerations of human moral choice are inextricably linked to cosmological cycles of fate, destiny, or predestination. The evil figure is the alienated figure, that is, a self determined by some force beyond itself.

Myth then proceeds toward *wisdom*—Ricoeur's next discursive category—to the extent that we not only recount the origins of evil but also seek to justify why such is the case for each one of us. In short, while myth narrates, wisdom argues.[9] It seeks to address the question not only of *why* but *why me?* The wisdom genre turns lament into a legal complaint. It tries to make moral sense of the monstrous. An exemplary case here is the Book of Job, where God and man engage in dialogue about the nature of creation and covenant. With such wisdom literature, the enigma of evil becomes less a matter of metaphysical giveness than of interpersonal relations (human–human or human–divine). In the conclusion to Job, arguments about retribution and justice are ultimately turned to a contemplative wisdom of love: Job learns to love Yahweh "for naught" in defiance of Satan's wager at the outset of the story.

Wisdom discourse gives way, in turn, to the fourth discursive account of evil listed in Ricoeur's critical genealogy, namely, the *speculative*. This discourse begins, Ricoeur argues, with the development of Christian theology. Augustine is the first great advocate of this position in his answer to the gnostics. In order to show that evil is not a substance implanted in the universe but a punishment (*poena*) for human sin (*peccatum*), Augustine invents a new category, "nothingness" (*nihil*). Evil is now construed as a deficiency in being that amounts to a privation of goodness (*privatio boni*). If there is evil in the world, therefore, it can only be the result of human action—that is, an act of turning away from the benign being of God toward a lack of being. Augustine thus proposes a radically moral vision of evil which replaces the genealogical question, *Unde malum?*, with the question of willful human wrongdoing, *Unde malum faciamus?* The cause of evil is not to be found in cosmology but in some form of willed action—the sins of the "bad will." This leads in turn, of course, to a penal view of history in which no one, in principle, should suffer unjustly. Everyone gets his or her reward, and all pain is a recompense for sin.

The difficulty for Augustine and subsequent theology was, as Ricoeur notes, how to reconcile this extreme hypothesis of moral evil with the need to give sin a "supra-individual" and historical-generic account in order to explain how suffering is not always justly apportioned as a retribution for individual sins. For in countless cases it is clearly excessive. In other words, if evil is something we as humans do, it is also *done to us*. It is, at least in part, something we inherit, something already there. Augustine thus sought to reinterpret the Genesis tale of original sin in order to rationalize this apparently irrational paradox: namely, we are responsible but not *entirely* responsible for the evil we commit or endure. Thus does Ricoeur attempt to respond to a paradox that remained unresolved in *The Symbolism of Evil*.

It was, Ricoeur observes, but a short step from these Augustinian speculations on original sin to the fully fledged theories of Western ontotheology. Here Ricoeur enters territory not covered in his earlier work. The thinking of Leibniz, for example, invokes the principle of Sufficient Reason to account for the judicious balancing of good with evil in the "best of all possible worlds." And if this balancing act of retribution and compensation is attributed to the infinite mind of God by Leibniz, it is dialectically humanized by Hegel and the German Idealists. Hegel's "cunning of reason" silences the scandal of suffering by subsuming the tragic into a triumphant logic where all that is real is rational. Here the hubris of systematic speculation reaches its untenable extreme: "The more the system flourishes, the more its victims are marginalized. The success of the system is its failure. Suffering, as what is expressed by the voices of lamentation, is what the system excludes."[10]

But Ricoeur is of the view that neither version of theodicy—Leibnizian or Hegelian—can provide a convincing answer to the protest of unjust suffering: *Why me?* This protest rightly and righteously continues to echo through the testimonies of evil from Job and Gethsemene to Hiroshima and Auschwitz. Nor can theodicy resist the debunking of "rational theology" in part three of Kant's *Critique of Pure Reason*. Indeed the greatness of Kant, for Ricoeur, was to recognize the need to pass from a purely "theoretical" explanation of evil to a more "practical" one. This move from speculative explanation to moral-political action liberates the insight that evil is something that *ought not to be* and needs to be struggled against. By de-alienating evil and making it a matter of contingency rather than necessity (cosmogonic, theological, metaphysical, or historical), Kant brought us face to face with the *responsibility of action.*

Ricoeur adds that if Kant freed us from the excess of rationalist speculation on evil, he also warned against the opposite extreme of drunken irrationalism (what he called *Schwarmerei*), the sort of mystical madness that submits to evil as an alien power that invades and overwhelms us at a whim. This latter view typifies not only belief in demonic possession but also the mystical profession of the "dark side of God" running from the Gnostics and Bruno to Boehme, Schelling, and Jung (e.g., *Answer to Job*). By taking the mystique out of evil, Kant removed some of its captivating power. He enabled us to see that evil is not a property of some external demon or deity, but a phenomenon deeply bound up with the anthropological condition. Evil thus ceases to be a matter of paranoid projection and sacrificial scapegoating and becomes instead an affair of human responsibility. Absolutist dualities are overcome. One's self becomes oneself-as-another and one's other becomes another-as-oneself. Ricoeur enthusiastically approves—at least thus far.

But even Kant, Ricoeur is compelled to admit, could not totally ignore the aporetic character of evil. For if Kant clearly called for a response within the limits of practical human reason, he could never completely deny some residual inscrutability (*Unerforschbarkeit*) of evil. At one point, Kant even states that there may be "no conceivable ground from which the moral evil in us could originally have come."[11] The lament of *Why? Why me? Why my beloved child?* remains as troublingly enigmatic as ever. Victims of evil cannot be silenced with either rational explanation (theodicy) or irrational submission (mysticism). Their stories cry out for other responses capable of addressing both the alterity and the humanity of evil.

So for all his endorsements of the anthropologizing of evil—in this 1985 essay as well as in *The Symbolism of Evil*—Ricoeur returns once again to the ultimately paradoxical character of evil. And, once again, he fully acknowledges here a radical ongoing challenge to both philosophical and theological reason. A challenge that, he suggests, can perhaps best be met by some form of hermeneutic understanding, attentive to the various aporias and enigmas that the expressions of evil expose. In the final part of this chapter, I will look at some ways in which Ricoeur's hermeneutics of narrative understanding might help us confront the problem of evil in history and memory.

NARRATING HISTORICAL EVIL

A key power of narrative, claims Ricoeur, is to "provide ourselves with a figure of something."[12] So doing, we can make present what is absent. Translated into the idiom of historical time, we are dealing here with the capacity to liberate ourselves from the blind amnesia of the "now" by projecting futures and retrieving pasts. Projection is an emancipatory function of narrative understanding, retrieval a testimonial function. Both resist the contemporary tendency to reduce history to a "depthless present" of "irreference."[13]

In the third volume of *Time and Narrative*, and again in *Memory, History, Forgetting,* Ricoeur analyzes the "testimonial" role of narrative when confronting historical trauma and evil. The whole problem of Holocaust testimony is central to this analysis. A hermeneutics of narrative, he maintains, must include a sense of ethical responsibility to "the debt we owe the dead."[14] We would not be able to respond to the summons of historical memory were it not for the mediating/schematizing function of narrative imagination, which provides us with "figures" for events that happened but are suppressed from memory. The responsibility here is twofold. On the one hand, narrative provides us with figural reconstructions of the past that enable us to see and hear things long since gone. On the other, it stands-in-for, by standing-for, these things as events that actually happened. Here we encounter the right of the past, as it once was, to incite and rectify our narrative retellings of history. We recall our debt to those who have lived and suffered evil. We remind ourselves, for example, that gas ovens and gulags did exist, that Nagasaki and Cambodia were bombed, that political crimes and injustices have been inflicted on innocent people over the centuries. These were not simulations. They actually happened.

The ostensible paradox here is, of course, that it should be narrative that responds to the ethical summons to respect the "reality of the past." It is ironic that it should be poetics that comes to the service of ethics as a means of recalling our debt to those who suffered and died (and are often forgotten). But this is the case. Narrative serves in this way to recall the neglected "others" of history, for, as Ricoeur remarks, "it is always through some transfer from Same to Other, in empathy and imagination, that the Other that is foreign is brought closer."[15]

This process of transfer, however, is by no means obvious. In addition to narrative reenactment—which reappropriates the past as present under the category of the Same—hermeneutic understanding has a duty to the otherness of the past by way of expressing the past precisely as past, that is, as something that is no more. We are dealing here with a dual fidelity to past suffering as sameness and difference. The hermeneutic act of *transfer by analogy* seeks to address this paradox. It enables us to transport ourselves into alien or eclipsed moments, refiguring them as similar to our present experience (failing which we would not be able to recognize them), while simultaneously acknowledging their dissimilarity as distinct and distant. In short, the narrative reappropriation of past experiences of evil operates according to a double responsibility: to the past as *present*, and to the past as *past*.

To the extent that it remains ethically responsible, the historical remembering of trauma refuses to allow reconstruction to become a reduction of the other to the self; it resists absorbing difference into sameness.[16] So when we talk of narrative providing us with "analogies" of the past as-it-actually-was, we do well to appreciate that the analogous "as" is a two-way trope of absence/presence. We should never underestimate the radically unique, heterogeneous and irreducible nature of the experience of those who suffered evil in the past. This alterity cannot be wished away by an act of facile imaginative "appropriation."

This point merits development. Narratives of the past comprise an interweaving of fiction and history. Once we recognize that historical narratives of evil entail a refiguring of past events, we can admit that the telling of history involves the deployment of certain literary practices—plot, composition, character, point of view, and so on. This is why the same text can be at once a great work of history and a great work of fiction. It can tell us about the way things actually happened in the past at the same time that it makes us see, feel, and live the past as if we were there. Moreover, this "fiction effect" of history can often enhance, rather than diminish, the task of standing-for. One thinks, for example, of holocaust testimonies by Elie Wiesel or Primo Levi, not to mention the countless more "novelistic" accounts by writers like Thomas Kenneally and Aharon Appelfeld. Otherwise put, narrative can serve historical experiences of evil, and this service entails ethical as well as poetical dimensions.

The deployment of novelistic techniques by historians and witnesses, as well as by fiction writers, to place some past event or personage vividly before the reader's mind was already recognized by Aristotle in the *Rhetoric*, under the title of lexis or "locution"—a way of making things visible *as if* they were present. The danger is, of course, that the figural "as if" might collapse into a literal belief, so that we would no longer merely "see-as" but make the mistake of believing we are *actually* seeing. This "hallucination of presence" (easily conducive to dogmatism and fundamentalism) calls, in Ricoeur's view, for ethical vigilance by historians in order to sustain a proper dialectical balance between empathy and distance.

But freedom from illusion is not the only ethical responsibility of narrative. Equally important is the responsibility to refigure certain events of deep ethical intensity that conventional historiography might be tempted to overlook in favor of a so-called objective explanation of things. In a case like the Holocaust, it would seem that such a practice of "neutralization" is quite inappropriate. The biblical watchword *Zakhor*, "Remember!" is more ethically fitting in such circumstances. This is something Primo Levi, a firsthand witness and survivor of the camps, makes hauntingly evident in his resolve to tell the story as it happened in the most vivid fashion imaginable. The recourse to narrative tropes and devices to achieve this impact is motivated throughout by an ethical imperative: People must never be allowed to forget this evil lest it happen again. Or as Levi himself put it in his conclusion to *Si c'est un homme*: "The need to recount to 'others,' to make the 'others' participate, acquired in us before and after our liberation the vehemence of an immediate impulse . . . and it was in response to such a need that I wrote my book."[17]

In such cases, "rememoration" of evil takes on an ethical character quite distinct from the triumphalist commemoration of history's great and powerful. Where the latter tends to legitimate ideologies of conquest, the former moves in the opposite direction, namely, toward a felt reliving of past suffering as if we (readers/listeners/spectators) had actually been there. The distinction is important for Ricoeur. The cause of the *tremendum horrendum* needs narrative to plead its case lest it slip irrevocably into oblivion. The horrible must *strike* us as horrible. "Horror attaches to events that must never be forgotten," writes Ricoeur. "It constitutes the ultimate ethical motivation for the history of victims. The victims of Auschwitz are, par excellence, the representatives in our memory of all history's, victims. Victimization is the other side of history that no cunning of reason can ever justify and that, instead, reveals the scandal of every theodicy of history."[18]

In such instances, the refigurative powers of narrative prevent historians from neutralizing injustice. It prevents historiography from explaining history away. And this ethical task of preserving the specificity of past suffering from sanitizing homogenization applies not only to positivist historians but also to the abstract speculations of certain philosophers. Ricoeur is perhaps thinking here of Hegel's Ruse of Reason or Heidegger's musings on the Destiny of *techne* (which put gas chambers and combine-harvesters into the same category).[19]

The ethical role of narrative understanding in remembering the horrible is tied to a specific function of individuation: namely, the need to respect the uniquely unique character of certain historical events. Dachau, Hiroshima, the Gulag, the Armenian massacre, Mai Lai, Bloody Sunday, the Killing Fields of Cambodia, Sabra and Chatilla, Tiananmen Square. Such historical horrors of our century cannot be explained away as cogs in some dialectical wheel. They are more than epiphenomena of the *Zeitgeist*. Yet it is just this tendency to relativize evil that our current culture of simulation evinces when it reduces narrative to a play of imitation devoid of historical reference. Frederic Jameson decries this tendency to eclipse the historically unique as a "postmodern cult of the depthless present."[20] But other commentators, Jean Baudrillard and Jean-Francois Lyotard among them, seem at times to celebrate this liquidation of reference. Lyotard claims that narrative forms of imagination betray the "irrepresentable" nature of the postmodern sublime, while Baudrillard hails the postmodern condition of "irreference" where even the reality of war is reduced to television games of spectacle and simulation.[21] We can no longer distinguish, some postmodernists hold, between what is real and unreal in the representation of things. And one is tempted to conclude that it is a short step from Baudrillard's kind of thinking here to the claims of revisionist historians like Faurisson or David Irving that the gas chambers never existed (or Nolte's claim that the Holocaust is not a unique event of evil, but merely one of a variety of similar events). In any case, what the postmodern cult of "irrepresentability" and "irreference" appears to put in question is the power of narrative to retrieve historically real events for our ethical consideration in the here and now.

Against such a position, Ricoeur replies: The more narrative singularizes historical experiences of evil, the more we strive to understand them (rather than simply suffer them as emotional trauma). It is not then a question of opposing "subjective" narration to "objective" understanding. It is a question of appreciating that the comprehension of evil without narration risks becoming inhuman, just as the narration of evil without hope of some possibility of understanding runs the risk of blind irrationalism. The refigurative act of standing-for the past provides us with a "figure" to experience *and* think about, to both feel *and* reflect upon. "Fiction gives eyes to the horrified narrator," as Ricoeur puts it, "Eyes to see and to weep. The present state of literature on the Holocaust provides ample proof of this ... one counts the cadavers or one *tells the story* of the victims."[22] If history-telling, therefore, forfeits this testimonial vocation, it risks becoming a spectacle of exotica or else a repository of dead fact. Neither option is acceptable. "There are crimes that must not be forgotten, victims whose suffering cries less for vengeance than for narration," Ricoeur protests. "The will not to forget alone can prevent these crimes from ever occurring again."[23]

This ethical task of testimony is not simply an individual responsibility. It is also a collective one. Here, it seems, the ethical debt to the dead joins forces with the poetical power to narrate. And we recall that the two modes of narrative—fiction and history—share a common origin in epic, which has the characteristic of preserving memories on the communal scale of societies. Placed in the service of the not-to-be-forgotten, this poetic power permits us to live up to the ethical task of collective anamnesis.

The ethical task of narrative understanding faced with the problem of historical evil may be summarized, accordingly, under the following aspects: (1) a testimonial capacity to bear witness to the reality of the past (with its often untold suffering of evil); (2) an analogizing capacity to make present those who are absent and "other" than ourselves (our debt to the forgotten dead); and 3) an imaginative capacity to project future possibilities where justice might at last prevail.[24]

In *Memory, History, Forgetting*, Ricoeur argues that forgiveness may release the historical past into a different, freer future.[25] For genuine amnesty does not and cannot come from blind forgetfulness (amnesia), but only from a remembering that is prepared to forgive the past by emancipating it from the deterministic stranglehold of violent obsession and revenge. Genuine forgiveness, as Ricoeur observes, involves not a forgetting of the events themselves but a different way of *signifying* a debt to the dead that paralyzes memory—and, by implication, our capacity to recreate ourselves in a new future. The proper task of amnesty is not to efface the memory of crimes. It is rather to remember them so as to dissolve some of the more crippling aspects of debt they may have accrued. "Forgiveness is a sort of healing of memory, the completion of its mourning period. Delivered from the weight of debt, memory is liberated for great projects. Forgiveness gives memory a future." Ricoeur claims accordingly that it is not a contradiction to say that amnesty is the strict corollary of forgiving memory even as it is the strict contrary of "repetition memory."[26]

Critical caution is clearly called for here. Narrative memory is never innocent. It is an ongoing conflict of interpretations: a battlefield of competing meanings. Every history is told from a certain perspective and in the light of specific prejudice (at least in Gadamer's sense). Memory, as previously suggested, is not always on the side of the angels. It can as easily lead to false consciousness and ideological closure as to openness and tolerance. One only has to recall the recent controversies around Holocaust denial to appreciate the stakes involved. This distorting power is sometimes ignored by contemporary advocates of narrative ethics— MacIntyre, Nussbaum, Booth—who, unlike Ricoeur, tend to downplay the need for a hermeneutic of critical suspicion. Nor is it properly appreciated by those advocates of the second of Nietzsche's *Untimely Meditations,* "The Use and Abuse of History for Life," who believe it is sufficient to "actively forget the past," to have done with it. Ricoeur does not share such a sanguine belief.

We may say, in summary, then that Ricoeur endeavors to balance (a) our duty to attest to the incomparable *singularity* of a unique event like Auschwitz, with (b) our duty to testify to the representative *universality* of good and evil. The truth is no doubt to be found in some kind of Aristotelian mean that combines both ethical impulses in delicate tension. That is what a practical wisdom (*phronesis*) of historical narrative requires in our age of easy forgetfulness—a proper balance between the dual fidelities of memory to the *uniqueness* and *communicability* of past events. As Ricoeur observes:

> We must remember because remembering is a moral duty. We owe a debt to the victims. And the tiniest way of paying our debt is to tell and retell what happened at Auschwitz.... By remembering and telling, we not only prevent forgetfulness from killing the victims twice; we also prevent their life stories from becoming banal ... and the events from appearing as necessary.[27]

Sometimes, in some places—Northern Ireland, Bosnia, Kashmir—it is important to let go of the paralyzing hold of evil suffered in order to surmount the instincts of resentment and revenge. At other times, in other places—Auschwitz being the time and place par excellence—it is essential to remember the past in order to honor our "debt to the dead" and to ensure it never happens again. Narrative remembrance, as analyzed by Ricoeur, can serve two functions: it can help us to represent the past as it really was *or* to reinvent it as it might have been. In fiction, the role of reinvention is what matters most—even in historical novels like *War and Peace.* In historical testimonies of evil, by contrast, the function of veridical recall claims primacy. Distinguishing between these two separate, if often overlapping, functions is, for Ricoeur, of crucial ethical import. As is discerning *when* it is right to remember and *when* it is better to forget. Or, indeed, *how much* we should remember or forget.[28]

CONCLUSION

How then can Ricoeur acknowledge the enigma of evil, laid bare by his various accounts, while still addressing Tolstoy's question: *What is to be done?* He proposes a threefold approach: (1) practical understanding (*phronesis-mimesis-praxis*); (2) working-through (*catharsis-Durcharbeitung*), and (3) pardon.

"Practical understanding" is the name Ricoeur gives to that limited capacity of the human mind to *think* the enigma of evil. He draws, it seems, from such varied models as biblical "wisdom" (discussed earlier), Aristotle's "practical wisdom" (*phronesis*), Kant's "practical reason" (indeterminate judgment), and his own original notion of "narrative understanding." What each of these models has in common is an ability to transfer the aporia of evil from the sphere of theory (*theoria*)—proper to the exact knowledge criteria of logic, science, and speculative metaphysics—to the sphere of a more practical art of understanding (*techne/praxis*), which allows for an approximate grasp of phenomena: what Aristotle calls "the flexible rule of the architect." Where speculative theory, epitomized by theodicy, explained evil in terms of ultimate causal or creationist origins, Ricoeur's model of practical understanding is geared toward a more hermeneutic comprehension of the indeterminate, contingent, and singular characteristics of evil—while not abandoning all claim to quasi-universal criteria (which might account for at least a minimally shared sense of evil). Such practical understanding borrows from action the conviction that evil is something that ought not to be and must be struggled against. In that sense, it resists the fatalism of archaeologies of evil to be found in both mythology and theodicy. And it does so in favor of a future-oriented praxis.

The ultimate response offered by practical understanding is to *act against* evil. Instead of acquiescing in the face of an origin that precedes us, action turns our understanding toward the future "by the idea of a *task* to be accomplished." The moral-political requirement to act does not, Ricoeur insists accordingly, abandon the legitimate quest for some minimal model of reasonable discernment. It in fact demands it. For how could we act against evil if we could not identify it, that is, if we could not critically discriminate between good and evil? In this respect, the genuine struggle against evil presupposes a critical hermeneutic of discernment. And such hermeneutic understanding retains Kant's insistence on a practical reason that seeks to think somehow the unthinkable. And to do so with what Ricoeur calls the "sobriety of a thinking always careful not to transgress the limits of knowledge."[29]

Our critical understanding of evil may never surpass the provisional nature of Kant's indeterminate (i.e., "aesthetic reflective") judgment. But it at least judges. And it does so in a manner alert to both the singular alterity of evil and to its quasi-universal character as grasped by the *sensus communis*. This is not exact or adequate judgment but a form of judgment, for all that, based on the practical wisdom conveyed by narratives and driven by moral justice. We may say, consequently, that practical judgment is not only "phronetic" but "narrative" in character. This overlapping of *phronesis* (Aristotle) and judgment (Kant) is neatly captured in Ricoeur's account of the ethical role of narrative:

> Ethics as Aristotle conceived it, and as it can still be conceived today, speaks abstractly of the relation between virtue and the pursuit of happiness. It is the function of poetry in its narrative and dramatic form, to propose to the imagination and to its mediation various figures that constitute so many *thought experiments* by which we learn to link together the ethical aspects of human conduct and happiness and misfortune. By means of poetry we learn how reversals of fortune result from this or that conduct, as this is constructed by the plot in the narrative. It is due to the familiarity we have with the types of plot received from our culture that we learn to relate virtues, or rather forms of excellence, with happiness or unhappiness. These "lessons" of poetry constitute the "universals" of which Aristotle spoke; but these are universals that are of a lower degree than those of logic and theoretical thought. We must nonetheless speak of understanding but in the sense that Aristotle gave to *phronesis*.... In this sense I am prepared to speak of phronetic understanding in order to contrast it with theoretical understanding. Narrative belongs to the former and not to the latter."[30]

If practical understanding addresses the action-response to evil, it sometimes neglects the suffering-response. Evil is not just something we struggle against. It is also (as noted earlier) something we undergo. To ignore this passivity of evil suffered is, Ricoeur concludes, to ignore the extent to which evil strikes us as shockingly strange and disempowering. It is also to underestimate that irreducible alterity of evil that myth and theodicy tend to overestimate. One of the wisest responses to evil is, on this count, to acknowledge its traumatizing effects and work them through (*durcharbeiten*) as best we can. Practical understanding can only redirect us toward action if it has already recognized that some element of estrangement almost always attaches to evil, especially when it concerns illness, horror, catastrophe, or death. No matter how prepared we are to make sense of evil, we are never prepared enough. That is why the "work of mourning" is so important as a way of not allowing the inhuman nature of suffering to result in a complete "loss of self" (what Freud called melancholia). Some kind of catharsis is necessary to prevent the slide into fatalism that all too often issues in despairing self-destruction. The critical detachment brought about by cathartic mourning elicits a wisdom that turns *passive lament* into the possibility of *active complaint, that is, protest.*[31]

The role played by narrative testimonies is, as we saw, crucial in this respect. For such narrative rememberings invite the victim to escape the alienation of evil, that is, to move from a position of mute helplessness to speech-acts of revolt and (where possible) self-renewal. Some kind of narrative working through is necessary, it seems, for survivors of evil not to feel crippled by grief or guilt (about the death of others and their own survival) or to succumb to the game of the "expiatory victim." What the catharsis of mourning-narrative allows is that new actions are still possible *in spite of evil suffered.* It detaches us from the obsessional repetitions and repressions of the past and frees us for a future. For only thus can we escape the disabling cycles of retribution, fate, and destiny: cycles that alienate us from our power to act by instilling the view that evil is overpoweringly alien—that is, irresistible. Working through the experience of evil—narratively, practically, cathartically—helps us to take the allure out of evil. And in so doing it enables us to distinguish between possible and impossible modes of protest and resistance. Working through is central to a hermeneutics of action in that makes evil *resistible.* In sum, by transforming the alienation and victimization of lament into a moral response of just struggle, Ricoeur's hermeneutics of understanding and action offers a powerful, if partial, response to the challenge of evil.

Finally, we return to the difficult—and often ostensibly impossible— issue of forgiveness. Against the "never" of evil, which makes pardon impossible, we are asked to embrace what Ricoeur calls the "marvel of a once again" which makes it possible.[32] But the possibility of forgiveness is a "marvel" precisely because it surpasses the limits of rational calculation and explanation. There is a certain gratuitousness about pardon due to the very fact that the evil it addresses is not part of some dialectical necessity. Pardon is something that makes little sense before we give it, but much sense once we do. Before it occurs it seems impossible, unpredictable, incalculable in terms of an economy of exchange. There is no science of forgiveness. And yet this is precisely when phronetic understanding, attentive to the particularity of specific evil events, joins forces with the practice of patient working through—their joint aim being to ensure that past evils might be prevented from recurring. Such prevention often requires pardon as well as protest in order that the cycles of repetition and revenge give way to future possibilities of nonevil. This is a good example of Ricoeur's claim that pardon gives a future to the past.

Cathartic narration can, Ricoeur concludes, help to make the impossible task of pardon a bit more possible. This is why, as we noted, amnesty is never amnesia. The past must be recollected and worked through so that we can identify, *grosso modo*, what it is that we are forgiving. For if pardon is beyond reason, it is never completely blind. And if it is mobilized by the gratuity of love—which calls for that element of extra or excess—it is never insensitive to the logic of justice. Or, to put it in Pascal's terms, pardon has its reasons that reason cannot comprehend. Perhaps only a divinity could forgive indiscriminately. And there may indeed be some crimes that a God alone is able to pardon. Even Christ had to ask his father to forgive his crucifiers: "Father, forgive them for they know not what they do." As man alone he could not do it. Impossible for us, possible for God. But here an ethics of pardon approaches the threshold of a religious hermeneutics.

If philosophy is to continue to address the perennial enigma of evil, it might do well to take a lead from Ricoeur's hermeneutic response—first, by conducting hermeneutic analyses of the principal discourses deployed in the history of theology and philosophy to represent the enigma of evil; and, second, by advancing new modes of recognition and renewal. We need both a hermeneutics of interpretation and an ethics of active forgiveness. For as Ricoeur continually reminds us, it is not enough to interpret our world of suffering and injustice, we must also try to change it.

NOTES

1. *The Symbolism of Evil* (Boston: Beacon Press, 1967), pp. 156f. See also Karl Simms, *Paul Ricoeur* (Routledge: London and New York), pp. 9–28.
2. *The Symbolism of Evil*, p., 15. Ricoeur goes on to argue that symbolic expressions are 'donative' in that a primary meaning gives rise to a secondary one that surpasses the first in its semantic range and reference. Further clarifying what he means by symbol, Ricoeur contrasts in to allegory. While an allegory relates one meaning directly to another, without residue or ambiguity, a symbol works by enigmatic suggestion or evocation—it designates a *surplus* of meaning that exceeds the obvious one. Allegories have one meaning, symbols two or more.
3. "Introductory Response by Paul Ricoeur" in *Hermeneutics and the Human Sciences* (Cambridge: Cambridge University Press, 1981). Cosmic symbols refer to a human's earliest attempts to read good and evil in the world. Here the human imagination interprets aspects of the world—the heavens, the sun, the moon, the waters—*as* signs of some ulterior meaning. At this most basic level, the symbol is both a thing and a sign: it embodies and signifies at one and the same time. Or, to put it in another way, when dealing with cosmic symbols of evil, we read the things of the world as signs, and signs as things of the world. As such, the symbolic imagination is already, at least implicitly, *linguistic*. Ricoeur makes this

clear in the following passage from *Freud and Philosophy:* "These symbols are not inscribed *beside* language, as modes of immediate expression, directly perceptible visages; it is in the universe of discourse that these realities take on a symbolic dimension. Even when it is the elements of the world that carry the symbol—earth, sky, water, life—it is the word (of consecration, invocation or mythic narrative) which says their cosmic expressivity thanks to the double meaning of the *words* earth, sky, water, life (that is, a) their obvious literal meaning as reference to things *and* b) their ulterior meaning, for example, water as a symbol of renewed spiritual life." Ricoeur can thus affirm that the "expressivity of the world comes to language through the symbol as double meaning" (*De L'Interpretation: Essai sur Freud*, Paris: Editions Du Seuil, 1965, p. 23). For a cosmic symbol of good or evil occurs whenever language produces composite signs where the meaning, not "content to designate something directly, points to another meaning which can only be reached (indirectly) by means of this designation" (p. 24). Illustrating this linguistic property of symbols, Ricoeur comments on the phrase from the Psalms, "The skies tell of the glory of God," as follows: "The skies don't speak themselves; rather, they are spoken by the prophet, by the hymn, by the liturgy. One always needs the word to assume the world into a manifestation of the sacred (hierophany)" (p. 25).

4. *The Symbolism of Evil*, p. 18.
5. Ibid., p. 19.
6. Ricoeur, *Figuring the Sacred: Religion, Narrative and Imagination* (Minneapolis: Fortress Press, 1995).
7. Ricoeur, *Figuring the Sacred*, 250.
8. As Aristotle noted in *Poetics* (London: Dent: 1963), 4, 1448b5–10: "There is the enjoyment people always get from representations ... we enjoy looking at accurate likenesses of things which are themselves painful to see, such as obscene beasts and corpses."
9. Ricoeur, *Figuring the Sacred*, p. 252.
10. Ibid., p. 257.
11. Immanuel Kant, *Religion within the Limits of Reason Alone* (New York: Harper, 1960), p. 38. Cited by Ricoeur, *Figuring the Sacred*, pp. 258–59.
12. Ricoeur, *Time and Narrative*, vol. 3 (Chicago: University of Chicago Press, 1988), pp. 184–85.
13. See my critique of this postmodern cult of "irreference" in the conclusion to my *Wake of Imagination* (St. Paul: University of Minnesota Press, 1988) and in chapter 6 and "Afterwords" of my *Poetics of Imagining* (London: Routledge, 1991), pp. 170, 232. See also Fredrick Jameson's critique in "Postmodernism or the Cultural Logic of Late Capitalism," *New Left Review* (1984): 53–91. For Baudrillard's own account of this sublime "irreference" of simulation, see *Simulations* (New York: Semiotext(e), 1983). For Lyotard's account of sublime "irrepresentability," see *The Inhuman,* trans. G. Bennington and R. Bowlby (Stanford: Stanford University Press, 1991), p. 136.
14. Ricoeur, *Time and Narrative*, vol. 3, pp. 185–86.
15. Ibid.
16. Ibid.
17. Primo Levi, *Si c'est un homme* (Paris: Juliiard, 1987). For further discussion of this ethical role of narrative memory see my *Poetics of Imagining* (London: Routledge, 1991), pp. 220–28, and Claude Lanzmann's review of *Schindler's List,* "Holocauste, la representation impossible," in *Le*

Monde, February 1994. In addition to the fictional and cinematic narratives of the Holocaust, it would be useful to consider how other narratives of traumatic events in history are retold in contemporary novels or films—Oliver Stone's retelling of Vietnam in *Platoon,* Costa Gavras's retelling of the Chilean coup in *Missing,* Gerry Conlon and Jim Sheridan's retelling of the Guildford Four injustice in *In the Name of the Father,* and so on. Be it a question of documentary drama, fictional history, or historical fiction, in each case we are concerned with an interweaving of fiction and history. No matter how "empirical" and "objective" a historical account claims to be, there is no denying its reliance on narrative strategies of selection, heightening, arrangement, invented speeches, and reconstructed events, not to mention its need for coherence and connection. As Hayden White puts it, the historian "must choose the elements of the story he would tell. He makes his story by including some events and excluding others, by stressing some and subordinating others. This process *of* exclusion, stress and subordination is carried out in the interest of constituting *a story of a particular kind.* That is to say, he 'emplots' his story" (*Metahistory: The Historical Imagination in Nineteenth Century Europe* (Baltimore: The Johns Hopkins University Press, 1975), p. 6.

18. Ricoeur, *Time and Narrative,* p. 187.
19. See Richard Wolin, *The Heidegger Controversy* (Cambridge: MIT Press, 1992).
20. See Jameson, "Postmodernism and Consumer Society," *in Postmodern Culture,* ed. H. Foster (London: Pluto Press, 1985).
21. See Jean Baudrillard, *Simulations.*
22. Ricoeur, *Time and Narrative,* vol. 3, p. 188.
23. Ibid., p. 189.
24. For a development of these three functions of narrative imagination, see the "Afterwords" to my *Poetics of Imagining* (New York: Edinburgh University Press/Fordham University Press, 1998).
25. Ricoeur, *La Mémoire, L'histoire, L'oubli,* (Paris: Editions du Seuil, 2000), especially the epilogue entitled "La Pardon Difficile."
26. Ibid., p. 23.
27. Ricoeur, *Figuring the Sacred,* p. 290.
28. Ricoeur, *La Mémoire, L'histoire, L'oubli,* especially Part 3 entitled "La Condition Historique."
29. Ricoeur, *Figuring the Sacred,* p. 259.
30. Ricoeur, "Life in Quest of Narrative," *On Paul Ricoeur: Narrative and Interpretation,* ed. David Wood (London: Routledge, 1991), p. 23.
31. See S. Freud, "Remembering, Repeating, and Working-Through," in *The Standard Edition of the Complete Psychological Works of Sigmund Freud,* vol. 12. Ricoeur elaborates further in this theme in *La Mémoire, L'histoire, L'oubli.*
32. Ricoeur, *La Mémoire, L'histoire, L'oubli,* especially the epilogue entitled "Le Pardon Difficile," pp. 593–658.

Paul Ricoeur and the Prospects of a New Humanism   5

William Schweiker

At the core of Paul Ricoeur's far-ranging corpus of work is sustained attention to the meaning and task of being human. Exploring human fallibility and also capability, he understood human beings as incomplete creatures who strive some kind of wholeness in their lives by means of cultural products and practices that endow life with meaning. It is hardly surprising, then, that Ricoeur examined questions of meaning in studies dedicated to metaphor, symbol, and narrative. Yet those studies are best seen as detours (so Ricoeur called them) on the way to the more basic concern for "capable man." Further, attention to human capability and fallibility, and thus the priority of action to consciousness, required a significant shift in thinking about being itself. "Should we not say," Ricoeur wrote in one essay, "to exist is to act? Does not being, in the first instance, signify an act?" "Being," he continued, "is act before it is essence, because it is effort before it is representation or idea."[1] The domain of representation and idea, the whole realm of human meanings, thereby reveals and also conceals the effort to be. The interpreter who wants to understand the human effort to exist must engage forms of representation in order to clarify the meaning of that struggle. Ricoeur thereby offers a reflexive, hermeneutical philosophy of human beings as acting creatures who express their effort to exist in labor, cultural artifacts, and language. He engaged in a grand and intricate interpretation of things human in order to clarify not only the significance of theories, symbols, and works of art, but to catch a glimpse of humanity *in via*, including the problem of evil that haunts the human adventure.[2]

Rather than exploring Ricoeur's hermeneutical theory, I want in this chapter to examine the connection in Ricoeur's work between the "effort to be" and his commitment to a form of humanism. Each of these aspects of his work has received considerable attention. The humanistic cast of his thought has long been evident. It reaches from his earliest writings for the journal *Esprit*, influenced by the personalism of its founder Emmanuel Mounier, to the last lectures and texts.[4] Many of the tributes to Ricoeur following his death similarly remarked on the humanistic cast of his life and work. There have also been fine studies on the importance of the effort to be, attestation, capability, and the "will" in his corpus. That focus on his work was natural insofar as Ricoeur undertook early in his career to write a "Philosophy of the Will" and ended his labors still speaking of human capability. All of these ways to enter into Ricoeur's sprawling and complex corpus of work are well known and obviously important. They have contributed to the assessment and appreciation of his thought.

What has not been sufficiently explored, I believe, is the precise way in which Ricoeur's humanism reflects his basic philosophical orientation to articulate human capability and fallibility, that is, the effort to be. The converse is also true. It has not been shown how his attention to the human effort to be determines the basic outlines of the form of humanism he judged viable and even required for the present age. The purpose of my inquiry is to gain some clarity about the connection between humanism and Ricoeur's account of the human effort to be, including some of his religious convictions. Besides exploring Ricoeur's work, my other intention in what follows is to advance contemporary humanistic thought, especially at the meeting point of philosophical, religious, and theological concerns. I will do so through sustained attention to a question that strikes to the core of the affirmation of our capacity or power to act: what is the limit on the capacity of human beings to be causal forces in the world? What is the measure of the human effort to be? How is it related to the dignity of human life, one's own and that of others? Is there a theological dimension to the measure of human power?

To answer these questions adequately, I need to show that an account of the measure to be is not only grounded in some account of human existence and power, but also, and its own way, opens up theological reflection within humanistic inquiry. Let me begin, then, by explaining the direction of my inquiry.

THE EFFORT TO BE AND ITS MEASURE

What does one mean by "the effort to be" or a "measure" and their relation? And why are these important ideas for contemporary humanists? To be sure, asking about the "measure" for the "effort to be" seems a rather abstract way of putting a question that is actually woven into the texture of every human life. The raw struggle for life, the pitch of human wants and desires for fulfillment against the onslaught of age, death, and suffering, and likewise the pangs of love that long to embrace the beloved beyond the sorrow of loss all testify to a *Wille zur Leben*, a will to life, in human existence. To be or not to be might be the question, as Hamlet thought, but, in fact, the desire to be, the sense that it is good to be, is a primitive datum of human existence linked to the struggle to live. The decision to end life, the act of suicide, is then always an intentional act that must overcome the more primitive desire to live. Albert Camus thought that "there is but one truly serious philosophical problem, and that is suicide. Judging whether life is or is not worth living amounts to answering the fundamental questions of philosophy."[4] But that problem is formulated in the order of critical judgment and philosophical reflection. More directly, more immediately, life makes a claim on us. While pessimism has been a seduction for some Western thinkers and always stalks the human psyche, most people most of the time love rather than hate life.

On the plane of actual existence arguably the more basic question than whether to be or not to be is rather about the measure or norm for our effort to exist. Is the mere preservation of one's own life or the life of those dear to one the good to seek? What claim, if any, do others make on my capacities, my power to act in the world? Which others matter? Is the measure of human capability just the increase of strength, the celebration of power and independence marked, say in Greek thought, by ideas of honor and glory and happiness (*eudaimonia*) rooted in the natural vitalities of existence? Is the norm for human action a command to care for the poor, the widow, and the stranger, a commandment of the God of the Bible, or is that command uttered simply and solely in the face of another suffering human being? How do these norms, whatever their content or origin, relate to the tenacity of the will to live that saturates our existence? Must one still the will to life in order to pay reverence to other forms of life?

These are hardly abstract matters even if they can be formulated in abstract terms. The question of the relation between the effort to be, the will to life, and its proper norm or measure presses on daily existence insofar as to be human, as Ricoeur insists, is to be with others and to live in shared institutions. Further, this question is at the center of current debates about humanism and Ricoeur's own response to competing philosophical positions. Put as a formula, Ricoeur's type of humanism arises from an attestation to being in the self and yet also insists that we are "human, *only* human." Acknowledgment of the limits on human thought and action, limits rooted in our finitude and the reality of others, are necessary to a proper grasp of our existence. Only when human beings repent of all idolatry about their own power and knowledge is the dignity of human life manifest. In this respect, Ricoeur contends that theological discourse and religious convictions use limit concepts to denote limit experiences. They specify the finite condition of human existence while also indirectly configuring an attestation to being.

As explored next, Ricoeur outlines this position in contrast to the Nietzschean formulation of "human, *all-too* human" and also Emmanuel

Levinas's humanism of the other, which I designate by the formula "human, *otherwise than* human."[5] Recall that Nietzsche mused "the world is beautiful, but has a disease called man." He sought to announce the coming man, the *Übermensch*, as a new form of existence. The daybreak of the *Übermensch* is the finality of human, all too human history. According to Levinas, the face of the other disrupts the drive to totality that is also the legacy of Western thought and life, especially under the dominance of Greek philosophy. The question of the limit and value of human power is thereby variously construed in these formulas. For Nietzsche, the will to power finds its limit only in the coming *Übermensch* and so after the time of "man." With Levinas, the power of the self is decisively limited by the advent of the other, the command "Thou shall not murder" uttered by the face of the other as if from Mount Sinai. According to Ricoeur, the limit to and value of human power is rooted in the attestation of *oneself as another* and the acknowledgment that we are human, *only* human.

These formulas constitute a typology of important expressions of contemporary humanism that I will elaborate in more detail later. Their full force for understanding current options in thought will thereby become clear as this inquiry proceeds.[6] They are also the opening to my specific constructive intentions that mark the far end, the horizon, of this chapter. Against Nietzsche's paradigmatically "Greek" affirmation of human power where the vitalities of will are to be ever increased and Levinas's insistence on the finality of the other rooted in his sensibilities about Jewish law, my argument enacts in thinking the reality of the "third man," as Ricoeur once called it. Neither dominated by forms of Greek thought, to which the Christian message went, nor the circle of Hebraic life, from which the Gospel arose, this " 'third man,' " Ricoeur notes, "this cultivated Christian, this believing Greek, is ourselves."[7] This is not to say that Greek or Hebraic forms of humanism are impossible or even invalid. Quite the contrary is the case. That is a reason to examine the positions of Nietzsche and Levinas. The point, rather, is that a Christian humanism, born from the tumultuous and yet exciting encounter of Greek and biblical modes of life, signifies yet another distinctive way of being in the world. It is the reality of the "third man" as a human possibility. While drawing on Ricoeur's thought precisely at this point, I also want to press beyond his argument to what is best called "theological humanism." This too will be a form of thought arising within the reality of the "third man," but now articulated in ways that transform Ricoeur's project and other contemporary expressions of Christian humanism.[8] The reasons for undertaking this turn of thought as well as some judgment about Ricoeur's assessment of that turn will also become clear in due course.

So, in what follows I will not only listen to but also deploy the resources of the Christian tradition in the service of understanding and orienting human life. At the conclusion of these reflections I will suggest a type of theological humanism developed from Christian sources.[9] The formula here is "human, *truly* human." The hermeneutical move that must be made, I judge, is from understanding the human "in the mirror of scripture," as Ricoeur emblematically puts it, to that of understanding existence "in Christ."[10] I hope to bring to articulation a form of humanism distinctive in its features but conversant with others' positions that, like Ricoeur's, attend to the effort to be. That intention, again, marks the horizon of this inquiry and thereby will not be developed in great detail.

I turn now to the current debate about humanism within strands of postmodern thought. This will enable us to develop in a further step of the inquiry the typology of positions announced earlier and thereby to specify the humanistic intent of Ricouer's philosophical project. I conclude, as noted, by outlining the project of theological humanism.

THE QUESTIONS OF HUMANISM

A survey of intellectual trends in early and late twentieth-century thought reveals that many of the convictions and values of traditional humanism fell to criticism. By the term "traditional humanism" I do not mean a specific set of thinkers or texts or even a particular period in Western intellectual history. While certain thinkers, notably Erasmus, Pico, More, or, later, Vico and Kant, and certain periods, especially the Renaissance and the Enlightenment, are often taken to define "humanism," I am much more concerned with a set of ideals or convictions that characterize a humanistic outlook. Tzvetan Todorov has noted that, for humanists, "Freedom exist and that it is precious, but at the same time they appreciate the benefit of shared values, life with others, and a self that is held responsible for its action."[11] Todorov formulates this outlook in terms of what he calls the autonomy of the I, the finality of the you, and the universality of the they. Put otherwise, the freedom of the self, the moral claim of others, and an inclusive moral community are basic humanistic values. And as Todorov further writes,

> Humanism is neither a 'naturalism' nor an 'artificialism'; it defends its values neither because they are embodied in the natural order, nor because the will of the most powerful has decreed it.... [For the humanist it is] because these values of freedom, respect for others, and the equal dignity of all impose themselves on him with the force of self-evidence, and seem to him more suitable to the human species than others."[12]

Correlative to these self-evident values, humanists also insist on human fallibility, and so humility in our appreciation of truth. And, finally, humanists believe, in Edward Said's words, that "human history as made by human action and understood accordingly is the very ground of the humanities."[13] Put most simply, for a humanist the purpose of thought and action is human flourishing achieved by means of the distinctive human power to act and so to create history, whatever other nonhuman purposes might obtain. These humanistic ideals reach a cultural height and prestige in the West during the eighteenth to nineteenth centuries.

Given these beliefs, it is not surprising that we are now amid a widespread debate about the viability of humanism. In an age of global dynamics, there is the possibility for expanded cosmopolitan or worldwide commitments, say to human rights, that challenge the tribalism of local loyalties and powers. Yet many now worry that humanistic ideals are the imposition of Western beliefs on other peoples and cultures. Further, the various forms of technology that characterize the global age are driven by anthropocentric values that endanger not only the natural environment but also myriad forms of nonhuman life. For many people, humanism cannot be reconciled with ecological sensibilities and concern for "animal rights."[14] Additionally, as Ricoeur foresaw, there are new threats to the dignity and worth of the individual person. Individuals are being subsumed into the working of massive, complex political, economic, and technological systems. Yet those systems, it would seem, can hardly be understood, let alone analyzed, if one clings to the traditional humanistic conviction that human beings and human beings alone "make" history. If we are to have a realistic grasp of the forces shaping the world, surely we must attend to the matrices of social power and the dynamics of complex systems freed from the humanistic bias for human agents.[15] All of these developments characterize the "postmodern" or global age. They put unique pressure on humanistic thinkers to defend their ethical commitments as well as to demonstrate the explanatory power of conceptions of history and society bound to human capacities for action.

Amid these challenges to humanistic ideals, one problem seems properly basic for my inquiry. The explosion of technological power in our age has rightly challenged the unchecked celebration of human freedom and power among earlier humanists. It is not surprising that the various kinds of "neohumanism" that dot the intellectual and cultural landscape insist that classical ideals about freedom, individual dignity, and the historical efficacy of human action must be grounded in and limited by the worth of the other. In order to preserve human dignity and expand moral sensibility, thinkers around the world and in various cultures have sought to revise basic humanistic ideals more attentive to the moral claim of others and an inclusive moral community.

In this light, Ricoeur's work can usefully be seen as part of the debate about the viability of humanism. In contrast to those who simply reject humanism, Ricoeur held, like other contemporary neohumanists, that all works of culture and society give expression, often indirectly, to the freedom of the human self. The dignity and freedom of the human self, or the autonomy of the "I," are perhaps the dearest of all ideas to humanists. It is a conviction that Ricoeur tenaciously defended. As he noted, "I look at my work as an attempt to provide a survey of the capabilities, so to say, of the very *I can* ... It can be read in terms of four verbs which the "I can" modifies: *I can speak, I can do things, I can tell a story,* and *I can be imputed*, an action can be imputed to me as its author."[16] In each case, the capacity of speech, action, historical understanding, and responsibility is predicated in complex ways of the "I" even as this "I" is only understandable in terms of these capabilities and their expressions. The effort to be, the *I can*, is basic to all representations of the self in speech, action, narration, and the imputation of responsibility. What about the limit on human capability? In his Gifford Lectures, *Oneself as Another*, Ricoeur's trajectory of thought about the limit on the "I can" comes to its highest expression when he explores the various forms of capability with respect to "aiming at the good life with and for others in just institutions." This maxim from the "little ethics" of that text summarizes, in terms parallel to Todorov, the neo-humanistic contours of Ricoeur's thought.[17] The maxim places Ricoeur's work within the larger agenda of those thinkers dedicated to reformulating humanistic ideas in ways appropriate to an age of the global spread of technological power and with it global endangerments to life.

It is beyond the purpose of the present inquiry to clarify in greater detail Ricoeur's place within the myriad forms of neohumanism. Insofar as my concern is the connection between the effort to be and humanism, it is much more important to examine Ricoeur's engagement with thinkers who, like himself, hold that will or desire or power is basic in human existence. In order to do so, I must develop further the typology of positions noted earlier, and this will likewise enable me to isolate the distinctive shape of Ricoeur's project. The typology likewise serves the further aim of these reflections to think with and beyond his work about the form of life of the "third man."

TYPES OF HUMANISM AND THE EFFORT TO BE

Ricoeur asserted his own humanistic outlook in an early essay, "What does Humanism Mean?" In that essay, Ricoeur wrote:

> Man is man when he knows that he is *only* man. The ancients called man a "mortal." This "remembrance of death" indicated in the very *name* of

man introduces the reference to a limit at the very heart of the affirmation of man himself. When faced with the pretense of absolute knowledge, humanism is therefore the indication of an "only": we are *only* men. No longer "human, all too human:" this formula still shares in the intoxication of absolute knowledge; but "only human."[18]

Careful attention to this passage enables us to isolate the contours of Ricoeur's humanism in contrast to the Nietzschean formula "human, *all too* human" and Levinas's humanism of the other and its summary formula "human, *otherwise than* human.

In Ricoeur's early essay, and also much later in *Oneself as Another,* he explicitly sets his thought against Nietzsche. In his Gifford Lectures, Ricoeur identifies Nietzsche with the diminution of the self. Interestingly, in the previous early essay noted, the Nietzschean formula of "human, all too human" is associated with an excessive confidence in absolute knowledge. Against that excess, Ricoeur insisted on the limits to human knowledge while in *Oneself as Another* he opposes Nietzsche's seeming reduction of the self to nonhuman causal forces. How can we explain the contradictory judgments about Nietzsche's thought and what are their significance for reading Ricoeur?

Ricoeur's point, in my understanding, is that humanism is inseparable from a perception of human beings as mortal, as death-bound. It is important to remember, as Tony Davies notes, the semantic density of the word "humanity." "The root-word is, quite literally, humble (*humilis*), from the Latin *humus*, earth or ground; hence *homo*, earth-being, and *humanus*, earthly, human."[19] To be earth-bound is, on Ricoeur's accounting, to be death-bound. There is a limit at the heart of the human project. Nietzsche's announcement of the coming of the *Übermensch* after a history dominated by the nihilism of human, all too human values aspires to a level of knowledge not possible for mortals. In other words, for Ricoeur, humanism necessarily expresses itself in a philosophy of limits and the Nietzschean project strives to exceed that mortal limit. "Man" cannot be overcome or transcended. We are human, *only* human, Ricoeur insists, and thereby we must forgo any pretense to know or to achieve a form of existence beyond "man."

This initial response to the Nietzschean agenda only partially captures Ricoeur's thought as seen from the beginning to the end of his corpus. He always argued that at the heart of human being is not simply the limit of mortality, but, much more, an attestation, a fundamental desire to be. Mortality, as the previous quote above stresses, is a limit but it is one *within* the affirmation of man himself. The desire to be, attestation to the goodness of being and not the *Wille zur Macht*, is what defines the human being.[20] The limit on that affirmation of self arising from within one's self is mortality, our awareness of death. While enduring the fact of mortality, there is nevertheless an attestation to the goodness of being "at the very heart of the affirmation of man himself." According to Ricoeur, this affirmation opens another horizon to human time other than the fate of death. Through the power of the imagination the desire to be reaches beyond mortality toward eternity in affirming its existence while also enacting its own limit. Nietzsche's attempt to reduce the human to the "will to power" no less than his hope in the coming *Übermensch* must be brought to criticism. If the formula "human, all too human" betrays an aspiration to absolute knowledge of the coming "man" not possible for finite creatures, the reduction of human existence to the "will to power" fails to grasp the desire to be in its depth or scope. In the end, Nietzsche suffers inconsistency, exuding epistemic confidence bound to ontological reductionism.[21] And that fact is, apparently, the reason for Ricoeur's seeming contradictory judgments about Nietzsche's agenda.

What then is the "limit" on the human effort to be? How, if at all, is it related to the ethical turn in contemporary neohumanism emblematically stated, in Todorov's words, as the finality of the "you" and the universality of the "they"? It is around this point that the ongoing encounter between Levinas and Ricoeur revolved, an encounter spanning many, many years. Levinas's claim, most boldly stated, is that the face of the other is the absolute limit on the drive to totality, that is, the drive of the self to subsume all being into the self.[22] The other utters a command as if from the height of Mount Sinai, the mountain of God: "Thou shall not murder." For Levinas, the self is a servant, a hostage, of the other, and so infinitely responsible for the life of the other. The limit on the self, the assertion of the ethical intentionality of humanism, is the face of the other and not in the heart of self-affirmation. "I" am, we might say, because the other commands me to be responsible.

In this respect, it is the death of the other, and not my own death, that discloses the unique singularity of human existence and designates the limit on human power. As Ricoeur notes in *Oneself as Another*,

> the face of the other raises itself before me, above me, it is not an appearance that I can include within the sphere of my representations. To be sure, the other appears, his face makes him appear, but the face is not a spectacle; it is a voice. The voice tells us, "Thou shall not kill." Each face is a Sinai that prohibits murder.[23]

To be sure, Levinas always acknowledged the significance of pleasure in human life and also the origin of language and representations in the face-to-face encounter. He likewise argued that in the domain of politics, reciprocal obligations of justice mean that I can make a valid claim on others.[24] Nevertheless, responsibility is an affirmation of the life of the other otherwise than the drive to totality arising from within the effort of the self. This is a humanism of the other.

It is at this juncture that Ricoeur sought to think through consistently the attestation to being. As he notes in the quote, mortality introduces a "limit at the very heart of the affirmation *of man himself*." What I find within myself is that through all the mediations of the desire to be, through labor, culture, and speech, I am also and always *as another*. There is an "otherness" at the core of the human self that, reciprocally construed, enables co-jointly an affirmation of self and other. Ricoeur specified this otherness in a number of ways: the fact of embodied freedom; the relation of *bios* and *logos* in symbols; the dual horizon of human time and eternity configured in narratives; the mutual co-inherence in subjectivity between *ipsem* and *idem* identity; and the moral injunction to love others *as* oneself. The explanation of the fine details of those arguments spanning Ricoeur's corpus are beyond this scope of this inquiry.[25]

How then does Ricoeur's argument differ from Levinas's position? The argument, if I understand him rightly, is that we are "only men," and that means, in distinction to Levinas, that human beings never escape, and, in fact, will never escape, the tenacity of the effort to exist. An encounter between beings who are "only men" always risks the reduction of other to self or the servitude of self to other. The asymmetrical relation of actor and patient in all human relations is the condition in which violence all too easily breaks forth. But the proper *aim* is a good life by means of responsibility for and with others within justice institutions. In order rightly to appreciate Ricoeur's point here, one needs to see a subtle shift in his consideration of "the affirmation of man himself," a shift I bracketed when considering Ricoeur's humanism in response to the Nietzschean project.

Ricoeur does not seek to establish the otherness of the other in terms of the *origin* of self-consciousness and thus the birthplace of the "I" and its representations. Levinas for his part does seek to isolate the origin of self-consciousness either in the totalistic drive of the ego or in the encounter with the face of the other. Ricoeur, having forsaken the search for a pristine origin of consciousness, specifies the trajectory or aim of responsible selfhood. If the defining fact of human being is not *cogito* (the thinking "I" as the origin of representations), but, more simply, the desire to be, then human beings in affirming themselves at one and the same time affirm the being of others, even while there is the possibility of fault and violence rooted in the power to act. The responsible life is the enactment of mutual respect with the aim of existence with and for others. This is why Ricoeur followed Kant and insisted on reciprocal regard in formulating the moral law: treat humanity in oneself or another always as an end and not merely as a means to some other end. The categorical imperative is the screen through which the search for the good life must necessarily move in light of the ever present possibility of violence. Any end that I seek, any conception of the good life, can only count as such if it meets the test of justice. To recall Todorov's phrase, Ricoeur insists on the finality of the "you," the moral claims of others.[26] Yet this moral demand does not escape, cannot escape, the human, only human character of the effort to be and the lurking threat of untold violence.

Now it is important that the moral demand that limits any pursuit of the good life is found, according to Ricoeur, "at the very heart of the affirmation of man himself." Contrary to Levinas, the limit that constrains the wanton use of power in seeking the self's good is not heteronomous to the self, it is not from the demand of the other, but, rather, arises within self-affirmation, the attestation to the desire to be in myself and all others. In a way decidedly different from Kant, on whom Ricoeur relies so heavily, the lawgiving power of (practical) reason is not the heart of autonomy, of freedom. Mindful of the danger of violence, Ricoeur reformulates the meaning of freedom. "Ethical freedom," he writes, "is not a claim which proceeds from me and is opposed to any control; it is, rather, a demand which is addressed to me and which proceeds from the other: allow me to exist in front of you, as your equal."[27] In a word, the limit is annunciated by the other to me, as Levinas rightly saw, but with respect to *equal dignity*, as Kant insisted. The moral demand is the prism though which an aim in life is to pass if it is to be justified. Yet the source of human dignity and its aim is neither the other as other (Levinas) nor the lawgiving power of reason (Kant) but in the desire to be, the attestation to being, in self and other.

Stated most succinctly, Ricoeur's humanism articulates the measure of human power not as the increase of strength to overcome all too human existence and thereby incarnate the *Übermensch*. The limit on power is not to be found in the ultimate perfection of power. Likewise, the measure of the effort to be is not a law announced in the face of the other that places the self on trial and instigates infinite responsibility for the other. From Ricoeur's perspective, these forms of humanism share an unsustainable premise, namely, that it is by the increase of power or within the encounter with the other the human as mortal and yet self-affirming will be transcended. According to Ricoeur, we are "only men"; our form of life cannot and will not be overcome either in the future or in the face of the other.

The full complexity of the desire to be and its limit must then be grasped if we are to understand Ricoeur's brand of humanism and also isolate the point of departure for thinking beyond him. The desire to be, we can now say, bears within itself an irresolvable tension and perplexity, an aporia. To desire being is at once to affirm being and yet to do so from within the lack of being; to desire is to affirm, to seek, within lack that is the mark of finitude. The limit on this desire arises from within mortality. It is why, as seen earlier, Ricoeur's humanism heralds "the remembrance of death." However, were that claim alone adequate for his brand of humanism, then privation, nothingness, sheer finitude would define the most basic contours of thought, and, further, being toward death, my own or that of the other, would be the necessary and sufficient conditions of thinking. Death is indeed necessary for valid reflection on human existence, but it is not sufficient. In facing death, as a finite end, there is also an attestation, an affirmation of life.

How might this aporia be represented so that through interpretation we can understand the full texture of the human project? In Ricoeur's judgment, death, as one temporal horizon of human existence, has its meaning in its other, that is, in the human capacity to imagine "eternity" as a horizon of meaning that exceeds finite limits.[28] Eternity, likewise, has its meaning for human beings in its other: the orientation toward death that is the limit in the heart of self-affirmation. The fact that *I can tell a story* represents, configures, within the order of discourse both the limit (death) and the affirmation (eternity) that is at the heart of self-affirmation. Narratives render productive the aporia of human existence in time.[30] The dual temporal structure of human being rendered productive in the capacity to narrate an account of one's life is, one must admit, an intuition, a grasp of (or being grasped by) a self-evident value, as Todorov noted.

The aporia of the desire to be, Ricoeur seems to be saying, imposes itself with the force of self-evidence and, when considered consistently, leads to a humanism of limits, the insight that "we are *only* men." This is where, as they say, the spade is turned. Ricoeur's account of the "third man," and with it the insight that we are human only human, claims for itself the same level of plausibility, equal force of self-evidence, as the *Wille zur Macht* for Nietzscheans and the face of the other on Levinas's account. That being the case, one cannot assume, I believe, that a definitive refutation of other forms of thought is possible or that a necessary vindication of one is likely to arise. That is why, we can now see, I could arrange these positions in a typology of forms of humanism focused on the effort to be. A genuine typology would not be conceptually useful if one could, in principle, establish the validity of just one position. So, what confronts us after having briefly surveyed Ricoeur's type of humanism in contrast to others is not the certainty of having validated one position. What confronts us, surprisingly, is a space of freedom, the possibility, that is, to choose among accounts of human existence. Yet if that is the case, has the argument simply regressed yet again to a celebration of human power without measure, without norm? Are we left just to choose? With these questions we reach the far end of this inquiry and also the opening to what can best be called *theological humanism* that attests to the truth of human existence as the power to be responsible with and for others, chastened by the depths of fallibility, and yet, in its religious impulse, thankful for the gift of life.

HUMAN, TRULY HUMAN

We have seen that Ricoeur's humanism of limits insists that human existence is always open both to the ever present possibility of death and yet in imagination, and so hope, to a horizon of meaning that exceeds finitude and death. Cultural forms, works of art, and religious symbols provide configurations of human temporal existence through which one can grasp via careful interpretation the outlines of basic structures and dynamics of human being. And those same works open a vision of reality in which human beings can find their own possibilities for life. Incomplete creatures we are, but we are also beings who create meanings in order to discover the truth of our lives and thereby endow existence with significance. There are no shortcuts to understanding human existence. Symbols, especially religious symbols, articulate the intersection of primal vitalities of life, of *bios*, with the rigors of thought, *logos*, and thus display an intelligibility of existence even in its brokenness. Narratives, as noted, configure the dual horizon of human time, death and eternity. Metaphors disclose the dynamic of meaning creation through the clash of literal and fictive claims rooted in human sensibility and imagination. A humanism of limits, we can say, simply articulates these aporias of human being in the world. The *meaning* of existence is attained through the interpretation of the manifold representations of the human effort to be. Not surprisingly, Ricoeur's philosophical project had to be undertaken through "detours" of interpretation in order thereby to articulate and understand the meaning of being human.

At this juncture in our reflections, a further question naturally arises. Are the types of humanism surveyed here exhaustive? Is there any other account that can make some claim to the force of self-evidence about the limit and value of the effort to be? The types, as we have seen, claim, on one extreme, that the limit on human power is with respect to its destiny of self-overcoming, the emergence of a new form of human life after our *human, all too human* existence. At the other end of the typology is the claim, appealing to the evidential power of the face of the other, that the limit on human power does not and cannot arise within the self's effort to be and thereby is, in this respect, *human, otherwise than human*. And, finally, Ricoeur, as we have seen, enunciates a type of humanism that, we might say, mediates these extremes. It is a strictly philosophical account of the reality of the "third man" made possible in Christian faith. He locates a limit to the effort to be "at the very heart of

the affirmation of man himself" and in the realization that we are
human, only human specifies the norm of human power in terms of the
demand to aim at the good life with and for others in just institutions.
Are these the only options available to a humanist who seeks to unfold
with the force of self-evidence the limit on the effort to be? More point-
edly, if one lifts the brackets Ricoeur places on theological thinking
within his philosophy, is there another possibility for considering the
reality of the "third man"? And what might that form of thinking
contribute to the current debate about the task of humanism in our age?

Another option is in fact possible. I want to conclude this inquiry by
outlining this possibility and how it indicates the stance I designate
"theological humanism." This too will be a vision of life for the "third
man," but it departs from Ricoeur, and so too Levinas and Nietzsche,
insofar as the limit on human power is not my own mortality, the death
of the other, or the end of human, all too human history. The limit on
human power, the measure of our effort to be, is the love of life, the
depth of which is the love of God. The possibility of this measure, and
so another form of humanism, arises from greater attention to a point
noted previously in these reflections and yet quickly suspended in order
to engage Ricoeur's argument. The point, recall, was that the hatred of
life, articulated in a systematic pessimism or the challenge of wanton
suicide, is not coequal, it does not bear the same evidential weight, as a
primitive love of life.[30] What if one attends to this love and its self-
evident force in human existence?

To be sure, Ricoeur seemed to have grasped this point and that is why
he insisted on the "affirmation of man himself." Yet, as we have seen,
because he specifies this "affirmation" within the "effort to be," rather
than with reference to the *love of life*, the limit of human power must be
found in the other of attestation to power, namely, in death as the end
of power and thus the end of the capacity for violence. This aporia, that
is, that the affirmation of life bears its limit in mortality, means that we
are human, *only* human. Ricoeur's humanism, we might say, demarcates
philosophically the space in which human existence can unfold within its
own finite limits. He insists on this point, as we have seen, because the
celebration of self-overcoming is finally beyond our capacities even as the
command of the face of the other can never quell our self-affirmation.
The question remains, however, if the "other" to the love of life that
forms the limit to human power is in fact mortality.

It is at this juncture that the narrative and symbolic resources of the
biblical traditions enunciate another possibility on the plane of representations, which, I wager, can be redeemed in terms of their
self-evidential power. Death may indeed form a limit to my power, so
too the command not to kill the other or even the emergence of a new
form of humanity. Yet none of those limits, rooted in mortality, the death

of the other, or the "end of man," limits the love of life by what exceeds human existence. They specify humanism not with reference to a love other than what is human, but just in terms of another human. The transcendence that marks the limit to human power is circumscribed by intrahuman relations. That is why, most simply, these are various kinds of humanism. Yet does it not also confront me with the force of self-evidence that the love of life is just that, a love of life that both exceeds and yet embraces human being, including the human will to life? How then to articulate this intuition? What representations that present the human effort to be can be used to articulate this love and its meaning for the limits on human power? Will this require a new type of humanism?

The biblical religions present in symbolic and narrative form the insight that the love of life finds its limit in the longing for the divine and thus intensifies human transcendence. In the love of God is disclosed a limit to the idolatry of any finite love, any elevation of self, other, or specific attachment to divine status. In the love of God, in other words, is represented the insight, the intuition, that we are human, *truly* human, only when our love for life embraces finite existence, our own and others, within a love, an attestation, to what exceeds the finite and yet endows mortal existence with distinctive dignity. We are, as Ricoeur rightly saw, human, *only* human; the love of life is the animating impulse of the effort to be. Yet when this love is embraced by a love of divine life, then, the biblical texts suggest, we are human, *truly* human. In fact, we might say, using Christian categories, that the "fall" into sin is precisely the regress from the *truly* human to being *only* human, to live limited by death rather than by the love of God. And in fact within the myth of the "fall," the account in Genesis, the connection is drawn between death and turning from God.

It is not surprising that the biblical texts formulate the law of life, the proper limit on human power, in terms of the complex relation and ordering between the command to love God with one's whole heart, strength, and mind and one's neighbor as one's self.[31] The great double love command, I suggest, specifies as a maxim of action the limit of love on human capacity. The self-evident force of this maxim is found not in our mortality and violence (Ricoeur) or power (Nietzsche) or the vulnerability of the other (Levinas). It is found in that the love of finite life is also and always a longing for the divine. St. Augustine and many others rightly captured this biblical insight by noting that in all loves what is co-loved is the divine, the living God. This insight must then be formulated not only as a type of humanism but also a kind of piety, a religious longing. One can specify it as *theological* humanism, whose basic formula is *human, truly human*.

That is not enough, however. Insofar as theological humanism is developed from Christian sources and with reference to the "third man" more needs to be said. One ought not to efface the "humanism" and the celebration of human vitalities through attention to the love of God.[32] In this light, the claim of the Christian message is that the "God" who is loved in all acts of the love for life is the God whose is the power of being and yet has been manifested in human time in the human Christ, a power made perfect in the loving service of others. That insight enables the Christian imagination to intensify the law of freedom initially inscribed in biblical discourse in terms of the double love command. As St. Paul puts it at Galatians 5:13, "For you were called to freedom, brothers and sisters; only do not use your freedom as an opportunity for self-indulgence, but through love become slaves one to another. For the whole law is summed up in a single commandment, 'You shall love your neighbor as yourself.' "

In a word, once life is seen "in Christ," then the double love command is intensified in the direction of love for the human other as the limit on human and even divine power. The contrast is no longer intrahuman versus extrahuman transcendence; there is an ingression of the love of God into mutual love of neighbors. This requires that Christian theological humanism articulate itself through predicates borrowed from christological formulas: one is called to be human, *truly* human in the freedom of love. Yet this formula, I suggest, is not without the force of self-evidence; it is not mere dogmatic assertion. As shown, the love of life, our own self-affirmation, the reciprocal claim of self and other, and a longing for the divine become articulate in the idea, the representation, of the Gospel of love. This is why the Gospel can resonate, can make sense, to "Greek" and "Jew"; it is the possibility of the "third man" who is neither slave nor free, Greek nor Jew, male nor female existing in a freedom other than the vitalities of nature or the giving of the law (Gal. 3:28).[33]

At the outset of this inquiry I noted that it is not at all clear that Ricoeur would reject this new formulation of a humanism of the "third man." However, it is also clear that he did not articulate his position in this way, owing, I suppose, to the strict division he drew through most of his career between philosophical and theological reflection. But my point is to note that within the reality of the "third man," that form of life marked as the believing Gentile, a type of humanism is possible wherein the limit on the effort to be is not simply the sting of mortality but much more the longing for the divine. Once this longing, itself at an attestation and a struggle, finds representation in the biblical witness, the limit on human power is the transformation of freedom in service and love to the other as oneself. Here is enacted, in a way contrary to Nietzsche, the overcoming, the perfection, of human existence. And this limit, manifest in the Christ, is also the claim of the Christian conscience whose force of self-evidence is no less than Sinai.

CONCLUSION

The destination of these reflections has been to enunciate the possibility of what I have called *theological humanism* drawn from Christian sources rooted in the love of life reformulated through the freedom of the Gospel. Yet, in concluding, it might be asked why this revision in the humanistic agenda is needed for Christians, for the "third man," in our age. In my judgment, the development of theological humanism around the formula *human, truly human* is required in order to accomplish a task that Ricoeur himself saw in the dawning of the global age and yet did not fully address. "The time in which we live," he wrote, "is one of planetary consciousness." And in this situation "what the theologian should rediscover here is that true Christian universalism which is a universalism of 'intention' completely distinct from the universalistic 'pretension' of the Christianity of the Constantinian Age."[34] Only when the humanism of the "third man" is formulated to respect and enhance the integrity of life rooted in the love of life and disciplined by the free service of others manifested in the Christ can it hope to speak to the needs and longings of an age riddled with endangerments to human and nonhuman life. By isolating a new formula for humanism, I have thereby sought to continue further along that path of thought and action Paul Ricoeur so brilliantly and faithfully sought to travel.

NOTES

I want to thank David E. Klemm for years of conversation about the subject matter of this chapter; we are currently writing a book on "theological humanism" (Blackwell, forthcoming).
  1. Paul Ricoeur, "Nature and Freedom," in his *Political and Social Essay*, ed. David Stewart and Joseph Bein (Athens: Ohio University Press, 1974), pp. 31–32.
  2. For an excellent account of Ricoeur's life and thought, see Chares E. Reagan, *Paul Ricoeur: His Life and His Work* (Chicago: University of Chicago Press, 1996). A volume of responses to Ricoeur's work in a host of humanistic disciplines is *Meanings in Texts and Actions: Questioning Paul Ricoeur*, ed. David E. Klemm and William Schweiker (Charlottesville: University Press of Virginia, 1993). A conference held in 1999 on Ricoeur's work at the University of Chicago, including the closing address by Ricoeur about the scope of his philosophy, is published as *Paul Ricoeur and Contemporary Moral Thought*, ed. John Wall, William Schweiker, and W. David Hall (New York: Routledge, 2002). These volumes also include important bibliographies of Ricoeur's work and scholarship on his corpus.
  3. For one of his last statements that underscores Ricoeur's humanistic concern, see his "Ethics and Human Capability: A Response," in *Paul Ricoeur and Contemporary Moral Thought*, pp. 279–90.
  4. Albert Camus, "The Myth of Sisyphus," in *The Myth of Sisyphus and Other Eessays*, trans. Justin O'Brien (New York: Vintage Books, 1991),

p. 3. On this point see also John Lach, *In Love with Life: Reflections on the Joy of Living and Why We Hate to Die* (Nashville: Vanderbilt University Press, 1998). It is instructive in this light also to consider again Leo Tolstoy's *A Confession*, trans. A. Maude (Mineola, NY: Dover, 2005).

5. The Nietzsche texts are well known, and Ricouer begins *Oneself as Another* with the contrast between Nietzsche and Descartes. Also see Emmanuel Levinas, *Humanism of the Other*, trans. Nidra Poller, intro. Richard A. Cohen (Chicago: University of Illinois Press, 2003).

6. Of course, any typology is fraught with dangers because it seeks to isolate the most basic contours of positions rather than to offer sustained analysis of any one position. And, similarly, a typology can appear to isolate merely logical rather than living options. Problems granted, it is still helpful to have some means to organize the contemporary intellectual scene and a typology is one way to do so.

7. Paul Ricoeur, "Faith and Culture," in *Political and Social Essays*, p. 126. Actually there is another problem here in Western thought that I cannot pause to explore, namely, the relation of "law" and "nature" in the guiding of human life.

8. In terms of Protestant Christian thought, the most powerful expression was given by Paul Tillich when he spoke of "ecstatic humanism." See his *Morality and Beyond*, foreword by William Schweiker (Louisville, KY: Westminster John Knox Press, 1995). For a brief examination of Tillich's project in our contemporary context, see Max. L. Stackhouse, "Humanism After Tillich" in *First Things* 72 (April 1997): 24–28. For a discussion of Protestant and Roman Catholic humanism, see R. William Franklin and Joseph M. Shaw, *The Case for Christian Humanism* (Grand Rapids, MI: Eerdmans, 1991).

9. On this see William Schweiker, *Theological Ethics and Global Dynamics: In the Time of Many Worlds* (Oxford: Blackwell, 2004). Also see the essays on theological humanism in *Literature and Theology* 18, 3 (2004).

10. On this see William Schweiker, "The Reason for Following: Moral Integrity and the Christological Summons," in *Faith and Philosophy* 22, 2 (2005): 173–98. Also see Robert P. Scharlemann, *The Reason of Following: Christology and the Ecstatic I* (Chicago: University of Chicago Press, 1991).

11. Tzvetan Todorov, *Imperfect Garden: The Legacy of Humanism*, trans. Carol Cosman (Princeton: Princeton University Press, 2002), p. 5.

12. Ibid., p. 42.

13. Edward W. Said, *Humanism and Democratic Criticism* (New York: Columbia University Press, 2004), p. 10.

14. For the most ardent expression of this point see Peter Singer, *Unsanctifying Human Life: Essays on Ethics* (Oxford: Blackwell, 2002).

15. One finds this argument made, on the one hand, by so-called systems theories, and, on the other, by theorists who explore patterns and circulation of power in societies. See, for example, Nikklas Luhmann, *Theories of Distinction: Redescibing the Description of Modernity*, ed. W. Rasch (Stanford: Stanford University Press, 2002) and Thomas E. Wartenberg, *The Forms of Power: From Domination to Transformation* (Philadelphia: Temple University Press, 1990).

16. Paul Ricoeur, "Ethics and Human Capability: A Response," in *Paul Ricoeur and Contemporary Moral Thought*, p. 280.

17. See Paul Ricoeur, *Oneself as Another*, trans. Kathleen Blamey (Chicago: University of Chicago Press, 1992).

18. Paul Ricoeur, "What Does Humanism Mean?" in *Political and Social Essays*, pp. 86–87.

19. Tony Davies, *Humanism* (New York: Routledge, 1997), p. 125

20. While it is beyond the scope of this chapter, this is the decisive reason why Ricoeur can endorse both Spinoza's idea of the *conatus* and also Aristotelian teleological claims while rejecting the metaphysics of the will found in the pessimism of Schopenhauer or the vitalism of Nietzsche. See, for instance, his essay "Nature and Freedom," in *Political and Social Essays*, pp. 23–45, as well as the collection *History and Truth*, trans. Charles A. Kelbley (Evanston: Northwestern University Press, 1965).

21. One can sense this contradiction build through the progression of essays in the famous *Genealogy of Morals*. See Friedrich Nietzsche, *The Birth of Tragedy and the Genealogy of Morals*, trans. Francis Golfffing (New York: Doubleday Anchor Books, 1956).

22. See Emmanuel Levinas, *Totality and Infinity: An Essay on Exteriority*, trans. A. Lingis (Pittsburgh: Dusquesne University Press, 1969).

23. Paul Ricoeur, *Oneself as Another*, p. 336. I think the equation of killing and murder in this passage from Ricoeur is confusing. I do not see in Levinas's work a general, even universal, prohibition of "killing," but more precisely the categorical prohibition of murder. In *Totality and Infinity*, Levinas wrote about ontology as a "philosophy of war," but it is not clear even there that overcoming "ontology" would mean the end of a conception of justified killing.

24. See Emmanuel Levinas, *Totality and Infinity* and also *Alterity and Transcendence*, trans. Michael B. Smith (New York: Columbia University Press, 1999).

25. So too I cannot pause to assess the adequacy of arguments by those who contend that his conception of selves "run[s] the risk of reducing otherness to selfhood" and thereby falls to Levinas's criticism. See Richard Kearney, "Narrative Imagination: Between Ethics and Politics," in *Paul Ricoeur: The Hermeneutics of Action*, ed. R. Kearney (London: Sage, 1996), p. 186. On this also see John Wall, *Moral Creativity: Paul Ricoeur and the Poetics of Possibility* (Oxford: Oxford University Press, 2005).

26. There is of course considerable scholarship on the forms of Kant's categorical imperative and also its meaning. On this see Christine M. Korsegaard, *The Sources of Normativity*, ed. Onora O'Neill (Cambridge: Cambridge University Press, 1996). Also see William Schweiker, *Responsibility and Christian Ethics* (Cambridge: Cambridge University Press, 1995).

27. Paul Ricoeur, "A Critique of B. F. Skinner's *Beyond Freedom and Dignity*," in *Political and Social Essays*, p. 63.

28. One might note here that Ricoeur has retained and yet revised Martin Heidegger's understanding of time as the "meaning of being." For Ricoeur, "time" is indeed that "upon which" we project our ownmost possibilities, but those possibilities, rooted in the effort to be, exceed being toward death.

29. This is of course the force of Ricoeur's theory of narrative. See his *Time and Narrative*, 3 vols. trans. Kathleen McLaughlin and David Pellauer (Chicago: University of Chicago Press, 1984–1988).

30. The question here is not the moral permissibility of suicide in extreme cases, but, rather, a question of principle. For a subtle discussion of these matters see James M. Gustafson, *Ethics from a Theocentric Perspective*, 2 vols. (Chicago: University of Chicago Press, 1984, 1988).

31. On this see William Schweiker, *Power, Value and Conviction: Theological*

Ethics in the Postmodern Age (Cleveland: Pilgrim Press, 1998). For Ricoeur's reading of the command see his "Ethics and Theological Consideration on the Golden Rule," in *Figuring the Sacred: Religion, Narrative, and Imagination*, ed. Mark I. Wallace (Minneapolis: Fortress Press, 1995), pp. 293–302.

32. A common criticism by some neohumanists, like Todorov, is that religious discourse, and especially Christian faith, is self-mutilating. That is, religious faith displaces proper concern for specifically human goods with a demand to love God in such a way as to demean human care. It should be obvious that my own formulation and Ricoeur's as well are not open to this charge.

33. There is of course considerable interest now in St. Paul, but this interest, as far as I can see, has not, sadly, been linked to any form of Christian humanism. See, for instance, Alain Badiou, *Saint Paul: The Foundation of Universalism*, trans. Ray Brassier (Stanford: Stanford University Press, 2003).

34. Paul Ricoeur, "From Nation to Humanity: Task of Christians," in *Political and Social Essays*, pp. 134, 151.

Ricoeur's Hermeneutical Phenomenology of Religion 6

Merold Westphal

Like Husserl, Ricoeur sees phenomenology as a descriptive task. To demonstrate is not to argue from premises to a conclusion but to show what can be "seen." Or rather, in the words of Heidegger, the task is "to let that which shows itself be seen from itself in the very way in which it shows itself from itself."[1] One must speak of presentation rather than representation because the agent of this showing is not the philosopher but the "thing itself." The philosopher plays a maieutic or ancillary role, a servant both of that which shows itself and of those who are helped to "see" its self-presentation. Knowledge is not power but service.

Like Heidegger and virtually every other post-Husserlian phenomenologist, Ricoeur has taken the hermeneutical turn. I want to propose five theses that summarize Ricoeur's epistemology of hermeneutical phenomenology.[2]

FIRST THESIS: UNDERSTANDING IS A MATTER OF INTERPRETATION RATHER THAN INTUITION.

This is the primal heresy vis-à-vis Husserl's "principle of principles," which states *that every originary presentive intuition is a legitimizing source of cognition*, that *everything originarily* (so to speak, in its 'personal' actuality) *offered to us in 'intuition' is to be accepted simply as what it is presented as being*, but also *only within the limits in which it is presented there*."[3] This attempt to made evidence, presentation, showing, and so on, a matter of intuition is the Cartesian Husserl speaking.[4] By contrast, the hermeneutical claim is that what is given to intuition, strictly speaking, underdetermines our perception or understanding. Wittgenstein makes use of Jastrow's duck-rabbit to make this point, namely, that all seeing is seeing-as in a context where other seeings-as are possible, and not just as mistakes.[5]

This is why Gadamer can say that "understanding is not merely a reproductive but always a productive activity as well."[6] He illustrates this principle with two analogies crucial to the argument of *Truth and Method*: understanding is like performing a play or musical composition, and it is like translating a text from one language to another. The "object" underdetermines its interpretation so that there is a plurality of interpretations of, say Hamlet or the Archduke Trio, or a plurality of translations of Dante that will be judged by the most discriminating reviewers to be superb. Multiplicity is not necessarily misunderstanding.

Appeals to intuition or, in the case of texts, the author's intention as the one genuine intuition of meaning,[7] are usually attempts to flee this indeterminacy and plurality out of the fear that unless we have a single, definitive construal, anything goes and every interpretation will be just as good as any other. But Gadamer's metaphors undermine this fear. While there are numerous ways of playing Hamlet superbly, he cannot say, "To fish or not to fish." Nor can the musician play a C# where the score has an F.[8] Similarly, just as there may be numerous excellent translations of Homer, or the Bible, or Dante, there are also bad ones and outright mistaken ones. While multiplicity does not necessarily signify misunderstanding and misconstrual, it may do so.

SECOND THESIS: INTERPRETATION TAKES PLACE WITHIN A HERMENEUTICAL CIRCLE.

It is Schleiermacher who introduces us to the notion of this circle, calling attention to the fact that our interpretation of parts of a text is shaped by our understanding of the whole, while the latter is subject to revision in the light of our reading of the parts. There is no independent variable but rather a circular relation of mutual determination between the two moments. While Schleiermacher presents numerous circles of whole and part within both the linguistic and the psychological dimensions of interpretation, not every circle has the form of whole and part. Thus the entire linguistic dimension stands in a circular relation with the entire psychological dimension.[9]

Heidegger reiterates this notion, insisting that interpretation is never presuppositionless, but is always guided by an a priori understanding that we already have in three modes, fore-having, fore-sight, and fore-conception. But this a priori is not the fixed a priori of Kantian transcendentalism; it rather stands in a circular relation with the interpretations to which it gives rise.[10] For Merleau-Ponty, the body is a prime source of our preunderstandings.[11] For Gadamer, the emphasis falls on language and on the cultural traditions that shape our prejudices (prejudgments), making us into *wirkungsgeschichtliches Bewusstsein*. Consciousness or the (transcendental) ego as the source and interpreter of meaning is always conditioned and blind to what goes on behind its back, as it were.[12]

It is for these kinds of reasons that Ricoeur sees the hermeneutical turn as "the dispossession of consciousness as the place and origin of meaning."[13] He speaks of

> a *decentering* of the home of significations, a *displacement* of the birth-place of meaning. By this *displacement*, immediate consciousness finds itself *dispossessed* to the advantage of another agency of meaning—the transcendence of speech or the emergence of desire ... We must really lose hold of consciousness and its pretension of ruling over meaning ... The necessity of this dispossession [is] ... aimed at making me completely homeless, at dispossessing me of that illusory Cogito which at the outset occupies the place of the founding act, *I think, I am.* [14]

These statements, to be sure, come from his account of the hermeneutics of suspicion, of which we have yet to take note. But, quite apart from the issue of repressed desire, this dispossession is already implied by the hermeneutical turn as such. This is why Gadamer can express his critique of philosophies of reflection by saying that "*the prejudices of the individual, far more than is judgments, constitute the historical reality of his being.*"[15] It is also why Ricoeur can preface his general project by speaking of the "shattered" and "humiliated" cogito."[16] He makes these comments in relation to Nietzsche, whom he also identifies as one of the "masters" of the "school of suspicion."[17] But we must not link them solely to suspicion; for Nietzsche's epistemology is not only a hermeneutics of suspicion but also a general perspectivism that is a major chapter in the history of the hermeneutical turn as such.

THIRD THESIS: THE HERMENEUTIC TURN TAKES PHILOSOPHICAL REFLECTION ON DETOURS THROUGH PREPHILOSOPHICAL TEXTS.

In *The Symbolism of Evil,* Ricoeur takes his phenomenology of religion not merely into the domain of language,[18] but, more specifically, the language of symbol and myth. In his interpretation of Freud's contribution to hermeneutics, where dreams and neurotic behaviors are heavily symbolic, Ricoeur recalls both his general thesis that reflection requires interpretation and that interpretation involves the recourse to symbols and offers these insights as justification for "the detour through the contingency of cultures, though an incurably equivocal language, and through the conflict of interpretations."[19]

We have here a triple finitude of interpretation over against "Cartesian" modernity.[20] First, instead of the quest for the intersection of universality and necessity we have the admission of historical contingency, along with the particularity and relativity this entails. It is important to remember here both (1) that we are indeed relative, conditioned by our historical situation and unable to occupy what Thomas Nagel has called the view from nowhere, and (2) that to acknowledge this is not to throw in the towel and say that anything goes, that all views are just as good as any other views. It is merely to acknowledge that since we are relative, our judgments and the justifications we give them are not absolute.

Second, in addition to the fact that the languages of both text and interpreter are historically contingent and particular,[21] language as such is inherently and thus incurably polysemic and at best ambiguous and metaphorical, if not outright equivocal. The Cartesian claim to possessing clear and distinct ideas and the Hegelian claim to operate in the pure ether of *Begriffe* uncontaminated by the *Vorstellungen* that are the currency of the cave are abandoned. Our predicament stems not only from our embeddedness in the history of culture, but also in the evasiveness of language.

Third, for these and other reasons that can be explored, hermeneutics involves the conflict of interpretations. This does not mean just that there will be disagreements but also that the very criteria by which we try to determine (1) when differing interpretations are complementary, (2) when they are mutually exclusive, and (3) which, in the latter case, is to be preferred are themselves contaminated by historical contingency and semantic ambiguity.

Two further notes about these detours. First, since these three conditions of possible understanding are changeable in their substance but not eliminable in their form, the detours are not merely temporary but define the place of philosophical reflection. "Ground" signifies not unsituated justification but the soil in which thought is rooted. There is a significant sense in which all philosophy, like all politics, is local.

Second, these detours put us in conversation with texts. Much of the time these are texts in the literal sense of the term. But, given Dilthey's extension of hermeneutics to the historical sciences and Heidegger's so-called pragmatism of everyday life, Ricoeur extends the concept of text to include the whole domain of meaningful action.[22] Thus, a hermeneutical phenomenology of religion will concern itself with practices as well as paragraphs and pericopes.

The next two theses concern the "antiphenomenological" dimensions of Ricoeur's hermeneutic phenomenology. But before turning to them we need to consider two questions raised by the account so far. The first concerns the apparent psychologism of the hermeneutics of *The Symbolism of Evil*. There Ricoeur is engaged in what is sometimes called a hermeneutics of recovery, a purely descriptive phenomenology that permits the believing soul to speak. The philosopher adopts provisionally the motivations and intentions of the believing soul. He does not 'feel' them in their first naïveté; he 're-feels' them in a neutralized mode, in the mode of 'as if.' It is in this sense that phenomenology is a *re-enactment* in sympathetic imagination."[23]

In its psychologistic dimensions, the "Romantic" hermeneutics of Schleiermacher and Dilthey had as its goal getting behind the text to the inner psychic life of the author so as to recapture, reconstruct, recreate, reproduce the *Erlebnisse* that make up the author's subjectivity.[24] Language and its texts are the public means of a mediation that "presupposes a primordial capacity to transpose oneself into the mental life of others."[25] When Ricoeur speaks of "re-feeling" and "re-enacting," he evokes this tradition quite strongly. But he is not unaware of Husserl's critique of psychologism in general and of Gadamer's specific critique of psychologism in hermeneutics. With explicit reference to this latter critique in *Truth and Method*, which appeared in the same year as *The Symbolism of Evil* (1960), Ricoeur abandons his early psychologism. Thus, in 1973, he speaks of "shifting the interpretative emphasis from the empathic investigation of hidden subjectivities towards the sense and reference of the work itself." When he speaks of the "autonomy of the text" he evokes Husserl's analysis of the independence of meaning as an ideality from the inner life of the consciousness that intends such meaning. Over against Romantic hermeneutics, he wants to focus on *what* a text says rather than *who* says it. Now "the text must be unfolded, no longer towards its author, but towards its immanent sense and towards the world which it opens up and discloses."[26] The provisional and "as if" character of interpreting and understanding, say, the symbols of defilement, sin, and guilt or the narratives of the origin of evil is not a matter of finding out what it was like to be an ancient Babylonian, or Hebrew, or Greek, and so on, but rather what it *would be* like for me to live, in New York in the twenty-first century, in a world of meaning shaped by these texts.[27] Thus, in a later attempt to find philosophical meaning in biblical texts, Ricoeur says that while the thinker need not share the faith of those whose communities are founded in these texts, imagination and sympathy are "the minimum condition for access to the meaning of these texts."[28] What is conspicuously missing here is the reference to reenactment and refeeling.

Our second question concerns the relation of the phenomenology of religion to the religious life, to theology, and to philosophy. For Ricoeur it is identical to none of these. While still speaking the language of reenactment, Ricoeur says that it is "no longer religious experience" and "not yet philosophy." The phenomenologist does not "feel" the "motivations and intentions of the believing soul ... in their first naïveté; he 're-feels' them in a neutralized mode, in the mode of 'as if.' "[29] Thus, even if the phenomenologist is a believing soul, seeking to articulate the meaning of religious experience and belief, to describe the world in which the believing soul lives is not immediate experience, belief, and life. To write an essay on the phenomenology of prayer is not to pray. To describe confession is not to confess. So the phenomenology of religion is not the religious life itself, and the phenomenologist need not be a believing soul engaging in the beliefs and practices being described (though that may be helpful).

Then there is the question of the relation to theology. It, too, is a reflecting activity one step removed from the" immediacy of belief" or "primitive naïveté" of religious life;[30] and the phenomenologist is interpreting the same quite particular and contingent texts that concern the theologian. So where is the difference? This question has been raised sharply by Dominique Janicaud, who accuses a number of thinkers of being wolves in sheep's clothing, of smuggling theology into philosophy in the guise of phenomenology. One of Janicaud's targets, Jean-Luc Marion, has responded by drawing a distinction Janicaud should have seen in Marion's earlier writings. In describing revelation in Christ as a saturated phenomenon, "I am not broaching revelation in its theological pretension to the truth, something faith alone can dare to do. I am outlining it as a possibility."[31] In other words, if there were to be epiphanies they would be phenomena of this sort.[32]

This is also Ricoeur's distinction. For him "understanding is not concerned with grasping a fact but with apprehending a possibility of being ... to understand a text, we shall say, is not to find a lifeless sense which is contained therein, but to unfold the possibility of being indicated by the text."[33] Precisely in understanding a religious world as a possibility of my being I can choose not to dwell in it. The believing soul and the theologian affirm this possible world as actual, as grounded in the real; accordingly, they seek to dwell in it. The phenomenologist, as such, does not. They take the texts being interpreted as normative. The phenomenologist, as such, does not.

Finally, there is the thorniest question, that of the relation of phenomenology to the philosophy that it is "not yet." Ricoeur holds that philosophy must eventually pose the question of truth, and he understands this as the move "from a simple 're-enactment' without belief to autonomous 'thought'." In this connection he speaks of "pure reflection" and a "direct exercise of rationality."[34] He begins to sound like an Hegelian who thinks that the transition from *Vorstellungen* whose symbols and narratives are embedded in the contingencies of conflicting traditions to the ether of pure concepts (*Begriffe*), whatever that may be, the home of autonomous, presuppositionless philosophy. The detours through cultural contingency are temporary.

But Ricoeur still insists, "There is no philosophy without presuppositions. A meditation on symbols starts from speech that has already taken place, and in which everything has already been said in some fashion; it wishes to be thought with its presuppositions."[35] Does this mean that he takes back his talk about "autonomous thought," "pure reflection," and "direct rationality" as soon as it is uttered?

Not quite. Through his notion of philosophy as a kind of faith seeking understanding he will preserve as much of these "modern" ideals as he can in a "postmodern" context. The believing soul and the theologian (who is also a believing soul) affirm the world of the sacred texts of their tradition as the actual, the real, and they treat the texts in question as authoritative. The philosopher, as such, does not, but rather can be described, where the symbol gives rise to thought, as one *deeply indebted* to the texts but *not deeply committed* to them. How is the philosopher's "faith" to be described?

Here is one account.

We must believe in order to understand: never, in fact, does the interpreter get near to what his text says unless he lives in the *aura* of the meaning he is inquiring after. As Bultmann very well says ... "The presupposition of all understanding is the vital relation of the interpreter to the thing about which the text speaks directly or indirectly."[36]

Here is another account.

I wager that I shall have a better understanding of man and of the bond between the being of man and the being of all beings if I follow the *indication* of symbolic thought. That wager then becomes the task of *verifying* my wager . . .[The being of the philosopher and of human life to be interpreted] may appear contingent and restricted. Why symbols? Why these symbols? But, beginning from this contingency and restrictedness of a culture that has hit upon these symbols rather than others, philosophy endeavors, through reflection and speculation, to disclose the rationality of its foundation.[37]

Whose rationality? we must ask. Can this rationality be any other than one already shaped by the symbols, the narratives, and the traditions to be interpreted and thus "contaminated" with the contingency and particularity of the texts themselves? The theologian also seeks to show the rationality of the world evoked by the symbols and narratives of the tradition, to show that the sense of the text makes sense. Does the philosopher who, through the work of the phenomenologist of religion, is so deeply indebted to the texts have any advantage over the theologian by continuing to talk about "autonomous thought," "pure reflection," and "direct rationality"? Isn't the conflict of interpretations in the final analysis a debate, quarrel, conversation, dialogue, call it what you will, among theologians? It is far from clear that Ricoeur has given a clear, much less a convincing answer to these questions.

Ricoeur's fourth and fifth theses can be termed antiphenomenological.[38] But at the very least they are dialectically linked to the detours that are the hermeneutics of recovery, integral parts of the whole project whose aim is "to let that which shows itself be seen from itself in the very way in which it shows itself from itself." It can be argued that while these themes are anti-Husserlian, they are essential parts of hermeneutical phenomenological as developed by Ricoeur.

If, for example, phenomenology is taken to be the study of intentionality, the hermeneutics of suspicion (fourth thesis) can be seen as the analysis of the ways in which intentionality is distorted by disguised desire. By the same token, inverted intentionality (fifth thesis) signifies that classical subject-object intentionality is not the whole story of the life of consciousness. Each of these theses signifies a reason why the language of consciousness needs to be replaced by a language not laden with assumptions about the self as a transparent center. The question, Who comes after the subject?,[39] is in part the question, How shall we think of ourselves after the deconstruction of the "modern" self by thinkers like Kierkegaard, Marx, Nietzsche, Freud, Sartre, Levinas, Derrida, and Marion.[40] Here the dispossession of consciousness already noted is deepened through further detours, first through the dark lens of disguised desire, and then through the call of the Other. The self is decentered by sources of meaning too deeply inside itself or too freely outside itself for it to be able to preside over them.

With these suggestions in mind, we can turn our attention to theses four and five.

FOURTH THESIS: THE HERMENEUTICS OF RECOVERY NEEDS TO BE SUPPLEMENTED BY A HERMENEUTICS OF SUSPICION. THE DELIBERATE ATTEMPT TO EXPOSE THE SELF-DECEPTIONS INVOLVED IN HIDING OUR ACTUAL OPERATIVE MOTIVES FROM OURSELVES, INDIVIDUALLY OR COLLECTIVELY, IN ORDER NOT TO NOTICE HOW AND HOW MUCH OUR BEHAVIOR AND OUR BELIEFS ARE SHAPED BY VALUES WE PROFESS TO DISOWN.[41]

In the hermeneutics of suspicion, the "re-enactment in sympathetic imagination" of the beliefs and practices of the believing soul is replaced by aggressive cross-examination. It is like the difference between the questioning of the witness by one attorney, who seeks to recover for the benefit of the jury what the witness heard and saw, and the questioning of the other attorney, who seeks to discredit the testimony of the witness not just in terms of capacity (Wasn't it really too dark to get a good look at the gunman's face, especially at that distance?) but especially in terms of hidden motivations to say what the first wants to hear (Hasn't the prosecutor agreed to lessen charges pending against you in return for your testimony? Isn't there a history of bad blood between you and the defendant?).

Suspicion seeks to discredit the believer and only indirectly the belief. It would be a genetic fallacy to assume that a belief is false just because the believing is the product of wish fulfillment (Freud), ideological need for justification (Marx), or resentment (Nietzsche). I may testify against the defendant because I want to see him go to jail even though I didn't in fact see much of anything. But he may still be guilty of the crime. So Ricoeur says of psychoanalysis what can be said of any mode of the hermeneutics of suspicion.

> My working hypothesis ... is that psychoanalysis is necessarily icono-clastic, regardless of the faith or nonfaith of the psychoanalyst, and that this "destruction" of religion can be the counterpart of a faith purified of all idolatry. Psychoanalysis as such cannot go beyond the necessity of icon-oclasm. This necessity is open to a double possibility, that of faith and that of nonfaith, but the decision about these two possibilities does not rest with psychoanalysis ... The question remains open for every man whether the destruction of idols is without remainder; this question no longer falls within the competency of psychoanalysis. It has been said that Freud does not speak of God, but of god and the gods of men; what is involved is not the truth of the foundation of religious ideas but their function.[42]

This is why the believing soul has at least as much good reason to explore the dark side of faith as atheists like Marx, Nietzsche, and Freud. In a tradition that extends from Paul to Augustine to Luther and Calvin and on to Kierkegaard, sin is an epistemological category for the believing soul. Lenten self-examination, whenever it may take place and whether it is personal or corporate, is a search for "a faith purified of all idolatry."[43] That is why Kierkegaard and those just mentioned with him seem to me to be "masters of suspicion" just as much as Marx, Nietzsche, and Freud.

One way of seeing suspicion as belonging to hermeneutical phenom-enology is to see it as "just" another of the detours that reflection must take in the search for self-understanding. The road block here is not merely cultural contingency but dangerous desire, desire shaped by a *conatus essendi*, a will to power blind to moral constraints. In theolog-ical language we are talking about the ways in which sinful self-assertion distorts our beliefs and practices. Hermeneutical phenomenology thus takes on a certain theological form. As a hermeneutics of finitude (contingency, plurality, conflict, etc.) it can be read as a commentary on the doctrine of creation, a reminder that we are not God, but finite and relative creatures. As a hermeneutics of suspicion it can be read as a commentary on the doctrine of the fall, a reminder that we are sinners and anything but pure reason or the good will. Thus, Marx, Nietzsche, and Freud can be read as secular theologians of original sin.

This second type of detour intensifies the "shattering" of the cogito of which Ricoeur speaks. After speaking of the major blows that human self-love has endured at the hands of Copernicus and Darwin, Freud puts it this way. "But human megalomania will have suffered its third and most wounding blow from the psychological research of the present time which seeks to prove to the ego that it is not even master in its own house, but must content itself with scanty information of what is going on unconsciously in its mind."[44] The same can be said of ideology critique and genealogy.

FIFTH THESIS: A HERMENEUTICAL PHENOMENOLOGY OF RELIGION INVOLVES A MOVEMENT BEYOND INTENTIONALITY.

Ricoeur writes that "if one takes intentionality to be the prisoner of representation, then one would have to say that [religious] feelings and dispositions mark the beyond of intentionality imprisoned by its representative limit."[45] To speak of this imprisonment is to speak of "objectivization, therefore of the subject's claim to mastery over the meaning of its experience," and Ricoeur notes that religious feelings and dispositions "can transgress the sway of representation and, in this sense, mark the subject's being overthrown from its ascendency in the realm of meaning."[46] This is a further "shattering" of the cogito, its exposure to meaning of which it is not the origin. But the issue here is not the *Wirkungsgeschichte* that requires a detour through the text and its cultural contingency. Nor is it the deeply disguised desires that require the "I think" to deceive itself about itself. It is the voice of the Other found in the call-and-response structure of the religious life. This call is "recognized, avowed, confessed" not only in prayer but above all in obedience.[47]

The structure of reverse or inverted intentionality invoked here is quite simple. It is central to Sartre's analysis of the Look and to Levinas's analysis of the face of the Other.[48] The idea is that meaning does not have its origin in my seeings-as, my acts of *Sinngebung*, but rather in the gaze or the voice of the Other. The intentional arrows that define the situation, give me my identity, and call me to a responsible response do not emanate from me but from the Other toward me. Here we have another radical dispossession or decentering of the ego.

One might call this appeal to an inverted intentionality antiphenomenological; yet both Sartre, who derives no ethicoreligious significance from the Look, and Levinas, who does, continue to call themselves phenomenologists. The move beyond intentionality in its original, Husserlian sense is best seen as a move to "an intentionality of a wholly different type,"[49] which turns out to be this inverted intentionality experienced in the face and in the saying of the Other. Just as my intentionality (consciousness, transcendental ego) arrives on the scene too late to be the origin of meaning because I am always preceded by both (1) the language and culture by which I have been formed and (2) the dark desires I manage to keep hidden from myself—so I arrive too late in relation to (3) the Others, human and divine, whose claim has always already placed me under obligation and called me to obedience. If there is anything to religion and morality that goes beyond clever *conatus essendi,* the therapeutic relation to self and the contractual relation to others, then such inverse intentionality will be necessary in order "to let that which shows it be seen from itself in the very way in which it shows itself from itself."

For a look at a substantive phenomenology of religion in the context of these theses, we might turn to Ricoeur's analysis of the symbols and myths of the meaning and origin of evil in *The Symbolism of Evil.* I turn rather to the reflections on the biblical texts that emerge in his later writings. In the "little ethics" that Ricoeur gives in the seventh through the ninth studies of his Gifford lectures, he defines the "ethical intention as *aiming at the 'good life' with and for others, in just institutions.*"[50] Although he insists on the primacy of the Aristotelian/teleological dimension over the Kantian/deontological aspect of this account, he has more to say about justice than about the good life in this text and others more or less contemporaneous with it. He especially concerns himself with the relation between justice and love, making a deliberate detour through various Jewish and Christian texts.

The phenomenological and philosophical tasks that we have seen him distinguish earlier on are here blended together. On the one hand, we have the description of a religious account of the normative "sieve"[51] through which any account of the good life must pass; on the other hand, and at the same time, Ricoeur's wager is that reflection on biblical texts will "give rise to philosophical thinking,"[52] in other words, will guide us to truth about who we are and how we should live, whether or not we are believing, practicing Jews or Christians.

Ricoeur tells us that love speaks a different language from that of justice.[53] So he contrasts the "poetics of love" with the "prose of justice."[54] The primary phenomenological move here is the contrast between what he variously calls the law, the logic, the economy, the pattern of equivalence, reciprocity, or exchange, and the law, logic, economy, pattern of excess, extravagance, superabundance, generosity, or gift.

Philosophical theories of justice, especially formal deontologies, tend to locate themselves in the context of the former. These are not without biblical equivalents. In other words, "the exegesis of the 'Ten Words,' in passing through the Golden Rule, finds its conceptual counterpoint in a contemporary reflection on law and justice."[55] The negative form of the Golden Rule is expressed by Hillel, "Do not do unto your neighbor what you would hate him to do to you," and the positive form is expressed by Jesus,"Treat others as you would like them to treat you."[56] In the Ten Words, the commandment against murder can also be read in this light: just as your value your own life, don't take that of others.

> But other biblical texts seek to preclude a "perverse" reading of these texts, one that through its demand for *reciprocity* remains within the parameters of the *lex talionis*: an eye for an eye, a tooth for a tooth. Understood this way, the golden rule just says, "I give *so that* you give" (*do ut des*). But is it not against this perverse interpretation of the golden rule that Jesus warns us in Luke: "If you love those who love you, what credit is that to you? For even sinners love those who love them.... But love your enemies, do good, and lend, expecting nothing in return" (Luke 6:32–35).[57]

These and other texts seek to bring about "a *conversion* of the golden rule from its penchant toward self-interest."[58]

The various ways in which this conversion resists the perversion of the Golden Rule involve the commandment to love one's neighbor as oneself, found first in Leviticus 19 and then repeated by Jesus (Mark 12:28–34). By itself, this could be understood in terms of the logic of equivalence. But the texts resist such a reading, and Ricoeur's detour through Jewish and Christian texts becomes a meditation on the tension between the ideals of love to justice. What follows are some of the stopping points along that detour.

To begin with, the Hebrew scriptures regularly require an extension of the concept of neighbor to include the widow, the orphan, and the stranger, precisely those from whom one could not expect an equivalent return. Loving the neighbor does not take place in the market, which is given over to contractual exchange of equivalents. Jesus pushes this "logic" even further with the command to love one's enemies.[59] Here generosity trumps equivalence and love prevails over justice.

Alongside this pushing of the concept of neighbor to its limits, Ricoeur describes another way in which the poetry of love challenges the prose of justice. It has three dimensions. First, love seeks to move us from the "disinterested interest" of which Rawls speaks, in which we seek to filter out bias in order to protect equivalence, to a sense of mutual indebtedness that takes us beyond merely being fair. Here Ricoeur evokes, without mentioning, Kierkegaard's analysis of "Our Duty to Remain in Love's Debt to One Another," based on Romans 13:8.[60] Love finds itself to be indebted not because of what it has received or hopes to receive (from the widow, the orphan, the stranger, or the enemy), but because of what it is able to give. This debt exhibits the "economy" of the gift, not that of exchange.

Second, love teaches justice to find its universality precisely in the exception.[61] Here Ricoeur evokes, without naming, Carol Gilligan's contrast between the ethic of justice as delineated in universally valid rules and the ethic of care that takes into account the particularities of the situation to which universal rules, ironically, can never do justice.[62] Thus, when Jesus in the Sermon on the Mount talks about turning the other cheek, going the second mile, and so forth, he is not formulating a rule but showing a pattern that through its extravagance and hyperbole disorients our complacency in order to reorient us to a new generosity whose model in Paul, Augustine, and Luther will be the excess of divine grace over the law of sin and its equivalent, death.[63]

Third, love counteracts the tendency of justice to treat others as faceless, as interchangeable, substitutable variables.[64] This third moment reveals the central point of the first two. Justice, because of the formalism of the logic of equality, tends to depersonalize the other. She is just another set of (possibly) competing interests; he is just another instance of a universal rule. In the process, the other is defaced. Love resists this "perverse" understanding of justice. The other becomes the one to whom I am asymmetrically indebted because (s)he is someone for whom I care. There can be no substitution of one neighbor for another.

In addition to (1) pushing the notion of neighbor to its limit, thereby transgressing the limits of justice and (2) giving a face, a unique personal identity to each other, including those unable or indisposed to be of benefit to me, love exceeds justice in a third way to which Ricoeur calls our attention. It concerns motivation. In biblical contexts love is the categorical imperative. You shall love the Lord your God, and you shall love your neighbor as yourself.[65] This gives rise to the question, How is it possible to obey this command? Whence the capacity for this generosity?

Ricoeur formulates the biblical answer this way: "Because it has been given to you, you give in turn."[66] He might have turned to John 4:19, "We love because he first loved us," but he turns instead of Rosenzweig to make the same point, quoting from *The Star of Redemption*.

Man can express himself in the act of love only after he has first become a soul awakened by God. It is only in being loved by God that the soul can make of its act of love more than a mere act, can make of it, that is, the fulfillment of a—commandment to love . . . The commandment to love can only proceed from the mouth of the lover. Only the lover can and does say: love me! . . . [To which the beloved responds] I still do not love nearly as much as I—know myself loved.[67]

Ricoeur shares this understanding. "A commanded interhuman love cut off from its source would be scandalous. Yes, the love that love requires is surprising, but it is not scandalous."[68] Divine love is the source of human love; before it is commanding love, it is enabling love. Among the gifts that enable gift love, Ricoeur mentions specifically creation, the exodus, the Torah, justification and forgiveness through the cross, and eschatological hope.[69] The superabundant generosity to which we are called has its ground in the superabundant generosity, what theologians call prevenient grace, which is always already prior to both the call (command) and our response. This world of gift and gratitude is indeed a different language game from that of justice, a game to which I may be motivated simply by fear of punishment or hope of minimized violence.

Ricoeur uses a rich vocabulary to describe what love does to justice. It helps, motivates, converts, infiltrates, extends, presses, reinterprets, protects, and assists justice to be or to become truly itself. In conclusion, two comments about this help.[70] First, it shows the virtual collapse in Ricoeur's thought of the distinction between hermeneutical phenomenology and philosophy *sensu stricto*. On the one hand, his account of the dialectic of love and justice is descriptive of what happens in the biblical texts through which he is making his detour. On the other hand, and at the same time, he is enacting his wager that this biblical material will help us better to understand who we are and how we should live, that it is, in other words, at once reasonable and true. We have seen him repeat the expectation that his detour through the contingency of texts and traditions, in this case biblical, will "give rise to philosophical thinking."[71] But there is no longer any reference to "autonomous thought," "pure reflection," or a "direct exercise of rationality" (SE 353, 347). It would appear that the lingering hope for a philosophical rationality not itself hermeneutically contingent and particular has been abandoned. He hopes to be persuasive, but not by being pure. He is phenomenologist and theologian at one and the same time.[72]

The second thing to notice is that the reference just now of the dialectic of love and justice was not incidental or accidental. To be sure, the logic of excess exceeds the logic of equivalence, but not in order to abolish it. Ricoeur insists that the two need each other. As we have seen, love represents a conversion of justice, and all our codes need to be tempered with compassion.[73] But this is not a one way street. Indeed, neighbor love is a "corrective" to the Golden Rule; but it is not a "replacement" intended to "eliminate" or "substitute" for the latter.[74] The ethic Ricoeur finds in the Bible and commends to his reader, whether Jewish, Christian, or neither, consists "in the tension between unilateral love and bilateral justice, and in the interpretation of each of these in terms of the other."[75]

This reference to tension is important inasmuch as Ricoeur calls attention to it but refuses even to try to resolve it. This means that in the final analysis he is Kierkegaardian rather than Hegelian. For Hegel, dialectic is the second moment of reason in which opposition, antinomy, and contradiction come to light. But this is only penultimate. Dialectic is followed by speculation in which the tension between opposed elements is resolved in an organic totality. With wonderful irony, Kierkegaard and his pseudonyms accuse Hegel of being insufficiently dialectical precisely because of the insistence on resolving all conceptual tensions. Ricoeur the phenomenologist finds no attempt to resolve the tension between love and justice, equivalence and excess in the biblical texts. Ricoeur the philosopher leaves things just that way.

NOTES

1. Martin Heidegger, *Being and Time*, trans. John Macquarrie and Edward Robinson (New York: Harper & Row, 1962), p. 58.
2. I say "epistemology" to resist speaking of method or methodology. These theses are not so much rules or procedures to be followed as they are an analysis of the nature and limits of human understanding in this mode. Thus, Gadamer can write, "My real concern was and is philosophic: not what we do or what we ought to do, but what happens to us over and above our wanting and doing." *Truth and Method*, 2nd ed., trans. Joel Weinsheimer and Donald G. Marshall (New York: Crossroad, 1991), p. xxviii. I leave aside here the question of the scope of hermeneutics that is central to the Habermas–Gadamer debate.
3. Edmund Husserl, *Ideas Pertaining to a Pure Phenomenology and to a Phenomenological Philosophy, First Book*, trans. F. Kersten (The Hague: Martinus Nijhoff, 1983), p. 44.
4. For Husserl's difficulty in holding to this move, see "Husserl's Departure from Cartesianism," in Ludwig Landgrebe, *The Phenomenology of Edmund Husserl: Six Essays*, ed. Donn Welton (Ithaca: Cornell University Press, 1981).
5. Ludwig Wittgenstein, *Philosophical Investigations*, trans. G. E. M. Anscombe (Oxford: Basil Blackwell, 1958), p. 194. On the relation of Wittgenstein and Heidegger, see Stephen Mulhall, *On Being in the World: Wittgenstein and Heidegger on Seeing Aspects* (New York: Routledge, 1993).
6. Gadamer, *Truth and Method*, p. 296. Heidegger writes, " 'Seeing' does not mean just perceiving with the bodily eyes, but neither does it mean pure nonsensory awareness of something present-at-hand in its presence-at-hand." The latter half of this denial undoubtedly refers to Husserl's theory

of categorical intuition in *Logical Investigations*. Heidegger concludes that "we have deprived pure intuition of its priority." *Being and Time*, p. 187.

7. In Schleiermacher's hermeneutics the mind of the author is to be grasped in an act of "divination," an intuition of an intuition, as it were. See my analysis in "Totality and Finitude in Schleiermacher's Hermeneutics," *Overcoming Onto-theology: Toward a Postmodern Christian Faith* (New York: Fordham University Press, 2001).

8. I'm bracketing the times when historical scholarship suggests that the textus receptus is the result of a copying error. But in that case, one is playing from a new score that calls for a C#.

9. For a more detailed analysis, see the essay mentioned in note 7.

10. See *Being and Time*, pp. 32 and 63.

11. In *The Phenomenology of Perception* and in the title essay of *The Primacy of Perception and Other Essays*.

12. For Hegel's hermeneutical phenomenology it is the *necessity* of the movement that transforms this blindness into *transparency* and this conditionedness into *absolutes Wissen*. This movement takes place "as it were, behind the back of consciousness." *Phenomenology of Spirit*, trans. A.V. Miller (Oxford: Clarendon Press, 1977), p. 56. For the hermeneutical phenomenologies of the twentieth century, this necessity and this transparency are pipe dreams. Their verdict on Hegel's project and Husserl's related aspiration for unconditioned transparency is negative, and hermeneutics signifies the humility of accepting the radical finitude of human understanding.

13. *Freud and Philosophy*, trans. Denis Savage (New Haven: Yale University Press, 1970), p. 494.

14. Ibid., pp. 422–23. All but final emphasis added. Cf. p. 424, where Ricoeur writes that "reflection, in order to get at the root of desire, must let itself be dispossessed of the conscious meaning of discourse and displaced to another place of meaning."

15. *Truth and Method*, pp. 276–77.

16. *Oneself as Another*, trans. Kathleen Blamey (Chicago: University of Chicago Press, 1992), pp. 11–16. Ricoeur does not think that the self is merely negated without remainder. He locates hermeneutics "at an equal distance from the apology of the cogito and from its overthrow . . . beyond the alternative of the cogito and of the anticogito . . . at an equal distance from the cogito exalted by Descartes and from the cogito that Nietzsche proclaimed forfeit" (pp. 4, 16, 23). Hermeneutics is not about "giving in to the vertigo of the disintegration of the self pursued mercilessly by Nietzschean deconstruction" (p. 19).

17. *Freud and Philosophy*, p. 32.

18. The hermeneutical turn and the linguistic turn are not identical, but they are like Venn diagrams that overlap considerably.

19. Ibid., p. 42. Ricoeur speaks of "the long detour of the signs of humanity deposited in cultural works" and of "the detour of understanding the cultural signs in which the self documents and form itself . . . [so that] reflection is nothing without the mediation of signs and works" *Hermeneutics and the Human Sciences*, ed. and trans. John B. Thompson (New York: Cambridge University Press, 1981), pp. 143, 158–59. In *Oneself as Another*, the detour is through the four Who? questions that structure the book. The self, so far from being the origin of meaning and the foundation of truth, is that which is sought in a reflection whose detours preclude total transparency. See pp. 16–19.

20. If it is surprising to hear Derrida refer to himself as "we, *Aufklärer* of modern times," it is no less surprising, though it should not be, given his anti-Cartesian posture, to hear Ricoeur say "we, postmoderns." See *Derrida and Negative Theology*, ed. Harold Coward and Toby Foshay (Albany: SUNY Press, 1992), p. 59, and André LaCocque and Paul Ricoeur, *Thinking Biblically: Exegetical and Hermeneutical Studies*, trans. David Pellauer (Chicago: University of Chicago Press, 1998), p. 121.

21. Philosophers all too often flee this finitude by presupposing their access to propositions that are externally related to natural languages. But this Platonism is not self-evident nor easily defended. See my "Taking Plantinga Seriously: Advice to Christian Philosophers," *Faith and Philosophy* 16, 2 (April 1999): 173–81.

22. See *Hermeneutics and the Human Sciences*, ch. 1, 5, and 8. These are also chapters 2, 5, and 7 in *From Text to Action: Essays in Hermeneutics, II*, trans. Kathleen Blamey and John B. Thompson (Evanston: Northwestern University Press, 1991. In fact, Ricoeur's phenomenology of religion focuses on texts in the narrower sense.

23. *The Symbolism of Evil*, trans. Emerson Buchanan (New York: Harper & Row, 1967), p. 19. Emphasis added. Cf. p. 9. On p. 3 it is "sympathetic re-enactment in imagination."

24. Ricoeur is aware of the complexity of the texts of Schleiermacher and Dilthey and that there is more than psychologism to be found in them. For my own analysis of this complexity, see "Totality and Finitude in Schleier-macher's Hermeneutics."

25. *Hermeneutics and the Human Sciences*, p. 49. Dilthey speaks of "trans-posing oneself into an alien spiritual life through linguistic, factual, and historical studies." "The Rise of Hermeneutics," in *Hermeneutics and the Study of History*, Vol IV of *Selected Works*, ed. Rudolf A Makkreel and Frithjof Rodi (Princeton: Princeton University Press, 1996), p. 242. Emilio Betti speaks of "transposition into the subjectivity of an Other." See *Contemporary Hermeneutics*, ed. Josef Bleicher (London: Routledge and Kegan Paul, 1980), p. 57

26. *Hermeneutics and the Human Sciences,* pp. 47–53. "What we wish to understand is not the fleeting event, but rather the meaning which endures" (134).

27. In other words, Ricoeur also agrees with Gadamer that application is ingredient in and not subsequent to interpretation. This presupposes that distance is not an obstacle to be overcome, since "historical consciousness seeks not simply to repudiate distanciation but to assume it." Ibid., p. 61.

28. *Thinking Biblically*, p. xvii.

29. *The Symbolism of Evil*, pp. 4 and 19.

30. Ibid., p. 351.

31. Janicaud's essay, along with essays from those he accuses of being theolo-gians in disguise, appears in Dominique Janicaud et al., *Phenomenology and the "Theological Turn": The French Debate* (New York: Fordham University Press, 2000). This version of Marion's reply is found in *Being Given: Toward a Phenomenology of Givenness* (Stanford: Stanford University Press, 2002), p. 5.

32. This 'if' echoes Ricoeur's 'as if'.

33. *Hermeneutics and the Human Sciences*, p. 56.

34. *Symbolism of Evil*, pp. 353, 347.

35. Ibid., p. 348.

36. Ibid., p. 351. On p. 357, Ricoeur explicitly refers to the "Anselmian schema" he is invoking. *Fides quaerens intellectum.*

37. Ibid., pp. 355, 357.

38. In *Freud and Philosophy,* Ricoeur regularly refers to what is here the fourth thesis in these terms.

39. This question is the title of a collection of probing essays edited by Eduardo Cadava, Peter Connor, and Jean-Luc Nancy (New York: Routledge, 1991). The question presupposes that the "shattering" of the cogito is not without remainder. Cf. Calvin O. Schrag, *The Self after Postmodernity* (New Haven: Yale University Press, 1997).

40. The latter four are mentioned here because of their analyses of inverted or reversed intentionality.

41. The quoted definition is from my own study, *Suspicion and Faith: The Religious Uses of Modern Atheism* (New York: Fordham University Press, 1998), p. 13.

42. *Freud and Philosophy,* pp. 230, 235. The reference to function shows that the hermeneutics of suspicion is not tied to a psychologistic understanding of motives. Ideology critique, for example, is about the function of beliefs, not the consciousness of believers, other than the claim that it is a false consciousness that knows not what it does, or why.

43. This is the argument of *Suspicion and Faith.* For a briefer overview, see "Taking St. Paul Seriously: Sin as an Epistemological Category," *Christian Philosophy,* ed. Thomas Flint (South Bend: University of Notre Dame Press, 1990).

44. *Introductory Lectures on Psychoanalysis,* Vol XVI of *The Standard Edition of the Complete Psychological Works of Sigmund Freud,* ed. and trans. James Strachey (London: Hogarth, 1953–1974), p. 285.

45. "Experience and Discourse in Religious Discourse," in *Phenomenology and the "Theological Turn,"* p. 129.

46. Ibid., p. 127.

47. Ibid., pp. 128–29. Ricoeur adumbrates this call to obedience in an earlier essay, where he writes that "the intended meaning of the text is not essentially the presumed intention of the author, the lived experience of the writer, but rather that the text means for whoever complies with its injunction." *Hermeneutics,* p. 161.

48. For Sartre, see *Being and Nothingness,* Part Three, Chapter One, Section IV. For Levinas, see *Totality and Infinity,* trans. Alphonso Lingis (Pittsburgh: Duquesne University Press, 1969). In speaking of "the beyond of intentionality," Ricoeur also alludes to Levinas's essay, "Beyond Intentionality." See *Philosophy in France Today,* ed. Alan Montefiore (New York: Cambridge University Press, 1983).

49. *Totality and Infinity,* p. 23.

50. *Oneself as Another,* p. 172.

51. Ibid., p. 170.

52. *Thinking Biblically,* p. xvi

53. Ibid., p. 125. *Figuring the Sacred,* trans. David Pellauer (Minneapolis: Fortress Press, 1995), p. 317.

54. Ibid., p. 324.

55. *Thinking Biblically,* p. xviii.

56. *Oneself as Another,* p. 219. The former is in the Babylonian Talmud, *Sabbath,* 31a, the latter in Luke 6:31 and Matthew 7:12.

57. *Figuring the Sacred,* p. 300. Cf. p. 328.

58. Ibid., p. 300.
59. *Thinking Biblically*, pp. 128–29.
60. *Works of Love*, trans. Howard V. Hong and Edna H. Hong (Princeton: Princeton University Press, 1995), pp. 175–204. The text for this meditation is Romans 13:8, "Owe no one anything, except to love one another; for the one who loves another has fulfilled the law."
61. *Thinking Biblically*, p. 128.
62. *In a Different Voice* (Cambridge: Harvard University Press, 1982).
63. *Figuring the Sacred*, pp. 280–83.
64. *Thinking Biblically*, pp. 131–32.
65. When Jesus summarizes the law in terms of these two commands (Mark 12:28–34, Matthew 22: 34–40, Luke 10: 25–28) he is quoting, respectively, Deuteronomy 6:4–5 and Leviticus 19:18.
66. *Figuring the Sacred*, p. 300.
67. Quoted in *Thinking Biblically*, pp. 121–22. Ricoeur adds, "The reader will not be surprised that this chapter in Rosenzweig ends with the parable of the Song of Songs ..." For Ricoeur's own related meditation on this biblical text, see pp. 265–303.
68. Ibid., p. 121.
69. *Figuring the Sacred*, pp. 299, 325.
70. No one of these terms seems privileged. I repeat the one that contingently appears first in the list just given.
71. *Thinking Biblically*, p. xvi.
72. Janicaud might object, but only if he could show that secular thought is neutral and embedded in no hermeneutical circle of its own.
73. *Figuring the Sacred*, pp. 301, 328.
74. Ibid., pp. 300–301.
75. Ibid., p. 301. Cf. p. 324.

Love Proceeds by Poetic Amplification 7

André LaCocque

To Paul Ricoeur, this token of my ḥesed, attachment, to his person
and way of thinking.

It can be said that civilization rests mainly on two pillars: justice and a
conceptual complex that the Hebrew expresses in one word *ḥesed*[1] and
which translates in English as love, goodness, compassion, generosity,
graciousness, and the like.

In this chapter, I intend to explore the Ricoeurian heuristic bracketing
of justice and love in the following oppositional comparison of the two
concepts: *Justice proceeds by conceptual reduction; love proceeds by
poetic amplification.*[2] I will reflect on the three pairs of contrasting
terms: justice and love; conceptual and poetic; reduction and amplification. In the final part, I will select the biblical book of Ruth as the
touchstone of my philosophical conclusion regarding the necessary
relationship of justice and love.

As a premise to any inquiry in more depth into Ricoeur's rationale for
bringing together justice and love, it seems experientially evident that
some manner of tie exists between the two, for each would demand the
presence of the other in order to be whole. Love without justice is a
sham; justice without love or compassion breeds oppression. But, if there
is indeed between justice and love a true relationship, this needs to be
explored so that their conjunction in society be conscious and carefully
grounded.

In Ricoeur's statement, there are three sets of opposition: justice and
love; conceptual and poetic; reduction and amplification. The first set,
despite the previously mentioned sentiment, could be ideologically
construed as in mutual exclusion. One does not expect the judge to love
the defendant, not any more than the physician is required to love her
patient. On the contrary, the judge is supposed to deal impartially and

dispassionately, and the doctor to treat her patient scientifically. Conversely, one could say that the lover is not necessarily moved by the justice criterion vis-à-vis the beloved. It may even happen—perhaps inadvisably or unacceptably—that one commits a crime for the love of someone else. Abraham is ready to sacrifice his beloved son Isaac (Genesis 22) in the name of a stronger love; Moses kills an Egyptian foreman for the love of his people (Exodus 2:12); "Sophie" prostitutes herself in the concentration camp to save her son;[3] Dietrich Bonhoeffer attempts at the life of Adolf Hitler in the name of compassion for the innumerable victims of the mad dictator....

An important step toward the dilemma's resolution is made, however, when one passes to the second set of oppositions: the conceptual versus the poetic. Justice, like science, is essentially conceptual. It weighs up the pros and cons after gathering as many relevant elements as possible to ground its judgment (evidence). Justice proceeds by cumulative judgments (jurisprudence). For justice is the adjudication of rights and punishments; it is discriminating between what is right and what is wrong; what is optimal for the *res publica*, and what is detrimental to it. Already at this elementary level, justice acquires a dimension of *Sorge* (care) and we come closer to an adumbration of love—although still a long way from a junction of the two. For, as long as one stays within the confines of the conceptual, there is little room for the realm of feelings, which the ideational rather looks at with suspicion.

So, a first serious limitation of the judicial must be taken into account. "Bare" justice finds itself divorced from an essential aspect of humanity, the psyche. The insistence on "facts" as opposed to "feelings" or *interpretation*—although a basic exercise of being human—is self-defeating if, indeed, justice aims at rendering to the victims the freedom to fulfill their life-goals.

Furthermore, the law is susceptible of laminating the human nuances and of codifying "acceptable" behavior patterns, that is, of defining as precisely as possible human *normality*. Such definition, however, leads to a "conceptual reduction," for it creates around the parameter of the "norm" a whole shaded zone of alleged abnormality or deviance, which the judicial may or may not tolerate.[4] We have thus arrived at a second and much more serious stricture in "justice." Justice indeed proceeds by *reduction*. Any codification of human existence cannot but curtail (cut the tail of) human autonomy and freedom.[5] Life transcends all definition of life; the self transcends all judicial confinement. For one is not just born a man or a woman (*Gabe*), one becomes a man or a woman (*Aufgabe*).[6]

Conscious of such a discrepancy between the innate or archaeological and the gerundive, Søren Kierkegaard sets forth the principle of a "teleological suspension of the ethical,"[7] that is, obviously, the suspension of the "norm." The ethical would lead Kierkegaard to marry Regina Olsen, as it is true of innumerable other love stories. Its suspension brings the Dane to renouncing her and—whether he was right or wrong[8]—to a *poetics* of human existence, that he expresses in his vast literary production.[9] In the eyes of "bare" justice, Kierkegaard has flouted the legitimate expectation of Regina. There is on his part something like a betrayal, a reneging on his pledge to her. To the extent that the legal is the normal, Kierkegaard's stance is not only abnormal, it is illegal.

His *intent* or *interpretation*, nonetheless, is a far cry from recklessness. On the contrary, he wanted to be an obedient servant of a higher justice principle, of a higher divine command. All his life, Kierkegaard tried endlessly to *justify* himself before the divine and human "court." For him, the religious calling to extravagance supersedes all other dictates. He was called to be unique, not to conform.

In a dialogical work coauthored with Paul Ricoeur, I have developed Franz Rosenzweig's heuristic distinction between law and commandment.[10] To the extent that the biblical revelation that God is a *living* God (and not a frozen "carved" idol) is to be taken seriously, it becomes imperative to make a clear distinction between the divine will as generally expressed in the Law (*Torah*), and the actual will given within the concreteness of the moment in the form of a unique commandment. Biblical examples abound: prostitution, for instance, is unlawful—but Tamar prostitutes herself to obtain justice (Genesis 38). In a strikingly daring move, the Gospel presents a genealogy of Jesus wherein four women are uniquely mentioned. All four are of questionable reputation: *Tamar* the Canaanite, mother by fornication of Perez; *Rahab* the professional prostitute of Jericho, mother of Boaz; *Ruth*, a citizen of Moab, a nation loathed in Israel as lewd and dastardly, is mother of Obed and grandmother of King David; the adulterous *Bathsheba* (called here "the wife of Uriah"), mother of King Solomon (see Matthew 1:3–6). Similarly, one of the most heinous crimes is certainly infanticide; it is abhorrent to the Law—but Abraham receives the commandment to kill his son Isaac (Genesis 22).

While the law reveals the divine economy, the commandment reveals the divine excess. The former orients life; the latter disorients (in order to reorient). The former demands an absolute obedience to the norm; the latter a punctual disobedience. The former is exemplified in the Gospel by the pragmatic Martha; the latter by the contemplative (and inefficient) Mary, her sister (cf. Luke 10:41). Mary, at any rate, underscores the unfinalizability and unpredeterminability of the human existence, as Mikhail Bakhtin so strongly insists. On the threshold, in the boundary (say, between this world and the kingdom of God, or, to quote Bakhtin again, between "man" and "the man in man"[11]), the commandment teaches that Truth is imponderable; it cannot be prescribed and is irreducible to any conceptual understanding of the human being. The commandment, by contrast with the law, compels one to realize that "the Sabbath has been made for man's sake, not man for the Sabbath" (Mark 2:27).

Of course, the law can be abused, and *a fortiori* the commandment can be abused. "The voice of Sam" allegedly ordered Samuel Berkovitz to kill. Thousands of people today claim that they have received the heavenly commandment to destroy the "ugly Americans." The "teleological suspension of the ethical" is an extremely dangerous *principium*, as it is open to erroneous and even lethal interpretations. But it is also the very condition for the human to become fully human, for the "man in man" to be blooming. "Without risk there is no faith," said Kierkegaard, an aphorism that we may paraphrase as, without risk there is no life. Only robots are programmed to evade all risks.

The Danish philosopher strongly emphasized the extravagance of transcending the law. The Christian, he said, is "the knight of faith who in the solitude of the universe never hears any human voice but walks alone with his dreadful responsibility."[12] The emphasis on "solitude" and "aloneness" is the ringing proclamation of the uniqueness of all human beings—a stance strongly supported by Martin Buber, for instance, most emphatically in his *I and Thou*. The "generality" of the law is a double-edged sword. It safeguards the *res publica*, but it also kills the particular. In the eyes of the law, the particular is dangerously edging on the extravagant and, as such, on the abnormal, the subversive, the "unlawful." In the name of the law, not only Kierkegaard but Socrates and Jesus must be condemned. Characteristically, Socrates is declared a "corrupter" and Jesus a "hooligan" (*lestes*).

Socrates' poisoning and Jesus' crucifixion are abhorrent. It is clear that the laws of fifth-century BCE Athens and of first-century CE Jerusalem were in need of being reinterpreted by way of alloying them with another ingredient (still to be defined here), lest they be a killing weapon in the hands of self-appointed guardians of morality or sycophants of the Establishment. The law alone proves insufficient. The "normative" is only a minimum required. It levels off the citizens by conceptual reduction to a common denominator. Collectively, this is a very serious matter. But individually, it is simply disastrous, for such a conceptual reduction at this level is an existential reduction of being; it produces a "minus-being." It does not honor people's humanness and bypasses the fact that those equalized citizens—all are equal before the law—are in reality less equals than "individuals of exception" because they are all "souls," as biblical anthropology affirms.[13] The equalizing law does not address the "soul," only the "flesh," in Saint Paul's vocabulary (using both terms inclusively).

If, in the words of Bruno Bettelheim, "love is not enough,"[14] it is at least as still true that justice is not enough. That is why, in a philosophical reflection so decisively prescription-oriented as is Rabbinic Judaism, Sages in the Talmud called at times to go *liphnim mi-shurat ha-din*, above and beyond the line of what is lawful.[15] This exhortation brings to mind Jesus' understanding of the *mitsvah*. I had, not so long ago the opportunity of reflecting on the famous parable of the traditionally called "good Samaritan" in Luke 10.[16] The law, in the case that Jesus submits to the judgment of the lawyer with whom he is dialoguing, is enmeshed in the definitional: "Who is my neighbor?" (verse 29). Is the wounded man on the road to Jericho worthy of being helped? Does he fill the requirements in the Leviticus definition of "neighbor"? How far, if such were the case, would the "love of the neighbor" go in his case? Why speak of self-love ("as thyself") when applying the commandment to love one's neighbor? Is the Samaritan's care of the injured man an excessive zeal—even an admission of guilt?—or is it the fulfillment of a *mitsvah*? But Jesus shortcuts the deployment of such intricacies by reversing the terms of the dilemma. He proceeds to a limitless amplification of "neighborliness" and calls to *be* the neighbor of anyone else, the needy, the sufferer, and even a Samaritan enemy (who, in the parable has, paradoxically, shown the way). For, while the law would be sorting out the proper categories for its legitimate application, the mugged man is dying! The heart of the matter does not consist in selecting who is and who is not a "neighbor," but to become the neighbor of anyone in need of help (and who is not?). Such is the spirit of the law, only capable to render his life to the wounded man, instead of "killing" him (or letting him die) through legally delaying succor.

And so is reached the high point where law and love do meet. [17]

Retrospectively, translating *Torah* by law was any way questionable. Because of the Second Temple period promotion of the law to the rank of a program of Jewish existence and of the highest principle of normative Judaism, the contemporary Greek translation of the Bible (LXX) referred to *Torah* as *nomos*,[18] and so does the New Testament also in Greek. In reality, however, the Hebrew term *Torah* does not mean anything like a code (although codes may be part of it), but is rather to be translated by "instruction, orientation, way of life." Fundamentally, the verbal root at the basis of the term *Torah* means "to shoot an arrow [in a certain direction]" (cf. 1 Samuel 20:36–37; Proverbs 26:18), then, figuratively, indicating a direction, universally symbolized by the arrow. *Torah* indicates the right way of life and, as such, is an existential paradigm. To *Torah* belong also narratives, myths of creation, genealogies, paraenetic exhortations. Under one of its aspects, namely, the prescriptive, *Torah* is summarized in a nutshell in the Decalogue ("Ten Words"), which, strikingly, is set, not in the imperative, but in the present/future of the indicative mode, thus collapsing prescription and description: "you shall (or, you will) not covet...."

Now, it must be conceded that a command like "Thou shalt not kill," for example, although showing the "magnetic North," so to speak, still says nothing about *how* not to kill. According to Jesus, for instance, the prohibition amounts ultimately to something as positive as to love, even to love someone I was about to kill or let die in her misery, passing her by with indifference or, maybe, with the judgmental feeling of her insignificance. In Jesus's parable, a priest and a Levite pass the half-dead man by on the road. They should have set an example of *ḥesed*, loving compassion, but instead they display an outrageous callousness. By not going beyond the letter of the law (for they can allege all kinds of reasons for their nonintervention), they have sterilized the law.[19]

Not to kill, as a commandment, has set the parameters of a vast area whose content is love. It says that anything less is still verging on murder. The nonassistance to the wounded man in the ditch is, for all practical purposes, condemning him to die. Even the enemy, says Jesus, must be loved, according to the commandment, if indeed the latter is not to be subjected to a casuistic of sorts. Thus, without the commandment (in the form of prohibition), any positive conclusion that not-killing means ultimately loving would have no basis whatsoever. When the modern Jewish philosopher Emmanuel Levinas states that, on the human face the begging, "do not kill me" is writ large, he is also poetically explicating the Sixth Commandment.

"Love proceeds by poetic amplification." Love, as a matter of fact, transforms justice into a poetic invention, into a poetic imagination. "All observance is training in the art of love," said Abraham Heschel.[20] For life is an art, by contrast with a "connecting the dots" according to a blueprint. The transition from law to love is like what happens in war and peace. War must be waged by the rules [the laws] of engagement. After the military victory, however, peace must be won through poetic imagination and invention. Without the rules of warfare, there is no advent of peace, but peace is so less the prolongation of war that it is its negation—a Pauline dialectic indeed.

As an application of what precedes, I should like to bring as a most beautiful example the book of Ruth.[21]

From the outset, the book of Ruth places us before a legal quandary that will reach a degree of *aporia* before its resolution at the end of the story. To our surprise, as a matter of fact, the action begins in the inimical and ostracized country of Moab and, although it soon continues in Bethlehem of Judah, Moab is, as it were, sticking with the plot in the person of "Ruth the Moabite," after whose name the book is known. By the way, it is the only document in the Bible bearing the name of a Gentile in its title, a sure sign of subversion.

This is our point of departure, for it conditions the argument of the whole book: Ruth is a Moabite in Judah. This fact is reiterated six or seven times, even in contexts that do not call for such a reminder.[22] It constitutes a very important background for the story, especially as the book was written during the (attempted?) "ethnic cleansing" by Ezra and Nehemiah in the fifth century BCE Jerusalem (cf. Ezra 9:11; 10:2; Nehemiah 13:28–31).[23] Now, the subversiveness of the story of Ruth becomes especially acute when the latter adopts her mother-in-law Naomi's people and God:

> Where you go, I will go;
> where you lodge, I will lodge;
> your people shall be my people,
> and your God my God.
> Where you die, I will die—
> there will I be buried.
> May the Lord do thus and so to me,
> and more as well,
> if even death parts me from you!
>
> (Ruth 1:16–17, NRSV)

At this point and unexpectedly, the Judeans of Bethlehem are facing a difficult legal problem: What is there to do with someone who "converts" to Israelite religion and nationality, when this someone "belongs"[24] to an inimical nation, loathed since the days when it refused entry to Israelite refugees fleeing the Egyptian slavery (Numbers 22–24; Deuteronomy 23:4–5)? In fact, the Israelite legislation is clear on the total exclusion for ever of the Moabites from the community (see Zephaniah 2:9 [seventh century]; Deuteronomy 23:4 [sixth century]; Nehemiah 13:23,25 and Ezra 9:1–2; 10:3 [fifth century]). By law, Ruth has no place in Bethlehem and she certainly is not a possible beneficiary of the legal provisions allowing the poor to glean behind the harvesters (but see Ruth 2). In fact, she is a nonentity where she settles with her mother-in-law. In Ruth 1:20–21, Naomi (diplomatically?) does not even hint to her presence at her side when speaking to the women of Bethlehem.

But there occurs a first encroachment to the letter of the law when Boaz, one of the pillars of the conservative community in Bethlehem, welcomes Ruth in his fields and showers her with surprising privileges. Boaz's rationale in doing so is explicitly based on Ruth's display of *ḥesed* (Ruth 2:11–12; 3:10). As previously stated, this Hebrew word is rich in meaning and is variously translated by "kindness, favor, goodness of heart, loving kindness" and the like. In short, what has proved able of disorienting and reorienting Boaz's understanding of the law is love. Ruth's love of her mother-in-law, of her people and her God, stirs a response of love on the part of Boaz—who as a result becomes a central character in the drama that unfolds.

For the plot dramatically intensifies. In one of the most risqué scenes of all biblical narratives, Ruth stealthily introduces herself one night into Boaz's "bed" and declares him the "next-of-kin redeemer" (one word in Hebrew) of a daringly assembled combination of Naomi and herself.

Now this is edging on the absurd: two women claiming to be legally treated as one unit, the younger one, a Moabite, substituting her sexuality to the older's, a Judean, so that when Ruth of Moab becomes a mother, her son is declared "officially" Naomi's son (Ruth 4:17); Boaz called to become the "redeemer" when in fact there is another man (called "So and so" in Ruth 4) who is the closest relative of Naomi or, rather, of her deceased husband, Elimelek, and is here bypassed; Ruth offering herself on the threshing floor to a man of her mother-in-law generation, because what is at stake is the perpetuation of *Naomi*'s clan.... All this is a expansive application of two different sets of laws in the Hebrew Bible—see below—according to the principle stated by the Sages of the Talmud, *liphnim mi-shurat ha-din*, above and beyond the letter of the law.

As if this were not enough, the story goes one step further toward the "poetic amplification" of understanding the law. In the court of assizes where Boaz confronts "So and so" before a jury of elders and a crowd of witnesses, the ostensible litigation is about a field that Naomi must sell but which could be redeemed by the closest next-of-kin (Ruth 4). The matter, however, is a complicated one because Naomi is too old to produce a successor to Elimelek's clan and heir to the redeemed property. The potential redeemer would thus acquire the field for himself rather than for Naomi and the alleged redemption is a sham. Hence, Boaz argues, who acquires the field must also marry Naomi's young substitute, Ruth the Moabite and produce through her an heir to the name and property of the deceased. This, of course, is highly "unorthodox." Two entirely different sets of laws are conveniently (from the point of view of Boaz) consolidated: the law of redemption and the law of leviratic marriage (by which, according to the letter of the law, the *brother* of a deceased man *without progeny* who *lived in the same house* must take his *sister-in-law* and legally consider the first born son of such union as heir of his *brother*'s name and "field" [Deuteronomy 25:5–10, my emphasis].)

None of the conditions envisaged by Deuteronomy 25 is met in Boaz's argument, which amounts to fiction rather than to a valid legal case, at least on the surface of things. And, to boot, there is no way that levirate marriage laws would apply to a Moabite woman, who, besides, is no sister-in-law of the potential Judean redeemer and cannot, by any stretch of the imagination, be considered as having "lived in the same house" with him.

Furthermore, as regards the second set of laws in question, namely, the principle of "redemption" (of persons or properties), it is operative only within strict limits of application. In the basic text in this respect, Leviticus 25:23 ff., it is a question of a "brother" impoverished and entitled to be succored by his closest next-of-kin. The latter is to free his relative by paying his debts (or ransom), by purchasing an alienated property of his kin, or by any other intervention that will guarantee the continuity of the family's name and estate. As to the resident-alien, although he or she must also be helped, it is not by "redemption," but through a kind of "social security" (verse 35).

All this, of course, "So and so" knows and he could easily dismiss on that basis Boaz's argumentation. He does not do so for the reason that the noncompliance with Boaz's demonstration leads to a blind alley. If the two laws are kept separate, Elimelek's clan, for all practical purposes, becomes extinct; Naomi remains a widow without support; the dead man's property is lost; Ruth is an "exorbited" satellite; Boaz has lost the benefit of Ruth's ḥesed (Ruth 3:10)—and, prospectively, there is no Obed (Ruth's son in the story), no King David (Obed's grandson), and no Messiah, descendant of David! *The law not fertilized by love kills instead of vivifying.*

What needs to be stressed is that love does not cancel off the law, despite the ungrounded but widespread opposition set in some Christian milieus between God's law (the "Old Testament") and God's grace (the "New Testament": ḥesed may also be translated by "grace"). The truth of the matter is that Ruth's love gives "Boaz's" law its validity. Justice is much more than meting out a commensurate penalty to the culprit and reward to the innocent. It is more than discriminating between the worthy and the unworthy; between who deserves to be rescued and who is to be left to die in the road ditch. Justice is "redemption," says the book of Ruth, that is, the restoration or the creation of conditions for the other's plus-being. True redemption means that Boaz will marry Ruth (by default of "So and so"); the field will be redeemed at the benefit of Naomi; the son born to Boaz and Ruth will be legally adopted as Naomi's own son (4:16); Elimelek's line will continue; it will even lead to the great King David and, beyond, to the future Messiah.

Thus, the establishment of justice in Ruth brings in joy and peace to all.[25] It redeems the past of the sour relationships between Israel and Moab;[26] it enlivens the present for all concerned; and it brightens the future of individuals like Naomi, Boaz, or Ruth, as well as for Naomi's or Elimelek's clan. Justice is a blessing for Ruth's progeny—the barren woman (cf. Ruth 1:4 f.) is now fertile (cf. Ruth 4:11–15) and for the nation and the world expecting "the son of David."

The conceptual reduction was only temporarily and transiently bringing the facts into focus, thus isolating them from the larger context to which they belong, for the sake of a close examination. Poetic amplification restores the whole picture of humanity. To take an example, if the exercise of justice can demonstrate that a defendant accused of being a wife-beater is indeed guilty, it may also be true that he was raised in a devastating milieu prone to violence, of which he has been the first victim. Or, to return to the case under consideration here, Moab is a stereotypical enemy characterized by profligacy and treachery (cf. Num 22–24)—but Ruth the Moabitess is a saintly woman redeeming the sins of her nation and succeeding in breaking up the "legal" stereotype (cf. Ezra 9:1–2; Neh 13:23–25). As a consequence of her breakthrough, a totally unexpected new history is initiated. The "old" was bogged down in the intricacies of casuistic, which almost forestalled a rebirth of the Judean community. For, according to the letter of the law, nothing but indifference was expected from Boaz as regards Ruth the Moabite (cf. Lev 25:23 ff.). No less than the commandment he receives in the concreteness of existence brings him to adopt a reverse attitude. It is a daring move on his part, but also a life-promoting one, on the model of Ruth's *hesed* that brought her to play the part of a wanton woman, like Tamar in Genesis 28, or like St. Mary-the-Egyptian in the fifth century.

The law without love kills! As Paul the exegete said, "the letter kills, but the Spirit gives life" (2 Corinthians 3:6). And another Paul, the philosopher, concluded, *"Love proceeds by poetic amplification."*

NOTES

1. Rendered in the Greek Bible by *agape*, and by the Latin Bible by *caritas*.
2. Personal communication.
3. William Styron, *Sophie's Choice* (New York: Random House, 1979).
4. An example of judicial lenience is displayed in what the French call "maisons de tolérance" (= brothels), tolerated as serving a more or less valid purpose in society.
5. Hence, for instance, the protest of some artists and politicians complaining in the name of freedom of speech about censorship.
6. In all brands of dictatorship, the intelligentsia is the enemy. Thinkers, poets, artists, always find intolerable the confusion of *Aufgabe* (duty, vocation, purpose) with *Gabe* (the given), namely, the automation of people into cogs of the state machinery.
7. Søren Kierkegaard, *Fear and Trembling* and *The Sickness unto Death*, trans. Walter Lowrie (Princeton: Princeton University Press, 1941), p. 64.
8. In an entry in the *Journal* (iv A 107; May 17, 1843), Kierkegaard writes, "If I had had faith, I would have remained with Regina."
9. Kierkegaard as husband of Regina would rejoin the generality and lose the particularity that makes him Kierkegaard.
10. Franz Rosenzweig, *The Star of Redemption*, trans. E. T., W. W. Hallo (Boston: Beacon Press, 1972), p. 177. André LaCocque and Paul Ricoeur,

Thinking Biblically (Chicago: University of Chicago Press, 1998), pp. 79 ff.

11. Mikhail Bakhtin, *Problems of Dostoevsky's Poetics,* ed. and trans. Caryl Emerson (Minneapolis: University of Minnesota Press, 1984), p. 59.

12. Kierkegaard, *Fear and Trembling,* op. cit., p. 90.

13. By contrast with Greek philosophy, the Hebrew worldview claims that the human being *is* a soul, he does not have a soul.

14. Bruno Bettelheim, *Love Is Not Enough: The Treatment of Emotionally Disturbed Children* (Glencoe, IL: Free Press, 1950).

15. See *Shabbat* 130a ; 131a; 132b–133a; etc.

16. André LaCocque, "Jesus's Hermeneutics of the Law, Rereading the Parable of the Good Samaritan," in Jiri Moskala, ed., *Creation, Life and Hope, Essays in Honor of Jacques Doukhan* (Berrien Springs: Andrews University, 2000), pp. 251–76.

17. The well-known storylike inquiry into the juvenile legal system by William Ayers bears the telling title: *A Kind and Just Parent: The Children of Juvenile Court* (Boston: Beacon Press, 1998).

18. *Nomos* as an ideal was endowed with the apologetic design of asserting to the Hellenistic world that the Torah is also the cosmic law that rules the universe as *oikoumene.*

19. In the Talmudic text of *Shabbat* 130 referred to, it is said that, when R. Eliezer ruled to go beyond the letter of the law, it was "only out of love for the precept." See note 15.

20. *The Wisdom of Heschel, selected by Ruth Marcus Goodhill* (New York: Farrar, Straus and Giroux, 1970), p. 256. He also said, "The goal is to live beyond the dictates of the law" (p. 255).

21. See A. LaCocque, *Ruth (A Socio-Legal Commentary). A Continental Commentary* (Minneapolis: Fortress Press, 2004).

22. See, e.g., Ruth 4:10.

23. However "justified" by political and economic issues in an isolated Judea within a regional hostile environment.

24. Cf. Ruth 2:5.

25. Remarkably, no one of the personages is blamed in the story, not even Orpah, the second daughter-in-law of Naomi who decides to go back to Moab, or "So and so," who does not seize the chance of furthering the history of redemption. Abraham Lincoln (a lawyer by trade), in his inaugural address as president, said, "With malice toward none, with charity for all."

26. There is no way anymore to associate Moab only with the regrettable events reported in Numbers 22–24. Ruth the Moabite has singlehandedly transformed the two nations' rapport.

The Challenge of the "such as it was": Ricoeur's Theory of Narratives

8

Pol Vandevelde

When Paul Ricoeur introduces the notion of narrative in order to offer a new approach to action, time, and selfhood, he offers a rather broad and provocative reformulation of two key phenomenological notions: the intentional relationship between consciousness and object, especially the Husserlian correlation between noesis and noema, and the hermeneutical circle, especially in its Heideggerean version. This reformulation not only accounts for how understanding works, but also how understanding is already part of the fabric of action, time, and selfhood. By qualifying life as having a prenarrative quality and action as a "potential narrative" (1991a, 30; 1984b, 74), Ricoeur in fact makes two different claims: (1) action and life are structured or organized in their being by narrative-like features, so that telling the story is not an after-the-fact reorganization of what took place, but the making explicit of what was already implicit in action and life; and (2) the understanding of what in and of itself asked to be so rendered takes the form of narratives and feeds on narratives.

While the second claim that understanding takes the form of narratives and is permeated by a cultural world itself made of narratives reformulates the hermeneutical circle, especially in its Heideggerean version, the first claim is significantly stronger. It is the view that the object must already be susceptible to being caught in a narration and thus must have a structure making it amenable to being talked about so that the process of narration "renders" the inchoate narrative structure at the heart of things, events, and people. Narratives are thus not mere descriptions of something that would be otherwise available independently of description, but are ontological layers, part and parcel of the paste of actions and experiences. Ricoeur believes that this second claim guards against idealism, whether textual or narrative. Ricoeur appeals to Husserl's notion of the correlation between noesis and noema and argues that the narrative is the noema of what took place.

By these two claims regarding the narrative character of understanding and the narrative structure of what is recounted, Ricoeur thus tries to accommodate the two different requirements, coming from hermeneutics and phenomenology: on the hermeneutic side, narratives are an interpretive mediation, but, on the phenomenological side, they provide the meaning content or noema of what is so recounted.

Ricoeur has applied his theory of narrative to different objects, especially time (Ricoeur, 1984a, 1984b, 1985) action (Ricoeur, 1986, 1991d), and selfhood (Ricoeur, 1990, 1992). We can already see significant differences among these objects and these differences already raise the question whether narratives fulfill the same function for each of these objects. Regarding time, Ricoeur does not claim to offer a theory of time, since he believes that time cannot be presented to intuition and can only be observed indirectly. His claim is that time becomes human and thus meaningful when articulated through narratives. He thus makes no ontological claim about time itself and does not attempt to render what time is. When he applies narrative to selfhood and uses the expression "narrative identity," he understands such an identity as "neither an incoherent series of events nor an immutable substantiality, impervious to evolution"; rather, it is "the sort of identity which narrative composition alone can create through its dynamism" (1991a, 32). Here there is an ontological claim, although weak, in the sense that selfhood is a matter of interpretation by the person, "whose being matters to him," as Heidegger says. But there are real constraints on how someone tells her own story. Facts, events, and deeds cannot be undone or ignored and other observers can point to missing links, gaps, or falsification. However, because the narratives about the self focus on the meaningfulness of facts, events, and deeds, we can see as nonproblematic the claim that the understanding of my own self needs the assistance of narrative. We can thus follow Ricoeur when he states: "It therefore seems plausible to take the following chain of assertions as valid: self-understanding is an interpretation; interpretation of the self, in turn, finds in the narrative, among other signs and symbols, a privileged form of mediation; the latter borrows from history as well as from fiction, making a life story a fictional history or, if one prefers, a historical fiction, interweaving the historiographic style of biographies with the novelistic style of imaginary autobiographies" (Ricoeur, 1992, 114).

However, with action and some types of experiences there seems be a lesser need of such narrative assistance, since action seems to have a self-identity of its own that time and self may not have so glaringly: we can recognize an action when we see one, initiate one, or prevent one without explicit reflection and thus without speaking. I will focus on this third realm of application for narratives and attempt to delineate the extent to which action and experience have a prenarrative quality. I will thus focus on the second claim Ricoeur makes that narratives can provide not only the meaningfulness of action or experience, in which case narratives are a tool for understanding, but also the meaning content, in which case narratives tell us what really took place. Let us start with the noema as applied to action.

NOEMA OF ACTION AS TEXT

The two claims previously mentioned, which Ricoeur does not distinguish, are manifested by the expression "to recount things or people such as they were," which Ricoeur discusses in the third volume of *Time and Narrative* (1985). The "such as" involves the genres of sameness, difference, and analogy. Sameness, because this is the claim of historians that any narrative about what took place is "the same" as what actually happened; that is what the word "such" represents: the claim to be adequate to what took place. Difference, because obviously what took place is not made of words, metaphors, or stories and needs to be recognized as heterogeneous to the order of narratives. And analogy, because there is a necessary mediation involved expressed by the word "as": what took place is not directly given, but has to be recovered. What gives us the past is the "such as it happened" provided by the accounts we have of it and which exert toward the past a function Ricoeur calls of *représentance* (representing) or *lieutenance* (stand-in), which he understands as the translation of the German *Vertretung*.[1]

The function of "representing" (*représentance*) offers an equivalent of what took place whereas the function of "signifying" (*signifiance*) points to the element of invention or fiction involved in a configuration. Ricoeur offers the notion of "debt" to lock the narrative configuration on the past and thus to keep the signifying function subservient to the representing function. In the case of the historian, she has a debt toward the past and is submitted, Ricoeur says, to "what once was the case" (Ricoeur, 1985, 204). Ricoeur appeals to Cézanne, who felt a debt "with respect to a *vision* which takes for him the significance of a logos which precedes him, which (pre)occupies him ... Added to this, the task of doing justice to the world has the value for us of being a hermeneutic key to the reading of phenomena" (Carr, Taylor, and Ricoeur, 1991, 187). Like a painter, the historian attempts "to render what is owed to what is and was (*rendre son dû à ce qui est et ce qui fut*, 1985, 220). But the historian only has a trace of the past. This trace has to become the representing of the past (*représentance* or *lieutenance*, translation of *Vertretung*) and makes the reference of history to the past an indirect reference. It is this indirect reference that has to be clarified.

Ricoeur dedicated several essays in the collection of articles *From Text to Action* (Ricoeur, 1986, 1991d) to showing that action is a text.

Although he does not use the word "narrative" in this collection of essays and only speaks of action as text, he mentions in *Time and Narrative* action as having a prenarrative structure (Ricoeur, 1984b, 60). I thus take text and narrative as analogous in their articulating or objectifying function.

Ricoeur establishes a correlation between action and text in terms of objectifications: the text makes visible and explicit what is implicit in action. Against Dilthey, who advocates a strong opposition between understanding and explanation, Ricoeur does not believe that we have to choose between an immediate meaningfulness, present in expressions of life, and indirect methods of quantification as in natural sciences. An objectification can be performed from the inside when implicit features and structures are made explicit.

In the case of writing, we have an objectification of oral discourse that is analogous to the objectification that takes place when an action becomes an object of investigation or of discussion, for example, when it is narrated. "Meaningful action is an object for science only under the condition of a kind of objectification that is equivalent to the fixation of a discourse by writing" (Ricoeur, 1991d, 150).[2] The objectification writing offers to oral discourse consists in (1) the fixation of meaning, so that meaning is no longer an event, but can be reidentified, (2) the dissymmetry between speaker's meaning and sentence's meaning, so that the text gains an autonomy oral discourse did not enjoy, (3) the liberation from the ostensive reference—the common situation of discourse—toward a projection of a world readers can inhabit, and (4) a universal range of addressees created by the text and no longer by the face-to-face situation of discourse.

We have something analogous in the case of action whose structure Ricoeur compares to the structure of a speech-act. This objectification is made possible by some inner traits of the action that are similar to the structure of the speech-act and that make doing a kind of utterance. The four traits of action, corresponding to the four traits of writing, are the following: (1) an action has a propositional content and an illocutionary force. The propositional content is, for example, "Brutus killed Caesar," and the illocutionary force is what counts as killing (Ricoeur suggests that the different forces are part of a typology or criteriology of action [Ricoeur, 1991c, 152]); (2) an action is detached from its agent and has consequences the agent may not have anticipated. This autonomy of action represents its social dimension. Only "with simple actions like those that require no previous action in order to be done, the meaning (noema) and the intention (noesis) coincide or overlap" (1991c, 153). The expression of an action leaving its mark or the notion of reputation or of criminal record indicate this social imprint of action;

(3) an action has an importance that goes beyond its relevance in its initial situation, so that the meaning of an action exceeds the boundaries of what agents knew and anticipated; and (4) an action is addressed to an infinity of readers so that an action is an open work and those who evaluate an action are not those who initiated it.

The advantage of Ricoeur's suggestion is that the objectification provided by writing and narrative respectively leads to explanation, but from within, on the basis of internal features. Similarly, when we move from action to text, we do not move from brute facts to signs, but we have a revelation of what was already intrinsic in action itself.

While there is indeed an analogy between these two types of objectifications, there is also something missing in Ricoeur's account. In the case of writing and oral discourse, we can speak of two different entities that can be identified independently of each other, but the relation between text and action is not a relationship between two different entities. It is rather that action can be "treated" as a text (1991d, 150) and is a "quasi-text" (1984b, 58). While the objectification in writing is a kind of fixation of what was already orally available, the objectification of action is the making explicit of what was implicit in action itself, but not available as such. Ricoeur himself feels that there is a missing term. He asks: "But if the 'sense content' is what makes possible the 'inscription' of the action event, what makes it real? In other words, what corresponds to writing in the field of action?" (1991c, 152). In *From Text to Action*, he appeals to the metaphor of an event leaving its marks on its time to show how "what is done is inscribed" (1991c, 152), so that action can be literally read like a text.

We can make the missing term appear if we pursue the analogy in the form of an analogy of proportion, which Ricoeur does not do, although he suggests it: writing is to oral discourse as X is to action. But can such an X work? I would have to say: "The reading I perform of an objectified written text which was originally oral is the same as the reading I perform of an action which was originally what?" The dissymmetry between writing as objectification of oral speech and narrative as objectification of action is due to the fact that what is objectified is not "the same." As mentioned earlier, the oral speech was available as such and it can be claimed that the writing provides the "meaning content" (what Husserl calls the noema of what was said). The "inscription" of action in the marks it left may provide the meaningfulness of the action in the sense of the significance, but not necessarily its meaning. Ricoeur himself acknowledges that there are two types of understanding involved in action: what agents understood at the moment of the action and what people after the fact understand, agents included. It is only because of the second feature that action is like a text, that it can be read, and not because of the first, since clearly agents did not "read" their actions at the moment they were performing them. They just performed them. And we know that agents can retrospectively read their own actions in ways not compatible with the intent they had at the time of action. Action, Ricoeur says, has a content and this content can be separated from its agent, so that it can have an importance that goes beyond its initial relevance; an action is open to a universal audience.

Ricoeur's solution to find the missing term consists in replacing the notion of inscription (in *From Text to Action*), which can only be metaphorical, with the notion of narrative. In this reformulation he appeals both to Husserl's correlation between noesis and noema and to Heidegger's hermeneutical circle. The narrative will be, on the one hand, a noesis as activity with emplotment as its correlate, that is, as the noema or meaning or sense content of what is narrated, and, on the other, an understanding, so that what is recounted was already pre-understood. This is what he presents in a difficult passage of *Time and Narrative*.

Ricoeur uses the word "mimesis," which he borrows from Aristotle, especially in his study of tragedy. Mimesis in Aristotle is not so much an imitation as a representation offering an analogon of what took place or of what could have taken place or can take place. Mimesis is thus an activity and Ricoeur plays with the ambivalence of mimesis as understanding and mimesis as the product of understanding (the actual narrative). Commenting on Aristotle's expression of *mimesis praxeos*, Ricoeur suggests that we understand the genitive *praxeos* (action) as the noematic correlate of a practical *noesis*. He reasons as follows: action is what is construed by mimesis; the construction consists in a *muthos*, a narrative. There is thus a noematic correlation between *mimesis praxeos* as an activity of construction (*noesis*) and the *muthos* as the ordering of facts construed (noema). He then writes—and this is his wager—"To report the same relation of correlation within the first syntagma, between *mimesis* and *praxis*, is then plausible, fruitful and risky" (1984b, 73). Ricoeur does not explain how it works. I thus try in the following to reconstruct his argument.

I understand Ricoeur as suggesting the following: Let the practical noesis be the noesis of the action and mimetic noesis be the noesis of that same action considered under the rubric of *mimesis praxeos*. Then what Ricoeur leaves unsaid is that the mimetic noesis objectifies the practical noesis so that the narrative as the noema of the mimetic noesis is at once the objectification—the text—of action and the noema of the practical noesis. Mimetic noesis is thus an analogon, literally, of action. We thus have the following relationships: In practical noesis, the noema is to action as in mimetic noesis the self-same noema is to its narrative.

Appealing to the hermeneutic circle, he can then call the practical noesis a pre-understanding, what in *Time and Narrative* he calls mimesis1, and the making of a narrative the understanding itself, so that the narrative as what understanding produces is the meaning or sense content of the pre-understanding, action itself. About writing Ricoeur says: "what we write, what we inscribe, is the noema of the speaking. It is the meaning of the speech event, not the event as event" (1991c, 146). Similarly, just as what is written is the noema (the what and the meaning) of what is said, the narrative as produced by mimesis is the noema of what is represented. And, as with writing, the narrative gives the "what" and meaning of action, not the event of action itself. It is the "such" as a content but "as," because of the objectifying transformation. "I should like to speak here of the noematic structure of action. It is this noematic structure that may be fixed and detached from the process of interaction and become an object to interpret" (1991c, 152). He also calls it, appealing to Husserl, the "sense content" (1991c, 152).

Because we have two noemata—action itself and a narrative—Ricoeur has to show how the analogical transfer works: how the move from practical noesis as pre-understanding to the activity of forming a narrative (mimetic noesis as understanding) preserves "the same" noema, namely, action as narrative, or how the narrative is an analogous noema to action. Ricoeur believes he can explain this through what he calls a threefold mimesis, which is his reformulation of the hermeneutical circle.

Ricoeur then transposes the ambivalence of mimesis as both activity of understanding and the very product of understanding to narrative itself. He can then claim that mimesis (and narrative) is both an understanding as well as a content of meaning.

THREEFOLD MIMESIS AS A HERMENEUTIC CIRCLE

In *Time and Narrative*, Ricoeur presents mimesis as an activity consisting of three stages that he calls mimesis1, mimesis2, and mimesis3. What is new in this version of the circle is that it is of a narrative nature through and through. It does not involve an immediate understanding of an action, experience, or author by trying to put oneself in the initial situation, and does not entail any act of reliving (*Nacherleben*) or reproducing (*Nachvollziehen*) what was experienced (as it was the case with Schleiermacher and Dilthey). Ricoeur's challenge is thus to show, among other things, that the level of life and experience, of action and suffering, is already in some sense a narrative order. Thus telling a story about life and experience, action and suffering will not just be Husserl's external garment of ideas (redundant compared to the action or experience), or a violence, but rather their rendering in the twofold sense of transposing them and doing them justice, "such as they were."

Mimesis1 is the level of life, action, and events that are already prenarrative. "This is not to say that practices as such contain ready-made narrative scenarios, but their organization gives them a prenarrative quality" (Ricoeur, 1992, 157). Ricoeur mentions three traits that make an action a story in its nascent state. First, there is a semantics of action (Ricoeur, 1991a, 28) in the sense of a conceptual network proper to action, differentiating action from physical movement. Action involves a goal, answering to the question, What?; motives, answering to the question, Why?; agents, answering to the question, Who?; circumstances, answering to the question, How?; and cooperation, answering to the question, With whom or against whom?

The second trait of action making it amenable to being told resides in a symbolics of action. Action is mediated by signs, rules, and norms that provide to action a readability (Ricoeur, 1984b, 58). This symbolic mediation "makes action a quasi-text for which symbols provide the rules of signification in terms of which a given conduct can be interpreted" (1991a, 28). Ricoeur gives the example of raising one's arm, which can be read by means of signs, rules, and norms as greeting or voting or hailing a taxi depending on the context (Ricoeur, 1991a, 29). Similarly, someone in a restaurant seeing a couple entering the same restaurant would have a good idea of the limited range of possibilities for what is going to happen: they will wait to be seated, be seated, given a menu, they will chat, place their order, and so on. "Before they are submitted to interpretation, symbols are the internal interpreters of action" (Ricoeur, 1991a, 29).

The third trait is the temporality of action itself: action unfolds in time and has a beginning and an end. These moments are not imposed by the description, but belong to the very dynamics of the unfolding of the action. If we use Augustine's distinction, there is an anticipation by agents of what will happen in a present of the future: from now on. There is also a present of the past, making it the case that the present course of action is prepared by the past: because of what took place. And there is the now of the action in a present of the present (1984b, 60).

Once Ricoeur has established mimesis1, his reformulation of the hermeneutic circle can work smoothly. While mimesis1 was a prefiguration, mimesis2 is a configuration as the explicit telling of the story through emplotment, what Aristotle calls *muthos* in the active sense of putting into a plot. "What Aristotle calls plot is not a static structure but an operation, an integrating process, which ... is completed only in the reader or the spectator, that is to say, in the *living* receiver of the narrated story" (Ricoeur, 1991a, 21). The story told provides intelligibility by making explicit what was implicit in action and the world of life. It is not a retroprojection, but a mediation between (1) the individual events and the story as a whole, (2) agents, goals, means, circumstances, and so on, and (3) the temporal characteristics so that the plot grasps the event in one temporal whole. The plot is "a totality which can be said to be at once concordant and discordant" (Ricoeur, 1991a, 21).

Mimesis3 is the return of mimesis2 to the world of action and life (mimesis1) but within a circle, so that they cross each other in a spiraling movement. "I would rather speak of an endless spiral that would carry the meditation past the same point a number of times, but at different altitudes" (1984b, 72). It is "the intersection of the world of the text and the world of the reader" (1991a, 26) so that the world of action becomes enriched by the narratives and stories readers have read. "What would we know of love and hatred, of ethical feelings and, in general, of all that we call the Self, if all this had not been brought to language and articulated by literature?"(Ricoeur, 1991d, 116). And this also explains how and why the world of fiction functions as a laboratory of moral judgments or a pool of possible scenarios for people to live their life and deal with their problems. At this level there is a resignification by narratives of the world of action. "Making a narrative [*le faire narratif*] resignifies the world in its temporal dimension, to the extent that narrating, telling, reciting is to remake action following the poem's invitation" (1984b, 81).

Ricoeur quotes several times the expression of Wilhelm Schapp that we are entangled in narratives (*in Geschichte verstrickt*), feeding on them and being influenced by them. Ricoeur goes so far as saying that "the world is the whole set of references opened by every sort of descriptive or poetic text I have read, interpreted, and loved" (1984b, 80) so that "what is interpreted in a text is the proposing of a world that I might inhabit and into which I might project my own most powers" (1984b, 81).

Ricoeur borrows from François Dagonet the expression of "iconic augmentation" to indicate the increase in meaning that has been provided by narratives.

> It will be recalled that our preunderstanding of the world of action under the governance of mimesis1 is characterized by the mastering of a network of intersignifications constitutive of the semantics of action, by familiarity with the symbolic mediations and the prenarrative resources of human acting.... The iconic augmentation in question here depends upon the prior augmentation of readability that action owes to the interpretants already at work here. Human action can be oversignified, because it is already presignified by all the modes of its symbolic articulation. (1984b, 81)

The expression of our "preunderstanding" of the world of action in the last quote reminds us of the ambivalence of mimesis1: it is both the level of what action, events, and life are in their ontological status and the understanding of actions, events, and life. Similarly, mimesis2 is (1) the actual telling of the story, (2) an explicit understanding of what was pre-understood in mimesis1, and (3) a productive activity providing an analogon or "stand-in" for what took place. The exclusive emphasis is on activity as creativity. Just as *poiesis* is active and "a dynamic operativity" (Carr, Taylor, and Ricoeur, 1991, 180), *mimesis* is "a kind of production" (181) that is both revelation and transformation (182). Ricoeur mentions approvingly the translation of *mimesis* by Else as "imitatings" (181), which is analogous to the "comparables" a translator is supposed to produce, according to Ricoeur (Ricoeur, 2004, 63ff).

Because mimesis2 is productive, Ricoeur very often speaks of it with reference to fiction. He dedicated the second volume of *Time and Narrative* to the configuration of time through fiction. It is also why he says that mimesis2 opens the realm of the "as if" (1984b, 64). But this in fact is quite troubling. For it threatens the "such as it was" and weakens it into an "as if": the analogon could in fact only be a feeble comparative.

It can be readily granted that an element of invention enters the making of a narrative; not only is there a selection of moments pertaining to the action—the sequence of these moments, and their causal link; there is also a choice of words, expressions, metaphors, which, strictly speaking, do not belong to the physical realm of actions and events. But our question is whether, granting this element of invention, we can still redeem the claim of the "such as it was" and pay off the debt we owe to what took place.

The productive ambivalence of the "as if" and the "such as it was" of mimesis1 and mimesis2 actually permits the dialectic to move to mimesis3, which is the impact that narratives and stories, historical or fictitious, have on the realm of action, since action is both of a prenarrative character and is understood through narratives. But Ricoeur's account of the "as if" of fiction threatens to turn this ambivalence into an ambiguity. If it is the case that mimesis2 is only an "as if" and cannot be locked onto mimesis1 with a strong "such as it was," the smooth movement from mimesis1, mimesis2, and back to mimesis3 would come to a halt.

Let us examine the first level of mimesis1, which is the most fundamental in Ricoeur's enterprise and, I submit, the most unstable.

THE UNSTABLE STATUS OF MIMESIS1

The ambivalence of mimesis1 and mimesis2 may turn into ambiguities if we do not find a mechanism that guarantees that the link between mimesis1 and mimesis2 is one of correlation, and not simply one of comparison—that the "as if" is indeed locked to the "such as it was." How can Ricoeur show that the "prenarrative structure of experience" (1991a, 29) or the "inchoate narrative" (1984b, 74) at the level of life are more than metaphorical, and really mean that, at the level of experience and action, we have a "potential narrative (1991a, 30; 1984b 74) in the ontological sense?

It is symptomatic that shortly after the publication of *Time and Narrative* Ricoeur's actual goal of linking mimesis1 (what is understood is narrative-like) and mimesis2 (the understanding is narrative-made) were missed by Hayden White and David Carr. It was tempting to understand, as Hayden White did, that for Ricoeur "it is their narrative structure that distinguishes historical events from natural events (which lack such structure). It is because historical events possess a narrative structure that historians are justified in regarding stories as valid representations of such events and treating such representations as explanations of them" (White, 1991, 142).

But equally tempting was the suspicion raised by Carr that Ricoeur may still side with the standard view that narratives belong to the discourse of the descriptor and should not be imposed on what is described. Carr points to Ricoeur's ambivalence in some of his formulations. On the one hand, there is the suggestion that the actual narrative brings into actuality what was potential in actions. But, on the other hand, Ricoeur ambiguates the notion of narrative with fictional narrative, suggesting that narratives give us access to a quasi-reality, acknowledging the gap between what actually took place and the manufactured narrative rendition of it. Carr quotes Frank Kermode's warning: "In 'making sense' of the world we ... feel a need ... to experience that concordance of beginning, middle and end which is the essence of our explanatory fictions," (Kermode, 1966, 35f, quoted in Carr, 1991, 160). But these fictions 'degenerate' 'whenever they are not consciously held to be fictive" (Kermode, 39, quoted in Carr, 1991, 160). Similarly, Louis Mink argues that "narrative qualities are transferred from art to life" (Mink, 1979, 557f, quoted in Carr, 1991, 161).

Faced with these rather opposite takes on his views, Ricoeur does not seem to understand what can motivate them and simply reiterates his position. "If ... every narrative configuration has a kind of retroactive reference, it is because life itself is an inchoate narrative; this is what I call the prenarrative character of life. This being so, I do not see what aspect of the circular character that I see between the three mimeses would lead me to the 'standard' theory" (Carr, Taylor, and Ricoeur, 1991, 180). Ricoeur claims that his distinction among three levels of mimesis is supposed to avoid the dichotomy of history either as a distortion of life or a representation of life. "I have attempted to produce a concept of mimesis which escapes the dilemma according to which either history falsifies life, does it violence, or reflects it" (Carr, Taylor, and Ricoeur, 1991, 180).

Ricoeur indeed convincingly shows that fiction cannot be simply opposed to history. The past has to be "rendered" such as it was, but the past is not given such as it was. An articulation is needed. "The 'having-been' causes a problem to the extent that it is not observable, whether it is the having-been of the event or the having-been of the testimony. The pastness [*passéité*] of an observation in the past is not itself observable, but memorable" (Ricoeur, 1985, 228). There is thus an element of invention or fiction in historical narratives. "History is quasi-fictitious since the quasi-presence of the events presented 'before the eyes' of the reader by an animated narrative supplements by its intuitiveness, its vivacity the elusive character of the pastness of the past, which the paradoxes of *représentance* illustrate" (Ricoeur, 1985, 277; my translation).

This element of fiction shows that action or experience is not coherent and structured enough to dispense with its retelling, so that the narrative is not redundant; at the same time, because the retelling is necessary for the "being" of experience and action, the selection made in the narrative and the medium of words and sentences are not heterogeneous to what they describe, and thus do not do violence to the self-identity of action and experience.

But is this fully convincing? There are many instances where Ricoeur suggests that the ambivalence of mimesis1 and mimesis2 is in fact an ambiguity. Let us review some of them. Speaking of an action, Ricoeur suggests, in one instance, that it is our understanding that turns action into texts. He treats "the imitated action like a text" (1985, 321). The text would be what we produce and not what action gives us to read. This leaves open the question of what action in reality is. In another case, trying to illustrate what he calls "a story not yet told," Ricoeur gives two examples: a patient in relation to a psychoanalyst and a judge attempting to understand a defendant (an example borrowed from Wilhelm Schapp—Ricoeur, 1991a, 30). These two situations, which Ricoeur considers analogous, in fact reveal a deep discrepancy between the object of understanding being narrative-like and the understanding being narrative-made. In the case of a patient, we can agree with Ricoeur that "with respect to analytical sessions . . . their aim and their effect is to allow the analysand to draw out of these story-fragments a narrative which would be at once more bearable and more intelligible" (1991a, 30). As previously mentioned about narratives applied to selfhood, we are dealing more with the meaningfulness of facts, deeds, and events than with their meaning. The patient's story aims at finding the meaningfulness of what took place and she reads facts and events in this light, so that her story may even significantly change in the course of time while still being hers, if, for example, what she saw as significant when she was sixteen now appears trivial. The aim is not to find out what took place, but rather what meaning the patient ascribes to what took place. And she is the one who can do that, the analyst being there to help her to cope. Of course there are constraints, but these constraints cannot reach the point of falsifying what the patient says. She looks for the significance and this is a matter of appreciation and evaluation, not of observation and testing.

Not so with the second situation of a judge "unraveling the skein of plots in which the suspect is entangled" (1991a, 30). Here the judge will be, well, the judge—and claiming to judge not which story is more plausible, but what actually took place, even if obviously it is only discursively that the judge and the jury can come to some conclusion. The "coefficient of adversity" (Sartre) is significantly stronger in this case because the judge or jury can be shown to be wrong and the decision can be appealed in most cases if counterevidence is presented.

One of the differences with the case of the patient is that a judge or jury makes the claim that the defendant is guilty or not; a judge or jury cannot qualify the verdict by saying that she found the story of the prosecutor more plausible than the one by the defense, even if conviction will be reached through stories and plausible stories are more convincing than others. But it is the defendant whom the judge or jury acquits or sends to jail and not the character of the prosecutor's or defense's narrative.

But the most intriguing ambiguity in Ricoeur concerns his presentation of the act of telling the story as a configuration of what was discordant and chaotic. Ricoeur borrows from linguistics the terms "paradigm" and "syntagma," the paradigm being what can be instantiated like verb, object, subject, and the syntagma being the actual concatenation of paradigmatic components in a sentence like "Brutus killed Caesar." Ricoeur considers the narrative as belonging to the syntagmatic order, but remarkably considers action as belonging to the paradigmatic order. This means, first, that only in the narrative does the action come to its full meaning, and, second and oddly, that, before, action was of the order of the discordant, chaotic, and unformed. Besides the fact that this seems to contradict Ricoeur's claim that there is a practical noesis in the world of action, it also clearly displays Ricoeur's confusion of meaning with meaningfulness. If action or experience is now on the side of the paradigmatic order, we only have in mimesis1 placeholders like rules and norms (semantics of action); goal, agent, and so on. (symbolics of action); and beginning, middle, end (temporal structure of action). But these are not even enough to constitute an object to be talked about. What Ricoeur suggests here is that narratives would then be absolutely productive, inventing life and actions by narrating them. This confirms our suspicion that the "such as" would lose its claim to preserving the same (such) and fall back completely on the fictitious "as if." And of course this entails that, of the two claims Ricoeur makes about narratives mentioned earlier, the first one, that narratives provide the noema of action, cancels out; the qualification of the prenarrative character of action and life would be strictly metaphorical as a retrospective understanding, without any ontological moorings. What is left is the second claim that understanding is narrative-made, but this claim, uncoupled from the first, is rather trivial and is not enough to make the hermeneutical circle work.

Let us examine this point more closely. The syntagmatic order is reached with the narrative, mimesis2. Ricoeur writes: "In passing from the paradigmatic order of action to the syntagmatic order of narrative, the terms of the semantics of action acquire integration and actuality. Actuality, because the terms, which had only a virtual signification in the paradigmatic order, that is, a pure capacity to be used, receive an actual [*effective*] signification thanks to the sequential interconnections the plot confers on the agents, their deeds, and their suffering. Integration because terms as heterogeneous as agents, motives, and circumstances are rendered compatible and work together in actual temporal wholes" (Ricoeur, 1984b 56–57). He adds: "This passage from the paradigmatic to the syntagmatic constitutes the transition from mimesis1 to mimesis2. It is the work of the configurating activity" (1984b, 66). This goes against the claim that the primordial character of action is to be symbolically mediated (1985, 321), but confirms his avowed goal to treat "the imitated action like a text" (1985, 321), so that it is not, strictly speaking, the action that is a text, but the action as imitated, that is, recounted. The text would belong to the process of analogical transfer, and thus not to the structure per se of action.

Of course this opens the question: how can an action be an action without syntagmatic order, without, in other words, an agent doing something with a goal in mind and taking circumstances into consideration as well as cooperation and opposition? The assistance of narratives would mean, in Ricoeur's scenario, that only when told can the action in actuality be an action, clearly identifiable and meaningful. This grants an almost exclusive articulating role to the narrative at the expense of, for example, agents. And this confirms that the prenarrative quality is a retrospective qualification from the perspective of an understanding and that the narrative does not really "represent" the action as action, but the syntagmatic order it imposes. The narrative only provides the meaningfulness of the action for "readers," not necessarily the "meaning" of the action. The "such as it was" has been unmasked as a mere "as if."

I do not mean to disqualify the "as if." There are different forms of "as if" narratives that are very useful. For example, in order to explain the problem my car seems to have to my mechanic, it may be easier to tell him that the car always wants to veer to the left. And I am confident that my mechanic will not laugh at me for thinking that my car is possessed by a ghost. The story I tell does not claim to make explicit the inner workings of my car, but only to be, as a manner of speaking, a description of the steering problem. Similarly, ethologists often have recourse to stories to explain to us the complex behaviors of animals. They tell us that when a ground-nesting bird feigns a broken wing, it is because the bird wants to lead the predator away from the nest and they can give the bird's soliloquy: "This approaching predator ... could be distracted by its desire to catch and eat me, but only if it thought there was a reasonable chance of its actually catching me (it's no dummy); it would contract just that belief if I gave it evidence that I couldn't fly anymore; I could do that by feigning a broken wing" (Dawkins, *The Selfish Gene*, quoted in Dennett, 1987, 258). But scientists know that birds do not have the brainpower to do geometry and use hypothetical conditionals. Still, the stories they tell us are explanatory and in this sense very useful. We thus have a narrative that explains fairly well what is going on between birds and predators, without ascribing to them the syntagmatic order the narrative reveals.

This, however, does not apply to action—at least not without further justification. When we speak, like Ricoeur, of "potential story" (1991a, 30; 1984b 74), there must be something narrative-like in action itself. Ricoeur insists that the importance of an action exceeds its relevance to the initial situation or that an action has an autonomy exceeding what the agents intended or expected. As White puts it, commenting approvingly on Ricoeur, "human actions have consequences that are both foreseeable and unforeseeable, that are informed by intentions both conscious and unconscious, and that are frustratable by contingent factors that are both knowable and unknowable. It is for this reason that narrative is necessary for the representation of 'what actually happened' in a given domain of historical occurrences" (White, 1991, 145). But this of course guarantees almost by definition that the meaningfulness manifested in the narrative will not fit what the agents did or what the contemporaries understood and the question remains whether this view can even claim to do justice to action. I submit that a readability granted to action gives readers and interpreters far too much leeway for making sense of what took place (1991a, 29) (Ricoeur insists on the capacity to follow a narrative, 1985, 231). For such a view prevents the action itself from exerting constraints on the possible readings interpreters can make. Ricoeur claims that it would be a mistake to see the multiplicity of possible interpretations as a threat to the unity of the action. His view is precisely that an action by its very nature is susceptible to different takes because it is separated from its agents, has an importance going beyond the initial situation, and is addressed to an infinity of readers. "It is possible to compose several plots about the same incidents (which thus do not deserve any more to be called the same events)" (Ricoeur, 1985, 358). But then what makes of an "event" the same as what is recounted? What in action itself can represent what Sartre calls the co-efficient of adversity?

It seems that among the three types of traits Ricoeur mentions in action that make it susceptible to be retold, the symbolics and the temporal structure are not enough. Signs, norms, and rules are not specific enough to individuate, if I may use the term, an action as this particular action performed by these particular agents in these particular circumstances. And the fact that an action has a beginning and an end is not enough either, since it does not alone differentiate a movement that is merely physical—like Brutus strolling in the streets of Rome in the vicinity of the Senate on March 14, 44 BC—from an action like murdering Caesar. Only, it seems, the semantics of action is left.

But the semantics of action cannot constrain narratives so that they will be about this particular sequence of movements and mental events and not about another sequence. The first reason is that, as Ricoeur stresses, the importance of an action exceeds what agents and contemporaries may think. We noticed earlier that Ricoeur considers the semantics of action to be of a paradigmatic order, not an articulation. The articulation comes from the narrative itself. In the case of Brutus' action, we know that Brutus did not believe that what was happening was his story. He and Cassius wanted to protect the Republic against Caesar's authoritarian rule. But Octavius turned him into a traitor to Rome, forcing Brutus to flee. Before committing suicide after the battle of Philippus he allegedly said "*Virtus nomen!*" ("virtue is just a name!"), realizing the vanity of his effort to save Rome and, we may suppose, the bitterness of his story not being recorded. Octavius, the future Augustus, won the narrative game.

The second reason is that the symbolics of action is only of the paradigmatic order of goal, agents, motives, and so on. This paradigmatic order is not even constraining enough to determine what the very beginning of an action and its end are. When did the murder of Caesar start? With the actual stabbing by Brutus or the plot with Cassius or even after the battle of Pharsalus when Brutus switched camp and sided with Caesar against Pompey? All this is up for interpretation. Even worse: the very fact that it is an action is also an object of interpretation. Those who revisit history do precisely that, denying that what was taken as actions or events ever took place and thus was not action or event.

In order to understand why Ricoeur remains entangled in this difficulty it may be useful to look at what he describes in one of his last books, *Sur la traduction* (Ricoeur, 2004). Ricoeur may have unduly extended to the problem of action what holds true of the problem of translation.

In the case of translation, faced with a text to translate, translators do not wonder how one identical meaning, which has been articulated in one way in the original, can be articulated in another way in the target language. The meaning that is the same is not given as if it were susceptible to many articulations among which to choose. Translators only have two terms: the original meaning and the meaning in the target language, both of which have to be found; the former has to be found in the sense of being understood and the latter has to be found in the sense of being invented, and this invention precisely occurs when the original meaning has been captured. As Ricoeur likes to play with the word, to render means both to produce something new and give back to the original. This is the notion of debt he uses in *Time and Narrative*.

Thus, the meaning that is supposed to remain the same in the original and the translation did not preexist its articulation in the original and cannot be invoked for judging its rendition in the target language otherwise than through another articulation. Since we cannot cross along a vertical axis and grasp the meaning itself before its articulation in the original, we can only move horizontally from one articulation (in the original) to another articulation (in the target language). The latter represents a rendering of the former in the sense that the translator makes the original meaning explicitly or reflectively conscious. Translation is thus what retrospectively contributes to establishing the meaning of the original (we can hear the extent of Benjamin's influence on Ricoeur). What the translation does is to offer an equivalent of the original and this equivalent is what the word or sentence or text "means." Using Husserl's vocabulary, translators reveal the noematic sense of the original. But clearly translators have to "invent" this equivalent, what Ricoeur calls a "comparable," a meaning that accounts for what is translated, interpreted, or discovered, a meaning that did not exist before in their target language (or community) and which gives access to what the original "means."

Ricoeur seems to believe that he can apply the same process of invention in his treatment of narratives. The meaning that is "the same" in the narrative and in the action or experience narrated is thus not simply discovered nor fabricated; it is "found," but in the creative sense of the word: it is "invented." Herder uses the word *er-finden* in this active sense of creating a correlate or comparable or equivalent. Heidegger, commenting on it, understands *er-finden* not as finding something by stumbling on something already there and not as making up something either. In Heidegger's terms, *er-finden* means "to make something available [*anfertigen*] which absolutely did not exist before" (Heidegger, 1999, 22). Without reference to Herder or Heidegger, it is this sense that Ricoeur tries to recover: "one has to return to the beautiful [French] word *inventer* (to invent) in its twofold meaning, which entails at the same time to discover and to create" (Ricoeur, 1975, 387–88).

Notwithstanding Ricoeur's provoking and fruitful insights, can we turn the "such as" that is the normal standard of recounting what took place into a "comparable" without derealizing what is recounted? The comparison of recounting an action with translating a text, which Ricoeur does not make but seems to have in mind, encounters the obvious difficulty that an action or an experience is not made of words, but of physical and mental motions. When we pass from action to a narrative we move vertically from a physico-mental realm to a linguistic realm. By contrast, in translation we move laterally from one linguistic medium to another. The invention translators have to achieve consists in combining some felicitous mix of the meaning of the original (that people knowing the language can also understand and check) and the meaningfulness the text can have in the translator's community (or, as some translators say, in the target language). They negotiate the obedience to two masters Rosenzweig mentioned: the original author and the translator's audience. (On the different types of negotiations, see Lefevere, 1975, 1982, 1992; Benjamin, 1968, Vandevelde, 2005, esp. 63–109). However, the situation is different for those who give narratives about the past and about experiences or actions. For they cannot perform the same kind of negotiation because one of the terms, the original intent or meaning, has not been explicitly articulated as the original meaning is articulated in the original text to translate; one of the terms is thus not available to those who try to recount it—as the original meaning of the text to be translated is available to those who can read it in the original text. As opposed to translators, authors of narratives have first to produce the meaning in the sense of articulating it. Thus, the debt an author of a narrative has toward the past or toward what took place is not the same debt a translator has toward the original; the rendering of an action is thus not the same as the rendering of a text.

Ricoeur's treatment of action as text and of narratives as a production of an analogon is thus doomed to conflate meaning and meaningfulness. In the case of action this conflation is manifested by Ricoeur's dismissal of the agents' intention at the moment of action and focus instead on how what was done can be understood in the sense of "read" either by the agents themselves or observers. The latter is what I call the meaningfulness and the former would be the meaning. But there is no necessity for this dismissal of the "original meaning" as what agents meant or intended and to take into consideration this original intent does not necessarily limit our understanding of action, as Ricoeur seems to believe. Ricoeur's view that pastness is not given, but has to be reconstructed does not entail, as he suggests, that the past cannot be distinguished from how it is recounted. For we can try to recreate the past or, as in a trial, to figure out why a defendant did what she is accused of having done; in the process of "reconstruction" we will still be able to distinguish the knowledge we can have of what took place and the knowledge of the significance of what took place.

Against Ricoeur, then, we have to reintroduce the missing term in the analogy of proportion I suggested before. This missing term is the action as the noema of the practical noesis Ricoeur mentions but to which he refuses to grant a self-identity. He considers such a practical noesis only as a pre-understanding—not of those who performed the actions and had the experiences, but of those who understand what is taking place, agents included, when placed in the position of interpreters of their own actions (this is the confusion between meaning and meaningfulness). If we restore the missing term of the analogy—action as the noema of a practical noesis—we have to reject Ricoeur's claim that action belongs to the paradigmatic level and show that action is in fact a syntagma: When an action is performed as a practical noesis—like the fact that Brutus killed Caesar with the help of Cassius on March 14, 44 BC—we have an articulation (the carving out of a chunk of physical movements and mental events) and a concatenation of these movements and events in a syntagmatic way. And this syntagma is the noema of action. When we use words to tell what took place, the retelling of the action would only make explicit what was already semantically articulated in the action itself. This semantic articulation would be what in action invites a narrative.

Let us imagine our Brutus free from bloody intent just briskly walking and passing by the Senate consumed in his contemplation of a knife he just bought at the Mausoleum flea market, a knife he was told belonged to General Nicias; Brutus proudly and firmly holds the knife in his right hand in front of him. And the next thing Brutus hears is, "*Tu quoque, Brute*"[3] ("You too, Brutus") and Julius Caesar falling on him, apparently having impaled himself on the knife Brutus held when Caesar embraced him. Of this scenario it is still true that "Brutus killed Caesar on March 14, 44 BC." But, as we say, it would have been an accident, not a murder. While it is true that we would have to tell a story to discriminate an accident and a murder precisely by appealing to the symbolics of action, still the choice of the narrative—accident or murder—is not constrained by the symbolics of action itself. Here we do not have two versions of what took place. The narrative of choice is itself predicated on a previous decision that it was an action or an event. And this decision made before the narrative, I submit, has to account for what agents intended to do. Of course, as Brutus seems to complain about on his death, the story told by Octavius can retrospectively present what took place in a light the agents would not recognize. But we now can surmise that Brutus had an intent to which the story told by Octavius did not do justice.

In this sense, Ricoeur is right to emphasize the power narratives have to resignify, and that it is part of the meaningfulness—that we can revisit what took place and tell a story that is history. But an action is not a story as history, it is an object of a narrative and the narrative has to show within itself what the constraining power of action is and account for it, so that the narrative can exert a function of "representing" (*représentance*) of the action or the past, and not merely a function of signifying (*signifiance*).

As mentioned at the beginning, Ricoeur alludes to how the difference between meaning and meaningfulness can be established by saying that historians have a debt to the past or that a narrative of action like a painting renders what took place, in the sense of giving back what is owed. "We tell stories because in the last analysis human lives need and merit being narrated. This remark takes on its full force when we refer the necessity to save the history of the defeated and the lost. The whole history of suffering cries out for vengeance and calls for narrative" (1984b, 75).

However, this will not suffice, for the debt is still on the exclusive side of the one who tells the narrative and historians may have, and in the course of time have had, rather different appreciations of what a debt involves. We have had several examples of autobiographies including fictitious elements in them or biographies and other memoirs fabricating parts of the material and claiming a literary license for so doing. Debt is essentially a recognition and it is hard to impute a debt to somebody if that person rejects it.

If we want to keep, as I believe we should, a difference between the meaning of an action and its meaningfulness, what has to be added to Ricoeur's notion of narrative is the notion of justification. I cannot here give a full account of what this would involve (I developed the argument of justification in the case of interpretation in Vandevelde, 2005, esp. 28–62). Let me only sketch how justification is a necessary component of a narrative.

The notion of justification is in fact already embedded not in the narrative itself—nobody asks a novel or a historical account to justify itself—but in the performance by a real person. Telling a narrative is not only articulating an understanding, but also engaging one's own responsibility regarding the "mimetic" link between narrative and reality, so that the narrator cannot hide behind a storyteller, but has, if prompted, to justify the account given. It is certainly possible for a while to refuse to justify oneself and to adopt the attitude of Barry Bonds who, when asked why he did not want to comment on a book reporting his use of enhancing drugs, replied something like, "Because I am an adult and I don't have to comment if I choose not to." But this refusal can only be temporary. There is in action not only something to be recounted, but also something asking to be justified. Justification is thus virtual in the action itself.

We can agree with Ricoeur that the action or event as the other of the narrative—what Ricoeur calls its *Gegenüber*—cannot simply command and order the narrative told about it. But the narrative cannot ignore the constraints coming from this *Gegenüber*. As mentioned above the constraints on narratives coming from time or selfhood are significantly less prominent than the constraints offered by actions and events. This justification embedded in narratives is actually what most people provide. They not only configure and articulate, but also offer evidence, proofs, and arguments implicitly acknowledging—something Ricoeur does not see—that the "such as it was" will be true as long as the justification for the analogon holds. The "such as it was" not only includes an analogical transfer, but also a claim to adequacy. The narrative thus not only involves a configuration in the manner Ricoeur describes, but also a grammar of justification.

NOTES

I want to thank John Meech for his comments on a previous draft.

1. "Representing [*représentance*] ... means in turn reduction to the same, recognition of alterity, analogizing apprehension" (Ricoeur, 1985, 229). In the case of the past, "things must have happened *as* it is said in the present narrative" (1985, 224. Ricoeur's emphasis), so that, in the relation of stand-in or representing the "reality [in the expression, 'The facts such as they really took place'] is only signified by the 'such as ...' " (1985, 225).
2. "My claim is that action itself, action as meaningful, may become an object of science, without losing its character of meaningfulness, through a kind of objectification similar to the fixation that occurs in writing" (1991d, 151).
3. Another tradition reports Caesar's words as "Et tu, Brute" (Suetonius).

WORKS CITED

Benjamin, Walter. 1968. "The Task of the Translator." In *Illuminations*, trans. R. Zohn, pp. 69–82. New York: Harcourt, Brace, and World.

Carr, David, Charles Taylor, and Paul Ricoeur. 1991. "Discussion: Ricoeur on Narrative." In Wood, 1991, pp. 160–87.

Heidegger, Martin. 1999. *Vom Wesen der Sprache: die Metaphysik der Sprache und die Wesung des Wortes. Zu Herder's Abhandlung "über den Ursprung der Sprache."* Oberseminar Sommersemester 1939, hrsg. I. Schüssler. Gesamtausgabe bd. 85. Frankfurt a. M.: Kostermann.

Kermode, Frank. 1966. *The Sense of an Ending: Studies in the Theory of Fiction.* London: Oxford University Press.

Lefevere, André. 1975. *Translating Poetry. Seven Strategies and a Blueprint.* Assen, Netherlands: van Gorcum.

———. 1982. "Théorie littéraire et littérature traduite." *Canadian Review of Comparative Literature* 9: 137–56.

———. 1992. *Translating Literature. Practice and Theory in a Comparative Literature Context.* New York: Modern Language Association.

Mink, Louis. 1970. "History and Fiction as Modes of Comprehension," *New Literary History*, vol. 1, no. 3, pp. 541–58.

Ricoeur, Paul. 1975. *La métaphore vive*. Paris: Les Editions du Seuil.

———. 1984a. *Temps et récit 2. La configuration dans le récit de fiction*. Paris: Les Editions du Seuil.

———. 1984b. "Time and Narrative. Threefold Mimesis." In *Time and Narrative*, vol. 1. Chicago: University of Chicago Press, 1984.

———. 1985. *Temps et récit 3. Le temps raconté*. Paris: Les Editions du Seuil.

———. 1986. *Du texte à l'action. Essais d'herméneutique II*. Paris: Les Editions du Seuil.

———. 1990. *Soi-même comme un autre*. Paris: Les Editions du Seuil.

———. 1991a. "Life in Quest of Narrative." In Wood, 1991, pp. 1–19.

———. 1991b. "Narrative Identity." In Wood, 1991, pp. 188–99.

———. 1991c. "The Model of the Text: Meaningful Action Considered as a Text." In Ricoeur, 1991d.

———. 1991d. *From Text to Action. Essays in Hermeneutics, II*. Evanston: Northwestern University Press.

———. 1992. *Oneself as Another*, trans. Kathleen Blamey. Chicago: University of Chicago Press.

———. 2004. *Sur la traduction*. Paris: Bayard.

Vandevelde, Pol. 2005. *The Task of the Interpreter: Text, Meaning, and Negotiation*. Pittsburgh: University of Pittsburgh Press.

White, Hayden. 1991. "The Metaphysics of Narrativity: Time and Symbol in Ricoeur's Philosophy of History." In Wood, 1991, pp. 140–59.

Wood, David (ed.). 1991. *On Paul Ricoeur. Narrative and Interpretation*. London: Routledge.

Ricoeur and Lyotard in Postmodern Dialogue: Symbol and the Sublime

9

Patrick L. Bourgeois

In recent postmodern conversations, much emphasis has been placed on the role of the imagination in relation to the sublime and to the symbolic in Kant's extension [*Erweiterung*] of his critical philosophy from 1781 to 1790. These conversations, needless to say, sometimes get quite confusing and misleading, attributing to Kant things that are not at all Kantian, but, rather emanate from the perspective of the interpreter enamoured by the Kantian sublime, thus paralleling Heidegger's now famous interpretation emerging from his own hermeneutical situation of the Being-Question.

The extensions within Kant's philosophy and Paul Ricoeur's appropriation of these in the development of his own philosophy in relation to and at the heart of the postmodern discussions on the Kantian imagination and the sublime are the concern of this present study. We will attempt to incorporate the roles of the symbolic and the sublime from Kant, going far beyond his sense of these, but in a way quite different from the tendency to extend the role of the sublime and its violence to the imagination as the paradigm for all thought today. In the attempt to fathom the depth of the significance of Kant's own extended role of these in the third *Critique*, we will take Kant as much as possible in his own context, thus doing justice to that pole in the hermeneutical arch before trying to appropriate its significance into our own context.

In this postmodern situation the role of the sublime and the symbolic emerges in such a way as to make the sublime central to the reduction of all philosophy to literature. In contrast to Lyotard's giving the sublime a central position in his collapsing of philosophy into literature, Ricoeur extends Kant's notion in another direction, that of the narrative function as a third kind of reflective judgment, but one seriously influenced by Kant's view of symbol rooted in the sublime. While Lyotard, expanding on the role of the sublime in Kant's aesthetics, explodes any rule orientation by means of his notion of invention, Ricoeur, extending the role of the reflective judgment itself, wants to keep a rule orientation in making this new type of reflective function determinative, thus going far beyond Kant's intent.

Although Kant's admission that the sublime extends the imagination in doing a certain violence to it lends itself to further extensions, it does not necessarily, even in these further extensions, support or emerge into an antilogocentrism. Indeed, as Cassirer says: "In Germany meantime, even where aesthetics was waging war for the autonomy and originality of the imagination, it never revolted against the dominion of logic but remained in an intimate alliance with this discipline. Aestheticians did not attempt to free the imagination from the predominance of logic; they wanted to discover a logic of the imagination.... It is clear from the central position which the Swiss school gives to judgment that it in no sense intended to sever the bond between logic and aesthetics—of the development which reaches its climax in Kant's *Critique of Judgment.*"[1] Ricoeur's extensions of the sublime and the symbolic function in the Kantian aesthetic, in relation to deconstruction, will be seen to make him one of the best voices at the heart of this postmodern conversation, incorporating these elements into a broader philosophy that is viable for the future. In opposing certain postmodern extremes, we attempt to find a certain quasi "logic of the imagination,"[2] rather than a use of the imagination to subvert all relation to logos or reason. We will attempt to follow Ricoeur in his tendency to extend certain elements of Kant's aesthetic. After treating Lyotard's appropriation of Kant especially relating to his own view of invention, we must first turn to Kant's treatment of the productive imagination in relation to the symbol, the sublime, and rules to mediate between Lyotard and Ricoeur. For we must consider what extensions beyond Kant are viable for a thinking adequate to the contemporary scene of continental thinking today. We will now turn to the expansion by Jean-François Lyotard of the role of the aesthetic reflective judgment in the direction of a primary prelogical dimension in contrast to the logic of the aesthetic presented by Kant.

Today the very extensions of Kant himself sometimes get interpreted in the light of making the sublime the end all and be all of his philosophy, so that the claim is made that "sublime is another name for the imagination itself" and that "*Erweiterung* is nothing other than the "disproportion" (*Unangemessenheit*) of imagination, which is its very definition."[3] "Kantian imagination—the image of which does not complete itself in imitating but in appearing—is the other name for Being, the Kantian name for Being."[4] And it should be noted that, since the sublime is another name for the imagination according to some thinkers, then it seems that the sublime is another name for Being. And Lyotard, rendering the treatment of the sublime in the *Critique of Judgment* as central, seeking to displace any conceptual rule, thus supports invention that displaces the whole "game" over the innovation that makes new moves within the rules of the game. He extends the indeterminate dimension of the limited role of the reflective judgment of the sublime in Kant's use to a paradigmatic role in thinking, leading to common antilogocentism with Derrida. Thus, there is an attempt on the part of both to supplant the primacy of the Kantian theoretical understanding in its knowing function in favor of a priority of language that renders the human role of imagination passive and secondary to that of the "other." Further, language in their employ loses its semantic priority in favor of semiological priority.

It is interesting that this tendency to extend the Kantian sublime, like much of the postmodern deconstructive orientation, has its roots in Heidegger's thinking, as is well known. In this context, Helfer, in commenting on Heidegger's *The Age of the World Picture*, indicates that work's change of paradigm from the notion of representation that structures the modern age to the gigantic that is making its appearance everywhere, intimating the sublime of Kant in that here "quantity becomes incalculable, a feature that imbues it with a special quality: greatness."[5] For Heidegger, it is this that brings us to stop representing, allowing the true essence of Being to emerge beyond representation, showing itself first as Nothing. Along these lines, Escoubas has also indicated from Kant's first Critique the category of nothing in the context of the nonobjectivity of the imagination and of the faculty of judgment. And this nonobjectivity is correlated with objective nothingness. "*Einbildungskraft* and aesthetic *Urteilskraft* are related, if not identical, by virtue of their common nonobjectivity. They coincide in the retreat [*retrait*] of the object.... The imagination gives itself out as the faculty of form at the heart of objective nothingness."[6]

Helfer goes on to indicate that, for Heidegger, the transcendence of representation is best accomplished through poetry, which is "prefigured and predetermined by the critical praxis of German Idealism and early German romanticism,"[7] as is the turn to the poetic to address the shortcomings of philosophical discourse. This is all caught up in the notion of *Darstellung* as a new type of presentation or representation opposed to the conceptions of mimetic or "'objectifying" representation (*Nachahmung, Repräsentation, Vorstellung*) prevalent in the late eighteenth-century critical discourse."[8] It is necessary to recall that, for Heidegger, philosophy, in a new sense of the word, is still employed in the coming to truth of Being, the sense of Being, as seen even in such later works as *Was ist Dass, die Philosophie?*[9] Thus, Heidegger does not simply turn to poetry or literature as many do today as the only direction for thought. Hence, Helfer, allegedly following Nancy and Lacoue-Labarthe, criticizes Heidegger for not being able to completely shake off this link with the representational of which he firmly accuses the modern era. "Heidegger's positing of a space withdrawn from representation in which the subject joins with a true Being that first reveals itself as 'Nothing' is a redaction of the conceptually powerful and tremendously alluring figure of the negative *Darsetellung* of the Kantian sublime. Paradoxically, then, Heidegger's modern age reaffirms its representation roots at the same time that it tries to escape them."[10] We will now turn to Lyotard's treatment of the aesthetic and the sublime that is aligned with these extremes.

Lyotard, in centralizing of the role of the sublime and the aesthetic reflective judgments, collapses philosophy into literature. For him, the aesthetic judgment, as tautegorical and domiciling, not only subtends the whole critical enterprise, but guides and directs it in such a way that this subtending level becomes primary, and the rest is at best *per accidens*. By tautegorical he means that the aesthetic is basically the feeling of pleasure and displeasure, and at once, gives information to the mind about itself. By domiciling he means that the critical philosophy as such requires this reflective dimension as concomitant in order to furnish a guide to Reason for the place of its concepts and the kind of activity entailed. While it is looking for concepts, and what kind of activity is entailed, it needs this prelogical level, which itself takes on the most importance. This level becomes the laboratory for thought, free of rules, and making the violence of the sublime paradigmatic. Lyotard's stresses invention as cultural transformation: "Here the aesthetic is the site of invention, where desire works free of the rule of truth. What is important here is the kind of invention of which art is capable." This is an invention that will "displace the rule of truth."[11]

Thus, sensation is seen to inform the mind of its state. Lyotard considers this to be a nuance [a state of mind, the *Gemütszustand*]. This nuance, affecting thought as it thinks, ranges from extreme pleasure to extreme displeasure, and all that is in between. Thus, "sensation, the *aisthésis*, signals where the 'mind' is on the scale of affective tints," and, in a sense, is already a judgment of thought upon itself that "synthesizes the act of thinking that is taking place before an object, with the affection that this act procures for it" [AOS, 10]. Thus, according to Lyotard, this affection is the reflecion of the act, and is like its inner repercussion. It is in this sense that he claims, as the main characteristic of reflection, that the occurrence of sensation accompanies all modes of thought: that is, that it is always there, accompanying any act of thought, so that as felt-thinking, feeling signals to thought its state. Thus, pure reflection itself is primarily the "ability of thought to be immediately informed of its state by this state and without other means of measuring than feeling itself" [AOS, 11]. Further, this pleasure is the law and object of this judgment, or, put another way, comprises the referentiality and legitimacy of this judgement. This is another way of putting the tautegorical aspect of such judgments, as the identity of form and content. Thus, in this context, it is clear that thought feels itself on every occasion.

Another way of putting this is that "the sensation is a simple sign for thought of the state of thinking this object. The sign provides an indication of this state every time that thought thinks" [AOS, 14]. Lyotard indicates the Kantian supplementary faculty, as the simple "capacity to feel pleasure or displeasure," as introduced by Kant to account for this disposition. "The term 'subjective' forces the critique to question what thinking feels when it thinks and what it cannot fail to feel in every case" [AOS, 15]. He refers to this occurrence as a "shadow" of thought thrown on itself, and not a substantial predicate. "In sensation, the faculty of judging judges subjectively, that is, it reflects the state of pleasure or displeasure in which actual thought feels itself to be" [AOS, 15]. "Reflection is the (subjective) laboratory of all objectivities. In its heuristic aspect, reflection thus seems to be the nerve of critical thought as such" [AOS, 26].[12]

The difference between Lyotard's invention and Ricoeur's semantic innovation, all of which innovation is considered to be modernist by such postmodernists as Lyotard, lies in Lyotard's radical distinction between paralogical invention previously referred to above and mere innovation, especially applied to art in *The Postmodern Condition*. The paralogical invention makes the unforeseeable or impossible moves that displace or destroy any rules, while innovation in art merely transforms within certain rules. Invention thus attempts to replace the rule of truth by fostering invention rather than truth, and art is thus pit against knowledge. In the context of Kant's third *Critique,* Lyotard indicates that the imagination is free in that it is not limited to givens in experience, but that it is really free only in the case of the sublime. He contrasts this role with its limitation in the first Critique, where the imagination "presents givens to concepts with the aim of knowing something of them."[13] Lyotard points out that we cognize something in the sublime that is impossible, "the presence of an Idea of reason, but at the same time something which should be possible becomes impossible, that is to say, the presentation itself by means of the power of imagination."[14] Lyotard points out that the relation between thinking and the object breaks down in the sublime of Kant, and thinking "grasped in the sublime feeling is faced, 'in nature,' with quantities capable only of suggesting a magnitude or a force that exceeds its power of presentation."[15] Lyotard goes on to reveal, in relation to the sublime, the direction in which he wants to take Kant's strict doctrine: "This powerlessness makes thinking deaf or blind to natural beauty. Divorced, thinking enters a period of celibacy. It can still employ nature, but to its own ends. It becomes the user of nature. This 'employment' is an abuse, a violence. It might be said that in the sublime feeling thinking becomes impatient, despairing, disinterested in attaining the ends of freedom by means of nature" [AOS, 52]. In contrast to, and as a corrective of, Lyotard's interpretation of Kant, Ricoeur's redirective interpretation leads to a fuller postmodern possibility. In order to establish this conviction, we must now turn to Kant's own treatment of the aesthetic in relation to rule.

Lyotard contends in an interview[16] that it is only in the Kantian sublime that the imagination is really free, for in all other cases of the productive imagination there is some connection to rule or law, even in the case of the judgment of beauty. And there is no doubt that what he states about the freedom of the imagination is quite true to Kant's texts. It might be beneficial, then, to begin our reflection on the aesthetic function of the productive imagination by contrasting it with the reproductive and other productive functions of the imagination. The reproductive function is bound by empirical laws of association, and the productive imagination is bound by categories of the understanding that determine according to rules. In a sense, neither of these functions enjoys freedom. The aesthetic function of the productive imagination is free in the sense that it is not determined by empirical laws or by categories. But it has to be seen that the freedom differs among its various manifestations: in the judgment of beauty, in the judgment of the sublime, and in its use in making fine art.

In the judgment of beauty, the imagination is somewhat bound by the form of the object about which the judgment is made, since the form of the object is a limitation; it is free, however, in relation to the understanding, since, as stated, there is no concept and thus no determinate relation, but only an indeterminate relation. Now in the case of the judgment of the sublime, it is precisely the formlessness and unlimitedness of the object that give rise to awe, so that there is not this limitation or bond with the form of the object; and there is the orientation to that which is beyond our world, beyond our sensibility, reaching to the ideas of reason. But again it is a relation of indeterminateness. We must examine this aesthetic judgment further.

Thus, it is clear that the aesthetic judgment of the beautiful does not enjoy the same free play as does the judgment of the sublime or those of sheer fancy. In the *Prolegomena*, Kant has stated that the imagination can be forgiven such flights into fancy, but not the understanding, which must adhere to limits. Here, it should be clear that there is a distinction between the imagination given to such fancy, not bound to the form of objects of experience, and that of the aesthetic judgment of the beautiful, which is so bound. Thus, this latter function of imagination is free, but it relates to the form of the object, as well as enjoys an indeterminate relation to the understanding and its principle of conformity to law in general. Since the imagination is a faculty of sense, it needs the understanding in this relation for there to be a judgment, but not a relation to a concept of the understanding, but only to its principle of conformity to law in general. Thus, the imagination (in the judgment of beauty) is not free in reference to two relations: first in its relation to the form of the object; second, in its relation to the principle of conformity to law in general. Now this is clearly a subjective, universal judgment that does not employ any objective law or category. That is, anyone should, on seeing this object, be able to judge it to be beautiful.[17] The judgment is regarded as an example of a universal rule that one cannot state, so that when one states that this object is beautiful, one is claiming that all ought to describe it as beautiful.

In order to contrast the free play of the judgment of the sublime with that of the beautiful, it is necessary to consider briefly the differences between the two.[18] Now these differences must be elaborated on, since they become the significant focus for Lyotard, and since the entire enterprise becomes significant for Ricoeur's expansion of the role of the productive imagination of Kant. First, the beautiful is connected with the form of the object, consisting in having definite boundaries, as seen earlier, while the sublime is found in a formless object, so to speak, so that boundlessness is represented in it, and totality is thought, entailing the ideas of reason considered as the faculty of indeterminate ideas of totality. And this brings us to the paramount difference: "Thus the beautiful seems to be regarded as the presentation of an indefinite concept of understanding, the sublime as that of a like concept of reason."[19] But the main difference between them Kant indicates as the fact that the sublime does violence to the imagination. On the apprehension of an object, what excites the feeling of the sublime appears in its form "to violate purpose in respect of judgment, to be unsuited to our presentative faculty, and ... to do violence to the imagination; and yet it is judged to be only the more sublime." The sublime exceeds what the imagination can form, is cut off from nature in a way that the aesthetic form is not, and, for Kant, relates to an indeterminate concept of reason instead of understanding, as in the case of taste.[20]

We must not, however, underestimate the importance of this transition from the beautiful to the sublime, for it is here that Kant shows how he has "circumscribed the creative role of the imagination."[21] And it is the sublime that challenges the human mind to unfathomable depths in shattering form and limits. This inadequacy of the images of the imagination, drives it toward reason, toward the totality of the realm beyond its own. Thus, the artistic imagination can serve as a symbol that directs us toward the mind's suprasensible province. Something becomes sublime, or, rather, elicits the sublime in us, to the extent that it produces symbols, analogues to the ideas of reason, which means something that our mind cannot actually grasp, drawing us to the awareness of something great in the mind itself.

Leading up to his famous treatment of the production of the work of art, Kant presents in paragraph 43 important distinctions and points for recent reappropriations of this doctrine, especially in distinguishing the production of a work of art from mere play. In distinguishing art from handicraft, which is employed not because it is pleasant, but rather for its effect or wages in contrast to art as pleasant and purposive as play. The significance of the end of this treatment is Kant's distinction of the art production as work from mere play, invoking a sort of mechanism or compulsion essential to handicraft, but now revealed as prerequired for art production. Kant is showing clearly here that for the artist or the producing of fine art there must be a backdrop of knowledge presupposed for this particular fine art: for instance, the poet must have a good knowledge of languages and, if classical, of the classical disciplines as prerequisite for his production. As Kant so tersely expresses this: "But it is not inexpedient to recall that, in all free arts, there is yet requisite something compulsory or, as it is called, mechanism, without which the spirit, which must be free in art and which alone inspires the work, would have no body and would evaporate altogether: e.g. in poetry there must be an accuracy and wealth of language, and also prosody and measure. [It is not inexpedient, I say, to recall this], for many modern educators believe that the best way to produce a free art is to remove it from all constraint, and thus to change it from work into mere play" [CJ, 147]. This insight, as Kant so well puts it for the end of the eighteenth century, is quite relevant today, especially in the case of some tendencies in postmodernism. For there we see the attempt to sidestep constraints, and thus do precisely what Kant warns against when he refers to spirit, without such compulsory element, as having "no body" and as evaporating altogether. Postmodernism, then, in some of its adherents, has done just that by subverting the role of the subject altogether, yielding to some force of language or chance.

There is a subtle and relevant point in the productive activity in the production of the work of art that becomes apparent in Kant's rigorous attempt to distinguish beautiful art from nature. It seems for Kant that beautiful art must look like nature even though we are conscious of it as art, as a product of art. It appears like nature in that it can be seen in agreement with rules that make it become what it ought to be, yet there is no trace of the rule capturing or hampering the artist. This insight springs from the difference between nature according to the rules of the categories and art as entailing, not a rule or a concept of understanding, but rather the general lawfulness or purposiveness of understanding without being hampered by the strict and specific rule. Thus, Kant can say that beautiful art looks like nature, even though we are acutely aware of it precisely as art.

At the heart of his treatment of the production of fine art is Kant's famous and enigmatic doctrine of genius as the (producer) productive capacity of fine art in paragraphs 46–51, culminating in paragraph 49. The first tentative and inadequate articulation of genius is that it is the talent of giving the rule to art, but this is obviously insufficient because one must be careful of the rule here, and the talent as well. Kant goes on to define genius as "the innate mental disposition (*ingenium*) through which nature gives the rule to art." [CJ, 150] [*Genie ist die angeborne Gemütsanlage (ingenium), durch welche die Natur der Kunst die Regel gibt.*][22] In Kant's sense, beautiful art must be considered as a product of such genius. This reveals something of the productive imagination that is of great interest to us. In further explaining genius, Kant is drawn to tie it down and to free it at once. For it is first original as a talent, an *ingenium*, an innate ability, one not taught or learned, of producing that for that "no definite rule can be given." It is, however, tempered or bridled, in that the unbridled imagination in fancy can produce total nonsense, while genius produces fine art which itself must serve as models that are exemplary, as seen earlier in the context of the necessity of everyone agreeing that a particular product is beautiful. Now the function of "exemplary" is also manifest in the other direction in the actual production of art on the part of genius. In this production, the imagination is tied down, although only minimally and not jeopardizing its free play by tying it to a rule or concept. Thus, genius is the inborn mental disposition through which nature gives the rule to art, all things above considered.

In the next paragraph, 47, Kant clarifies a glaring ambiguity in this account of genius regarding the rule prescribed by a quasi–nature in the artist, or by the disposition endowed by nature for the prescription of such a rule. Kant further stipulates that this is not a precept or a formula, for the aesthetic judgments of the beautiful would be determinative judgments according to rules, which he cannot admit. The rule must hence be "abstracted from the fact, i.e., from the product" [CJ, 152] so that others might imitate its aesthetic production, but not copy it, according to their own innate talent. "The ideas of the artist excite like ideas in his pupils if nature has endowed them with a like proportion of their mental powers" [CJ, 152]. But again Kant does what we have already seen: he emphasizes that even beautiful art, basically distinguished from mechanical art, still does have a modicum of the mechanical element that can be followed as rules, since in such art some purpose must be conceived. If there were not this element, it would not be the product of art, but rather of chance [CJ, 153].[23] While the artist who merely copies produces art with no soul or animating principle, in contrast, the artist who throws off all relation to rule produces fancy and nonsense that is not fine art at all, and to whom Kant refers as "shallow heads."

At the outset of his famous paragraph 49, Kant attributes to genius, as the productive capacity of the imagination in producing fine art, the enigmatic and illusive power of spirit (*Geist*). This is the very animating principle of the mind [*im Gemüte*], the very faculty of presenting aesthetical ideas [*als das Vermogen der Darstellung asthetischer Ideen*] [CJ, 157].[24] In the process of unfolding the sense of the aesthetical ideas, the fuller sense of genius and artistic production of the productive imagination in relation to the other powers will become clearer. For the aesthetical idea is the product of the imagination in the interplay of other elements, and a rather enigmatic interplay. The aesthetic idea is "that representation [presentation] of the imagination (*Vorstellung der Einbildungskraft*) which occasions much thought, without however any definite thought, i.e. any concept, being capable of being adequate to it" [CJ, 157]. Hence, this aesthetic idea cannot ever be made completely intelligible in language. It is the counterpart of a rational idea. Thus, while the rational idea is one to which no intuition, or representation of the imagination, is adequate, the aesthetic idea is a presentation of the imagination to which no concept can be adequate.

Kant focuses on the productive imagination as the power of producing from the material given us by "actual nature" a quasi second nature, by which we "remold experience, always indeed in accordance with analogical laws, but yet also in accordance with principles which occupy a higher place in reason" [CJ, 157]. He is quick to point out that these principles are laws that are just as natural to us as the ones by which understanding comprehends empirical nature. Thus, there is the freedom that is not jeopardized, yet there is the relation to law without which genius in unbridled and produces sheer fancy or nonsense. We feel the freedom from the empirical laws of association that bind the empirical employment of the (reproductive) imagination, "so that the material supplied to us by nature in accordance with this law can be worked up into something different which surpasses nature" [CJ, 157]. And this material by means of which spirit animates the soul puts the mental powers purposively into swing, that is, "into such a play as maintains itself and strengthens the mental powers in their exercise" [CJ, 157].

In explaining the aesthetic ideas as ideas, Kant clarifies to some extent precisely what they are. These presentations [*Vorstellungen*] of the productive imagination are called ideas in part because they strive or reach to something beyond the bounds of experience, seeking to approximate to a "presentation (i.e., exhibition, *einer Darstellung*) of concepts of reason"[CJ, 157, 247] or intellectual ideas. In this striving, they give to the intellectual ideas the appearance of objective reality. They are called ideas also because no concept can be fully adequate to them in internal intuitions. Poets venture to "realize to sense, rational ideas of invisible beings, the kingdom of the blessed, hell, eternity, creation, etc." [CJ, 157].

And in dealing with things of experience, such as death, vices, love, fame, and so on, the poet uses the imagination in emulating "the play of reason in its quest after a maximum, to go beyond the limits of experience and to present them to sense with a completeness of which there is no example in nature" [CJ, 158]. Kant contends that it is in the case of the poet that the faculty of aesthetical ideas manifests itself in its "entire strength" and then adds that it is properly a talent of the imagination.[25]

Kant attempts to clarify the interrelation of the faculties functioning in the aesthetic idea considered earlier in another way. He points out that the forms, as approximate representations of the imagination, which do not constitute the presentation of the given concept, but only "express the consequences bound up with that concept and its relationship to other concepts" are what he calls "aesthetic attributes of an object whose concept as a rational idea cannot be adequately presented" [CJ, 158]. It is as a rational idea that this concept cannot be adequately presented. And these forms do not constitute the exhibition or presentation of the concept itself, but, rather, are supplementary representations [Nebensvorstellungen] expressing the concept's implications and its kinship with other concepts. These aesthetic attributes yield or furnish an aesthetic idea, substituting for or taking the place of the logical presentation for that rational idea. Its proper function, however, is to quicken or enliven [beleben] the mind by opening up for it a "view into an immense realm of kindred presentation."[26]

Thus, genius is seen to be a talent for art in which rules clearly determine the procedure. And, as such a talent, it presupposes a determinate concept of the product as its purpose and hence presupposes understanding. But "it also presupposes a representation (although an indeterminate one) of the material, i.e. of the intuition for the presentment of this concept, and, therefore a relation between the imagination and the understanding." This genius shows itself more in the "enunciation or expression of aesthetical ideas which contain abundant material" for accomplishment of the proposed purpose in a presentment of a definite concept than is actually accomplishing that purpose in a presentation; consequently, it "represents the imagination as free from all guidance of rules and yet as purposive in reference to the presentment of the given concept" [CJ, 161]. Finally "the unsought undesigned subjective purposiveness" in the free harmony of the imagination with the lawfulness of the understanding "presupposes such a proportion and disposition of these faculties as no following of rules, whether of science or of mechanical imitation, can bring about, but which only the nature of the subject can produce" [CJ, 161]. The product given rise to by such genius is an "example" for another kindred spirit or genius in whom is awakened a like productivity, and hence shows that the work of genius is truly "exemplary."

In leading to his conviction that the beautiful is the symbol of the morally good, Kant dedicates more than half of paragraph 59 to the "presentation" of concepts to the imagination in the dynamics of symbol and analogy in contrast to that of schemata. In this contrast, he focuses on the mode of presentation of concepts in each, showing especially the uniqueness of symbolic presentation, which does not entail schemata, but rather a following of the procedure for providing the schemata to intuition. It is clear that, in these processes, all intuition supplied to concepts a priori are either schemata or symbols. Each of these contains the presentation of the concept, but each in its own way. The schemata entails the direct presentation of the concept, while the symbol is an indirect presentation of the concept, by means of an analogy, with the judgment exercising a "double function" [CJ, 197], one that applies the concept to the object of a sensible intuition, and then "applying the mere rule of the reflection made upon that intuition to a quite different object of which the first is only the symbol. In this latter, even empirical intuitions are employed.27 Thus, for Kant, presentation, as *"subjectio sub adspectum"* or sensible illustration, what he calls *hypotyposis*, comes about either as schematical or as symbolic. Elaborating further on the symbolical than done immediately above, we can now add that this symbolical has an intuition supplied with which "accords a procedure of the judgment analogous to what it observes in schematism, i.e., merely analogous to the rule of this procedure, not to the intuition itself, consequently to the form of reflection merely and not to its content" [CJ, 197]. Thus, Kant finds it necessary to distinguish his use of symbol from a misuse of it by logicians according to whom it is distinguished from intuition rather than a mode of intuition.28

Although Ricoeur does not centralize the role of the sublime as Lyotard does, his development of the role of symbol acts to bridge the gap between him and Lyotard to some limited extent. For his emphasis on this can be seen to have some reference to the sublime in Kant, but in its relation to the symbol and analogy rather than to the violence it does to the imagination. Ricoeur expands on the fact that, for Kant, the artistic imagination serves as a symbol directing us toward the "minds supra-sensible province." I follow Richard Kearney's29 interpretation of Kant in affirming that "art can be considered to become sublime to the extent that it produce 'symbols (analogous to the ideas of reason) which signify something which our mind cannot actually grasp," thus hinting at some kind of rapport between the ideas of reason and the aesthetic ideas of the imaginative genius, as seen previously. These latter ideas, it must be recalled, have no concept or definite thought of understanding, yet they induce much thought, or, as Ricoeur puts it, the symbol gives rise to, contributes to, thought.30 These aesthetic ideas seem to function as symbols for Kant.

Ricoeur's appropriation of the Kantian productive imagination, in stark distinction from the role of imagination in Lyotard's view, gives it a central place without jeopardizing the role of reason. The most intense role, continuous with that in symbols, is in the creativity of living metaphor, is continued in narrative. This extension from Kant regarding semantic innovation must be distinguished from those that invoke an "invention" rather than innovation, breaking completely from any rule of purposiveness, thus directly opposing rather than extending the Kantian project. Here we do see Ricoeur extending and completing the role of the productive imagination beyond anything Kant conceived, and in a more integrated and whole philosophy than anyone else today. His view of imagination in these various roles and expressions allows him to inter-relate any number of cognate disciplines, and to do so while preserving the fullness and mystery of human existence in its vital tension with the tendency toward rational ordering and expression. We must begin by looking at these various expressions of the productive imagination in Ricoeur's philosophy, which is so central as to lead to the whole gamut of his writings in the past five decades. We will focus therefore on those aspects that are directly related to our project of a dialogue with post-modern deconstruction. Thus, it will be necessary for us to focus on the productive imagination in the creativity of language. This development will highlight the differences with other postmodern thinkers, especially deconstructionists.

A preliminary remark is in order about Ricoeur's placing ethics, or more precisely, an extended ethics, in the center of his entire philosophy. Such an extended ethics, with its role of evil in freedom and existence, gives rise to the view of hope and thus the necessity for speculative philosophy and its possibility as emerging from the innovation of meaning that is engendered by the productive imagination and its exten-sion. This entails a further extension of Kant, of the notion of regeneration of the freedom and the will in practical action. Ricoeur's entire philosophy is thus bound to the interplay among imagination, understanding, and reason. For it is the imagination that is presented by reason with ideas. His philosophy recasts the Kantian view of the demand on the part of reason for totality as well as reason's placing of a limit on experience, in terms of his own development of a view of the quasi-transcending of this limit through indirect expressions such as symbols, metaphors, and narratives. Thus, in contrast to the position clarified earlier, Ricoeur's view goes beyond Kant's strict doctrine, while remaining as true to some of its essential tenets as possible for a post-Hegelian and contemporary philosophy.

Within the sphere of poetics, in metaphorical and narrative discourse, semantic innovation is placed in the Kantian productive imagination in its extended role of schematism, which, for Kant, is symbolization.

Explicating Kant a bit more clearly than Kant himself does, Ricoeur contends that it is the work of the productive imagination to perceive resemblance in terms at first seen apart and then brought together by inaugurating the similarity between them. "This consists of schematizing the synthetic operation, of figuring the predicative assimilation from whence results the semantic innovation."[31] Ricoeur, however, in this context wants to cut beneath the imaginative synthesis of providing schemata for the rules of understanding in unifying the manifold of sense for objective knowledge. This role of creative imagination cannot be separated from the connection between symbols and metaphors for Ricoeur, and the relation between the symbol and metaphor is essential regarding creativity in semantic innovation of the imagination. Symbols are bound to spirit and to desire. Continuous with symbols, metaphors stress the unbound creativity in expressions with double meaning in the overall context of polysemy. Thus, looked at from that direction, the imagination in its role of schematism is the source of semantic innovation.[32] This, of course, entails both an extension of the Kantian role of schematism and the collapse of the distinction between the determinative and the reflective judgments. And now following Kant more strictly, looked at from the perspective of reason, it is reason (spirit) that gives to the imagination the ideas that stimulate the understanding to creative thought, which, in "thinking more," cannot ever be adequate to the idea. Thus, the demand for totality within the context of a bond to existence, through desire and spirit, allows a glimpse again at the infinite quest within a finite situation. It is beneficial to pursue this line of thought further in the direction of the productive imagination extended in schematism, for it is here that we see Ricoeur's own philosophic framework, both as Kantian and as contemporary, undercutting and underlying all of his philosophy of the will and myriad excursions into dialogue with other philosophies.

Ricoeur compares the "grasping together" characteristic of the act of configuration to judgment as understood by Kant, reminding us somewhat of Heidegger's "gathering" of reason. Still following Kant, Ricoeur compares the production of the act of configuration to the work of the productive imagination understood as a transcendental, and not a psychological, faculty. And Ricoeur indicates, following the third *Critique* to some extent, that the productive imagination is not only rule-governed, but also constitutes the "generative matrix of rules."[33] Along this line, Ricoeur reminds us that in Kant's first Critique, the categories of the understanding are first schematized by the productive imagination, and that the schematism has this power because the productive imagination fundamentally has a synthetic function, connecting understanding and intuition by engendering syntheses that are intellectual and intuitive at the same time. Applying this creativity to his own project, we see that, for him, emplotment[34] also engenders a mixed intelligibility, gathering together what he calls the point, theme, or thought of a story, and the intuitive presentation of circumstances, characters, episodes, and changes of fortune that make up the denouement. In this way, we may speak of a schematism of the narrative function. "This schematism, in turn, is constituted within a history that has all the characteristics of a tradition. Let us understand by this term not the inert transmission of some already dead deposit of material but the living transmission of an innovation always capable of being reactivated by a return to the most creative moments of poetic activity." In Ricoeur's understanding, traditionality enriches the relationship between plot and time with a new feature.

He says further: "However Kant only recognized those determinations of time that contribute to the objective constitution of the physical world. The schematism of the narrative function implies determinations of new genre which are precisely the ones we have just designated by the dialectic of the episodic characteristics and the configuring of emplotment."[35] Thus, we see Ricoeur expanding on the Kantian determination of time to include, within the context of indirect expressions, the whole of the narrative function, which allows for expressing new worlds in texts. This in general is what he means when he says he denies the Kantian distinction between the determinative and reflective judgments in this context. Such expression is correlated to the other end of the hermeneutical arch as the original appropriation of the latent world of the text, expanding the world of the reader or listener. Such ontic aspects of existence must be further investigated in terms of the ontic access to the Sacred explored in earlier works by Ricoeur, and culminating only now in his most recent works dealing with the world of the text and narrative discourse. In overcoming the supposed phenomenological subjectivism of Husserl, Ricoeur has refocused on the openness and rootedness of existence, and exposed the significance of the decenteredness of the Cogito in terms of its twofold dependence upon desire and on spirit. This ontic existential dependence has its roots in a further dependence on the ultimate telos and arche, the Sacred, as the prelinguistic level subtending language. And, it is metaphorical function that takes the ambiguity and polyvalence to the linguistic creative level.

Metaphoric function is not a part of conceptual thinking (IT, 57). As mentioned earlier, the theory of metaphor leads the theory of symbols into the neighborhood of the Kantian theory of the schematism and conceptual synthesis. Metaphor is the place in language, understood as discourse, where this creativity comes about. It is distinguished from, but rooted in, the symbolic level of discourse and expression, and, as living metaphor, gives rise to conceptual thought.

Ricoeur expresses this insight in the following text, indicating the direction toward the logos of rationality: "Metaphor would be the place in discourse where this emergence may be detected because sameness and difference are in conflict. If metaphor can be treated as a figure of speech, it is because it overtly presents in the form of a conflict between sameness and difference the process which is covertly at work in the construction of all semantic fields, that is, the kinship which brings individuals under the rule of a logical class."[36] However, Ricoeur also stresses the break, the discontinuity or epoché between the metaphoric and the speculative levels of discourse: "One passes from one discourse to the other only by an epoché"[37] But, despite this rupture, speculative discourse gets its possibility from the semantic function of metaphor in that the gain in signification is a demand in the concept but not a knowing by the concept.[38]

In two recent works,[39] Ricoeur, expanding on Kant with all of these themes, brings together time with the semantic innovation of the productive imagination and schematism. Narrative fiction[40] takes on a central role because by means of it "we reconfigure our confused, unformed, and at the limit mute temporal existence."[41] It is this that makes possible the "intersection" of the world of the text and the world of the reader, "wherein real action occurs and unfolds its specified temporality."[42] The culmination, however, of the relation of time and narrative is reached within Ricoeur's project as a whole when the "refiguration of time by narrative" is achieved, when "referential intentions of the historical narrative and the fictional narrative interweave. Our analysis of the fictive experience of time will at least have marked a decisive turning point in the direction of the solution to this problem that forms the horizon of my investigation, by providing something like a world of the text for us to think about, while awaiting its complement, the life-world of the reader, without which the signification of the literary work is incomplete."[43]

We can see that Ricoeur has followed Kant concerning the boundary of theoretical knowledge, the limits of thinking and speculation, and has expanded on these through the use of symbol and semantic innovation of the third *Critique*. His extensions on Kant in these areas collapse the distinction between reflective and determinative judgment, so that the poetics of the semantic innovation and its schematism, all extending beyond Kant in an attempt to find the quasi logic of the imagination, does not fall prey to the same pitfalls as does most postmodern deconstruction today. For Ricoeur's incorporation of an extended semantic innovation does not buy into an antilogocentrism or a paralogical experimentation, even though he does understand the decentering of the cogito and the need for constant openness to the excess of sense for renewal of thought. Within these extensions, we have seen how Ricoeur still respects semantic priority in semantic innovation and in language theory in general, and maintains a unique role of reason without collapsing it into the imagination as the romantics and deconstructionists have done. In addition, he has expanded on the limited a priori of time in Kant's strict doctrine, broadening its scope to include not only lived time, but the time of narration and of poetics.

In this context, Ricoeur seems to admit the need for an indirect access to the question of the whole, in thinking beyond the boundaries of knowledge and of problematic reflection. In fact, most of his reflections on existence and being take place within a certain domain going beyond the boundaries of the Kantian limit—that is, the total and full existence beneath and beyond the realm of a strictly theoretical reflection—the domain of existence, which for Kant must remain unknowable. And Ricoeur constantly speaks of the need for indirect language of myth, symbol, metaphor, and narrative in general in order to prevent idola-trizing what is reflected on here. Must not philosophers admit that we cannot really free ourselves from some key images—for example, that of heaven as the abode of the blessed—provided that we show that these images are bound up with the conditions of existence that belong to a wayfaring creature, and that they cannot accordingly be considered as literally true? This is so. Thus, Ricoeur's expansion on Kantian limit and imagination leads to a full context of thinking and philosophy. We see clearly that today we do not necessarily end up substituting literature and poetry for serious philosophical endeavors, but, rather, must move forward with the serious task at hand of following a path of a perhaps renewed reason.

NOTES

1. Ernst Cassirer, *The Philosophy of the Enlightenment*, trans. Fritz C. A. Koelln & James P. Pettegrove (Boston: Beacon Press: 1951), pp. 332–33.
2. Ibid., p. 333.
3. Éliane Escoubas, "The Simplicity of the Sublime," in *Of the Sublime: Presence in Question*, trans. Jeffrey S. Librett (New York: State University of New York Press, 1993), p. 69. This statement follows the statement: [quoting from Kant, #25, 89, 87] "it is not a matter of a satisfaction [*Wohlgefallen*] occasioned by the object [*am Objekte*], as for the beauty... but of a satisfaction occasioned by the extension of the imagination itself [*an der Erweiterung der Einbildungskraft*]."
4. Ibid.
5. Martha B. Helfer, *The Retreat of Representation: The Coincept of Darstellung in German Critical Discourse* (New York: State University of New York Press, 1996), p. 2.
6. Escoubas, "The Simplicity of the Sublime," p. 56.
7. Helfer, *The Retreat of Representation*, p. 3.
8. Ibid.
9. Martin Heidegger, *What Is Philosophy?*, bilingual edition, trans. by William Kluback and Jean T. Wilde (New York: Twayne, 1958).
10. Helfer, *The Retreat of Representation*, p. 4.
11. Bill Reading, *Introducing Lyotard: Art and Politics* (London: Routledge, 1991), p. 72.
12. This puts the aesthetic feeling in the singularity of its occurrence in the

prominent role in the critical enterprise, for here the aesthetic feeling is reflective judgment or pure subjective thinking. Lyotard interprets Kant to call the subject the subjective aspect of thinking and "as such consists entirely in the tautegory that makes feeling the sign, for thought, of its state, thus the sign of feeling itself because the 'state' of thinking is feeling; or else the subject is the ground zero where the synthesis of concepts is suspended (in the first *Critique*) or is the ever receding horizon of the faculties' synthesis (in the third *Critique*).... It is precisely through reflection, using the subjective state as a guide for thinking, using the feeling that accompanies it in all its acts, that one can locate this appearance and restore all proper domiciliations. And when the act of thinking is directed to the subject, it is with reflection again that one can critique the notion of subject" [AOS, pp. 24–24].

13. "Links, the Unconscious, and the Sublime: An Inter-Phrase with Jean-François Lyotard," ed. Tim Craker, Michael Strysick, and Bretchen Topp, *Ellipsis* I, 1 (Spring 1990): 125.

14. Ibid., p. 126.

15. Jean-François Lyotard, *Lessons on the Analytic of the Sublime*, trans. Elizabeth Rottenberg (Stanford: Stanford University Press, 1991), p. 52.

16. "Links, The Unconscious, and the Sublime," pp. 125–26.

17. Kant invokes a "common sense" [*ein Gemeinsinn*] in this relation, but not in the usual sense of *sensus communis* of the medieval philosophy, which is an inner sense unifying what is given in external senses. Rather, for Kant, the common sense is employed to distinguish the "universal" principle of aesthetic judgment of the beautiful from a logical principle, that is, the common sense is the presupposed commonness bringing about the judgment. This is the effect of the free play of the cognitive powers in their harmony, which can and should be experienced by all on the occasion of experiencing this particular beautiful object. Thus, there is a sort of necessity of assent on the part of all, which Kant calls "exemplary."

18. Immanuel Kant, *Critique of Judgment*, trans. J. H. Bernard (New York: Hafner, 1951), p. 82. Henceforth CJ in the text. Kant, in focusing on these differences, first refers to their agreements: that they both please in themselves, and neither presupposes a judgment of sense or a judgment logically determined, but rather, a judgment of reflection. Also, they are both singular judgments, even though they "announce themselves as universally valid for every subject," in the feeling of pleasure and not in the cognition of an object.

19. Ibid.

20. Kant makes an important point about the "independent natural beauty" as making us see a "technique of nature" analogous to art, thus overcoming a closed and absolute nature as purposeless mechanism. This conjures up the principle of the purposiveness as a regulative and subjective principle, extending our concept of nature without extending our cognition of natural objects, so that nature can be considered as art and not merely as mechanism. Kant concludes, which will become important later: "Hence, we see that the concept of the sublime is not nearly so important or rich in consequences as the concept of the beautiful; and that, in general, it displays nothing purposive in nature itself, but only in that possible use of our intuition of it by which there is produced in us a feeling of a purposiveness quite independent of nature" (*Critique of Judgment*, p. 85). Thus, because of this separation of the sublime from purposiveness of nature, and the fact that it only involves a purposive use that imagination makes

of its representation, Kant considers the theory of the sublime a "mere appendix" to the aesthetic judging of that purposiveness.

21. Richard Kearney, *The Wake of the Imagination: Toward a Postmodern Culture* (Minneapolis: University of Minnesota Press, 1988), p. 174.

22. Immanuel Kant, *Kritik der Urteilsdraft* (Stuttgart: Philipp Reclam, 1966), p. 235.

23. This remark regarding chance can help to clarify Jacques Derrida's effectively scuttling the creativity of imagination in favor of this chance.

24. Kant, *Kritik der Urteilsdraft*, p. 246.

25. In this further account of the aesthetic idea in relation to concept and presentation, we begin by focusing first on the representation [*einer Vorstellung*]. This representation of the imagination itself presents or exhibits a concept, and is placed under that same concept. Now, when this very representation, provided for that concept, prompts more thought than it is possible to comprehend in a definite concept, thus enlarging aesthetically the concept itself in an unbounded fashion [*auf unbegrenzte Art*], the imagination is then creative, bringing reason, as the faculty of intellectual ideas, into motion. This representation [*Vorstellung*] gives rise to more thought, which thought does belong to the concept of the object, than can be grasped or made clear in it. Thus, for Kant, it is precisely the creativity of the productive imagination that prompts reason into action in the process of aesthetically enlarging the concept, and the representation gives rise to thought that can not be adequate for the concept, as seen earlier.

26. Here I follow the recent translation of Kant's *Critique of Judgment: Including the First Introduction*, translated, with an Introduction by Werner S. Pluhar (Indianapolis and Cambridge: Hackett, 1987), pp. 183–84.

27. We must remember that empirical concepts have intuitions that Kant calls examples [CJ, 198].

28. Kant's example in giving an account of a symbol is that of a monarchical state represented by a living body if it is governed by laws that spring from the people, and by a machine (such as a hand-mill) if governed according to the individual, absolute will of an autocrat. Thus, Kant bases his idea of symbolism on analogy, which means that the similarity is between the relation between two relations, and not between objects. For the second example, it is not the question of the hand mill that is similar to a despotic state. Rather, the relation between the hand mill and its causality, that is, how it operates, is related to the relation of the state to its causality, that is, the causality of the despotic will as absolute cause. And the question arises, what are the points of analogy between the aesthetic and the moral judgments, or between the beautiful and the morally good, that justify our looking on the beautiful as a symbol of the morally good, keeping in mind that what is similar is the relation between two relations, each entailing the relation between two objects? In his own example, the first relation is that between the monarchical state and its government by the laws of the people, and the living body and its rules of operation; and the second relation is between the monarchical state and its government by the will of the autocratic monarch, and the hand mill and its causality. The first relation he calls a living body, and the second relation he calls a machine.

29. Kearney, *The Wake of Imagination*, p. 176.

30. Ricoeur expresses this as: "*Le symbol donne à penser*," playing on the twofold meaning of "*donne*" in this context, and meaning that the symbol

gives rise to and gives to thought: Paul Ricoeur, *Symbolism of Evil*, trans. by Everson Buchanan (New York: Harper & Row, 1967).

31. Paul Ricoeur, *Time and Narrative*, vol. I, trans. by Kathleen McLaughlin and David Pellauer (Chicago: University of Chicago Press, 1984), p. x: *Temps et recit* (Paris: Editions du Seuil, 1983), p. 12.

32. "But if we follow Kant rather than Hume, I mean the theory of schematism and that of productive imagination, we have to look at imagination as the place of nascent meanings and categories, rather than as the place of fading impressions.... And could we not say by anticipation that imagination is the emergence of conceptual meaning through the interplay between sameness and difference? Metaphor would be the place in discourse where this emergence may be detected because sameness and difference are in conflict." Paul Ricoeur, "Creativity in Language," *Philosophy Today* 17, 2 (Summer 1973): 109.

33. Ricoeur, *Time and Narrative*, I, p. 68: *Temps et recit*, p. 106.

34. Although he denies this Kantian distinction, Ricoeur contends that the kinship between emplotment and the reflective judgment that Kant opposes to the determining one, in the sense that it reflects on the work of thinking at work in the aesthetic judgment of taste and in the teleological judgment, applied to organic wholes. One could say that the act of emplotment has a similar function inasmuch as it extracts a configuration from a succession.

35. Ricoeur, *Time and Narrative*, vol. I, p. 244, footnote 18, p. 106, footnote 1.

36. Ricoeur, "Creativity in Language" pp. 109–10.

37. Paul Ricoeur, *The Rule of Metaphor*, trans. Robert Czerny et al. (Toronto: University of Toronto Press, 1977), p. 300. Hereafter cited within the text as RM. Although the citations are from the English edition, some of the translations from the original French are my own. *La Metaphore vive* (Paris: Editions du Seuil, 1975).

38. Ricoeur, *The Rule of Metaphor*, pp. 296–97.

39. *The Rule of Metaphor* and *Time and Narrative* (cf. Vol. I, p. ix).

40. Regarding "fictional narrative" Ricoeur remarks: "Remaining faithful to the convention concerning vocabulary I adopted in my first volume, I am giving the term 'fiction' a narrower extension than that adopted by the many authors who take it to be synonymous with "narrative configuration.... I am reserving the term "fiction" for those literary creations that do not have historical narrative's ambition to constitute a true narrative. If we take "configuration" and "fiction" as synonyms we no longer have a term available to account for the different relation of each of these two narrative modes to the question of truth. What historical narrative and fictional narrative do have in common is that they both stem from the same configurating operations I put under the title mimesis2. On the other hand, what opposes them to each other does not have to do with the structuring activity invested in their narrative structures as such, rather it has to do with the "truth-claim" that defines the third mimetic relation."

41. Ricoeur, *Time and Narrative*, vol. I, p. xi.

42. Ibid.

43. Ricoeur, *Time and Narrative*, vol. II, trans. by Kathleen McLaughlin and David Pellauer (Chicago: University of Chicago Press, 1985), p. 160. It is in volume III, which constitutes Part IV of *Time and Narrative*, on "Narrated Time," that this project is culminated.

Paul Ricoeur's Hermeneutics: 10
From Critique to Poetics

Olivier Abel

R icoeur is definitely regarded as the leader of the French hermeneutic
school. And yet he does depart from it in two main instances: the
role of language and historical critique, and the poetic performance of
reference. Here I intend to emphasize both of these particularities. But to
make it clearer how Ricoeur orients hermeneutics as a *critical* hermeneutics and redirects it toward a *poetic* hermeneutics, I would like to start
with where he comes from, why he went over to hermeneutics, and how
those two gestures may have their origins in his phenomenological experience. This seems important to me, as we are here in a place where the
history of phenomenology does matter.

HERMENEUTICS AS LEARNING FROM PHENOMENOLOGY

When, in 1940, Ricoeur was taken prisoner of war by the Germans, he
knew Husserl only through his reading of the *Logical Investigations*. He
managed to hide a pencil and a copy of the first volume of *Ideas
Pertaining to a Pure Phenomenology and Phenomenological Philosophy* (the books of the old master of Marburg were forbidden: he was
a Jew), and this is how he came to translate the text, in minuscule hand-
writing, in the margins of the book. This translation of Husserl put
Ricoeur among the first to introduce phenomenology to France, and
indeed it is this *method* that he applies to the topic of the will (a
geometric crossroads of different themes like subject and choice, but
also desire, the tragic, or affirmation), directly paralleling Merleau-
Ponty's work during the same years. As we see very clearly in the
collection of articles entitled *A l'école de la phénoménologie,*[1] the
difference is that Ricoeur analyzes the ethical subject, the willing and
desiring subject (*le sujet du "vouloir"*), the praxis of subjectivity,
whereas Merleau-Ponty analyzes the theoretical or aesthetic subject,
the perceiving subject.

The Question of the Acting Subject

Why did Ricoeur meet with phenomenology from the angle of the willing, suffering, and acting subject? I think it has to do first with his formative period in the French university system between the two wars, marked by a reflexive neo-Kantianism in which Descartes and Kant ceaselessly intervene in a central question: What does it mean to be a subject?[2] And what does it mean for a subject who carries in himself the disproportion between will, knowledge, pleasure, and suffering, and so on? It is in this universe that Ricoeur acquired the critical gesture with which he distinguishes genres (for the same statement does not always have the same meaning, as this depends on the sort of question it is responding to: descriptive, moral, aesthetic, judicial, loving, and so on). It is a sort of Wittgensteinian discipline that does not prevent, but rather permits the posing of the true question: What is it to say "I," what is the unity of the subject across this disparity of genres, languages, and experiences?

But it has also probably to do with encountering Existentialist thought; that of Gabriel Marcel, that of Karl Jaspers (to whom Ricoeur devotes his first book), and that of Heidegger as well. And of course the thought of Kierkegaard, which allowed him to radicalize originary affirmation through anguish, through a broken dialectic that proposes no synthesis but designates a singularity in the margins of all discourse. The central reflection here bears upon the existential decision.[3] How does the project take shape, what does it mean to choose, to decide and to choose myself among the possible, despite that which limits and diminishes my choice? This is the dominant question, from a few short texts of the prewar period to the great treatise on *The Voluntary and the Involuntary* published in 1950.[4] In other words, that treatise links him to a mode of thought where being is life, as opposed to a mode in which being is a thing. What is a being, having remained desire, a tension bearing within itself its own alteration, its own nonbeing?[5] What is a being that is able to give birth to another being? We find echoes of this fundamental intuition, it seems to me, even in Ricoeur's most technical works on what he calls the "live metaphor."[6] This motif may have something to do with the "poetic" orientation of his hermeneutics, and notably with the way he agrees with the phenomenological theme by which there is a point from where the act of the subject must be apprehended in its naïveté, in its capacity to be born and to give birth, to initiate initiative, and not to be satisfied with merely reproducing the conditions of its own appearance.

The Phenomenological Sense of "Aporia"

How might we characterize the phenomenological experience? What dominates Ricoeur's thought is the failure to discover an originary experience in which consciousness is a presence to itself. With Ricoeur, this absence of the subject to itself is translated primarily through an anthropology of fragility: What becomes of the identity of the subject when it is dislocated by time? What becomes of will, when it bears within itself the opacity of evil? Besides, there is a remarkable fact: a pure phenomenological reflection on time and evil presupposes the experience of pure passivity regarding time and evil, an experience that escapes us. The subject's activity is always already interfering with the subject's passivity: that is why, here, experience becomes a narrative.

But this aporia, which Husserl displays in the quest for a passive pregiven layer, setting it out in *Experience and Judgment*, is redoubled by the one displayed in *Crisis*. In his inquiry into the transcendental ego, at the deepest levels of phenomenology, Husserl is led in his *Crisis* into an impasse: the subject always already belongs to a "*Lebenswelt*," a lifeworld. Incidentally, let us note how Ricoeur is always on the lookout for the limits of any method, and for how the impasses themselves are fruitful for true philosophical thinking. Ricoeur says, for instance, when speaking about witness and on the topic of the ascription or attribution to oneself of an action: "As is generally the case with the most intractable aporias, these aporias of ascription do not bring a verdict of condemnation against the philosophy which discovers them. On the contrary, they should be reckoned to its credit." And Ricoeur adds in a note: "*Time and Narrative 3* is entirely constructed around the relation between an aporetics of temporality and the response of a poetics of narrativity."[7] It is this fundamental aporia that, for Ricoeur (as for many others), determines the hermeneutic turning point of phenomenology. Thus he writes:

> As soon as we start thinking, we discover we are already living in and by the means of worlds of representations, idealities, norms. As far as that goes we move in two worlds: *the* pre-given world which is the other's limit and ground, and *a* world of symbols and rules through which the world has already been interpreted when we begin to think.[8]

The World as Interpreted

So the lifeworld (Lebenswelt) is always already there before any interpretation; but it is also always already given in a language-world. This ambiguity—impossible to overcome—requires two quests: one points toward critical hermeneutics and the other toward a poetic reorientation of hermeneutics.

The first requires giving up the attempt at thematization of all that is "precomprehension" in our use of words and things; all sedimented metaphors, all abandoned metaphors, all this thickness of prefigurations and schematisms set down by the history and prehistory of our signs and images. We must explain them as far as possible, but none of this can be fully explicated by us, and this is probably where Ricoeur puts up some resistance to Habermas: there are experiences, questions, and convictions that are not open to full explication or argument. One may even ask if this aporia is not transcendental, constitutive. About the critique of ideology, Ricoeur writes:

> perhaps it is impossible for an individual, and still more for a group to formulate, everything, schematize everything, pose everything as an object of thought. This impossibility—to which I shall return at length in criticizing the idea of *total* reflection—makes ideology by nature an uncritical instance. It seems that the nontransparence of our cultural codes is a condition for the production of social messages.[9]

In that way, the 'response'-questioning is an endless task, because we are looking for the universality of *the* pregiven world when having no access to this universal, other than through this symbolic network of the worlds of prefiguration and precomprehension. Our universals are always still rooted in languages, stories, metaphors; and the most universal and abstract concepts still bear the trace of metaphors that have helped to produce them.

The Poetic Interpretation of the World

In the second quest, the metaphorization that enlivens the sedimentary layers is not satisfied with a kind of rhetorical adaptation to common presuppositions or admitted metaphors. Far from being confined to the language of tradition, in the figures of an already set precomprehension, the live metaphor tries to shake them up, to reshape them; it suspends and reorients, it refigures the world and recasts the parts, trying to offer a new world in which to dwell and act, a world where dwelling and acting would be possible. The first movement was primarily concerned with hermeneutic critique, the second one is rather more concerned with a poetic reorientation:

> Conversion of the imaginary, that is the central aim of poetics; through it, poetics moves the sediment universe of consensual ideas, the premises of rhetorical argument. This same breakthrough of the imaginary at the same time shakes the order of persuasion, as it is more a matter of breeding a new conviction than of settling a controversy.[10]

And this is what we find repeatedly in *Time and Narrative*, with the idea that the reader changes worlds through the confrontation with possible worlds opened up to him by the text: the narrative configuration transforms the prefiguration structures; and this makes possible a refiguration of the world of the reader. We could even balance what we noted earlier about the metaphoric anchorage of universal concepts. Moreover, live metaphor is an anomaly of language, but a normal anomaly, so to speak, a vital anomaly that allows language to repair the loss of singularities expended by the conceptual and linguistic structuring of the real:

> As a process, individualization can be roughly characterized as the inverse of classification, which eliminates the singular under the name of the concept.... It is because we think and speak in concepts that language has to repair, as it were, the loss caused by conceptualization.[11]

If, then, metaphor is a live speech devoted to *telling all the residual singularities* that remain unsaid on the edge of language, this singularization cannot be isolated from the general structuring of language.

Variations as Interminable Detour

In the preface to *The Conflict of Interpretations*, Ricoeur writes: "My aim here is to explore the paths opened up for contemporary philosophy by what one could call the grafting of the hermeneutic problem onto the phenomenological method." In fact, onto each subject taken up by will, evil, subject, meaning, metaphor, narrative, history, political thought or ethics, law, and so on, Ricoeur grafts several methods, convinced apparently that only a hybrid method can rise to the complexity of the subjects chosen. This metaphor of grafting is quite frequent, and we find the idea that "this conjunction among phenomenology, linguistics, and analytical philosophy in its least logicalist aspect, provided me with resources for hybridization to which I owe a great deal."[12] In other words, one can only understand a text, a doctrine, or a theory if one understands them as responses to questions, as Gadamer said, and if one accepts the irreducible diversity of possible questions. "A hermeneutical philosophy is one which accepts all the demands of this long detour and renounces the dream of a total mediation, at the end of which reflection would enjoy intellectual intuition in the transparence to itself of an absolute subject."[13]

Texts and human works, as well as dreams and myths, and even great institutions, can be the objects of rival hermeneutics, each probably as legitimate as every other, and all of them needing to renounce their claims to exclusiveness. In other words, we are condemned to the conflict of interpretations, from which we cannot hope to emerge via a hermeneutic philosophy. If phenomenology, through the method of eidetic variations, wanted to reach invariant essences, it is the absence of these invariant meanings that sends us back to variations, to their rules and irregularities. And the theme of identity of the subject needs to be sought in its variations, as we will see later.

THE DOUBLE ORIENTATION OF HERMENEUTICS

Having reached that hermeneutic turning point by which we discover that "we appear in the very midst of a conversation already on its way and in which we try and find our own bearing so as to contribute when our turn comes,"[14] we shall now take up again the two themes we signaled: the former, Ricoeur expounds with his "critical hermeneutics," and the latter we gather up under the title "poetics of the world as interpreted" (i.e., poetics of metaphor, narrative, and so on).

A Critical Hermeneutics

The disparate varieties of hermeneutics, of types of interpretation, can be brought together in terms of a simple principle that can be stated as follows: "the meaning of a text is a function of the implicit question it is meant to answer." I will call this principle the "principle of the *implicit* question." The question is, so to speak, invisible. But there are two ways of showing this "invisible," one that goes around the block, and an immediate one: the implicit question may turn out to be the concrete problem of the context, or the human being's foundational questioning. So, when we insert this principle of the implicit question into the conflict of interpretations, we recognize that all the heavy machinery of hermeneutic theory can be arranged in terms of two quite simple functions: (1) to indicate the distance between our context and the text; and (2) at the same time, to indicate that the one who interprets belongs to the same "question" as does the interpreted text. If the hermeneutics of the implicit question is to find both its rhythm and its full scope, it must not mix up these two functions, and so it must operate between two poles: that of a critical hermeneutics and that of an ontological hermeneutics. These poles correspond, to the two ages of hermeneutics, as distinguished by Paul Ricoeur: the one, regionally and epistemologically oriented (as in Schleiermacher and Dilthey), the other, more general and ontological (as in Heidegger and Gadamer).

The Hermeneutic Distance

According to Ricoeur, the first move made by hermeneutic thought is to say that if our understanding is confused or distorted, this is because certain conditions for communication have not been met. For example, the language is foreign, the culture unknown to us, the age far removed from our own. In this way, hermeneutics was conceived of as consisting essentially in a "critique" of the linguistic and historical conditions necessary to communication. Hermeneutics recognized the *distance* introduced into understanding by language and time. It corresponds to a "geographic" sense of this distance. The necessity to proceed methodologically corresponds to this distance, which is not due to error or weakness but constitutes the very structure of interpretation, the moment we have to deal with the traces of the absent (written texts, works and monuments, but also dreams, etc.).

Ricoeur tries to integrate Habermas's critique of ideologies into the hermeneutics of communication, so as to be able to spot, and if possible amend, its distortions. But Ricoeur rejects any approach that turns ideological criticism into the path of free and unimpeded communication. To simplify greatly, Ricoeur reproaches him for neglecting the obstacle (or opacity) that is imposed on this communication by the fact of the interpreting subject's *belonging* to a world of language, to a form of life and to a complex of traditions. Even the critique of traditions has its tradition: the European Enlightenment. And, for instance, how does one prevent the ethics proper to debate from being reduced to be a code of pretentious-sounding argumentation? How does one ensure that debate be such as to allow the participants not to leave their convictions behind, outside the debating chamber? It is thus necessary to be hermeneutically modest enough to recognize this ontological belonging, and not be too quick to think that it has nothing to do with oneself.

The Hermeneutic Belonging

The second hermeneutic move consists in acknowledging that human beings, considered both as individuals and socially, identify themselves and understand themselves as *belonging* to a single meaningful world, even when they may not be aware of this world. There is a hermeneutic relation to the world as shaped by language, which precedes us with its traditions and its writings. In the wake of Husserl, we can say that the thinking and speaking "subject" discovers that she already belongs to this "lifeworld," and that this world is always and already a language. We have pointed out that this radicalization of criticism was probably the occasion for Ricoeur's resistance to Habermas, but we cannot explicate and discuss everything here.

According to Heidegger, to exist is a way of understanding or being understood as if in a world that is a way of speaking. Hermeneutics thus belongs to an "ontology" of understanding, where understanding is a way of belonging to the world. Hermeneutics tells us that the interpreting subject belongs irreducibly to the world he or she interprets. This apparently vicious methodological circle (stated in terms of a subject–object relation) is in fact an unsurpassable ontological structure. The hermeneutic circle is constitutive of all understanding. We must not try to escape this circle but, on the contrary, correctly situate ourselves within it, for a *"presuppositionless"* interpretation is impossible.

Then, we must also recognize a difference with post-Heideggerian hermeneutics. Indeed, with Ricoeur, hermeneutics ceaselessly insists upon the historic and linguistic *distance* introduced by time and by contextual differences, and the necessity for critical methods that allows us to map this distance. In this respect, Ricoeur reproaches Heideggerian hermeneutics with being less intent on resolving problems of historical and social knowledge than on dissolving them in the mere comprehension of self (i.e., of being). This is why, instead of the short route leading directly to an analysis of *Dasein*, Ricoeur always chooses the longest detours, those that demand the most diverse methods: the better, it would seem, to mark out the diversity of distances, the diversity of alterities.[15]

It is this double movement that characterizes what Ricoeur calls *hermeneutic criticism* that distances him both from the hermeneutics of Hans-Georg Gadamer (Ricoeur would never oppose truth and method, understanding and explanation) and from the critique ideology of Jürgen Habermas. All this is probably very well known, but it is not easy think both the linguistic and historical *distance* and the irreducible *belonging* of the interpreting subject to the lifeworld. One can say that the different kinds of hermeneutics correspond to the different answers to this problem. I think that, for Ricoeur, this equation between distance and belonging determines a tension that should offer the right distance for a perfect reading because the reader plays, between distance and belonging, with the text world.

In *The Rule of Metaphor*, Ricoeur speaks of "the work of resemblance" (or of similarity "through the dissimilar"). And he recalls this formula, quoted by Jakobson: "*Aixo era y no era*" (it was thus and it was not thus), a formula that ended Majorcan tales. It expresses very well the same double move and tension between: (1) the ontological vehemence that says that "it was"; (2) the critical distanciation that says that "it was not," both neutralizing the reality as designated by the narrative and thus opening onto the field of the possible.[16]

The Poetic World

This first polarity within hermeneutics is made more complex by a second one that we can characterize by drawing up the difference between the "hermeneutic essays" of Paul Ricoeur. In the first, published under the title *The Conflict of Interpretations*, the work has to do with the attempt to find the meaning or truth as that which is hidden "behind" the object of interpretation. The meaning or the truth of a text in some sense precedes the text, and answers the question that produced it.

In the second set of "hermeneutic essays," published under the title *From Text to Action*, to interpret means to imagine a world or worlds possibly unfolded by the text. The imagination "plays" with this world just as a musician performs a score or a preacher interprets a biblical text. Hermeneutics, therefore, operates in the open space "in front of" the text. It unfolds the possible mode of being that is found in the text. The meaning or the truth of a text comes after it, in the world made by it, and by the work of its reception. For Ricoeur, the text breaks away from its author's intention, its original social and cultural setting, and from its original audience as well. That a text can become autonomous in this way is attested to by its depth, its breadth. And a text is able to "open" up new spaces in front of itself, other worlds than the world to which it first responded.[17] But this autonomy of the text not only makes for the obligation of a methodical distance. It also creates the possibility of new meanings opening up new worlds.

And that is what keeps Ricoeur from being considered as part of the hermeneutic school: after having been considered the leader of this school in France, he redirected hermeneutics toward a poetics of meaning, of narrative, and so forth. This began with the encounter and the first debates with structural semiotics, Claude Levi-Strauss, of course, and Roland Barthes, but particularly Algirdas Julius Greimas, the true master of the method in its most essential form.[18] Ricoeur shows, as regards both live metaphor and fictional narrative, the suspension of the world of literal reference to the benefit of an opening in the direction of what we can call a metaphorical reference. The place of analytic philosophy in this argument may be outlined.

But this idea of "suspension," or of "neutralization," is probably a modest echo to the phenomenological "epoche," "reduction." Following Ricoeur, we can say, "Hermeneutical distanciation is not unrelated to the phenomenological *epoche*";[19] but he also writes, "The *epoche* is the virtual event, the imaginary act that inaugurates the whole game by which we exchange signs for things."[20] What makes the liveliness of a metaphor is the double movement by which a poetical utterance first suspends the ordinary meaning of words, their first descriptive reference, so as to open up, soon, a new space of meaning and of descriptive reference.

In a way, we have to do, here, a propos the metaphor, with this microphenomenology of Gaston Bachelard in his *Poétique de la Rêverie*, where each poetical image as read and received by the reader is a kind of microprocess of suspension of the ordinary world and an unfolding of the poetical world; it has indeed the capacity to suspend all the semantic, descriptive, and explanatory sedimentation that makes our knowledge and prejudgments, so as to give us the naïveté and birth of a world yet unheard of. From that image, the reader receives a kind of naïve identity: what Bachelard calls a "poetic cogito," which lies near Ricoeur's "poetic subject." Here there is something like a posthermeneutic and postcritical phenomenology. And because we started by reducing the literal reference to the world, we can see that the poetical text does not lack a reference, rather it opens onto a world, it proposes possible worlds for us. Similarly, if narrative can break up our usual temporal framework (if it suspends the present), it does so in order to open another temporality to us, another space. It opens what we could call a quasi-time, a quasi-space, which are like variations on the theme of our world and the opening on to another world in front of us. Ricoeur writes:

> What is to be interpreted in the text is a proposed world which I could inhabit and in which I could project my ownmost possibilities.... Reality is, in this way, metamorphosed by means of what I shall call the "imaginative variations" that literature carries out on the real.[21]

The phenomenological method of "eidetic variation," by which one varies the profile of a thing in order to seize its being or essence, is here taken up again, but reversed: far from searching for an invariable identity, it is in the variations, in the very conflict of interpretations, that existence is to be interpreted. It is all as if after a first move of the phenomenological inquiry, by which reduction aimed at establishing invariants through eidetic variations, the same inquiry found as invariant this only interrogation about eidetic invariants. As from this problematicity, this aporetics, the inquiry reroutes itself through the imaginative variations themselves, without an attempt to find behind them, through elimination, something that might remain identical.

The main idea of *Time and Narrative* is that identity must be sought in a narrative but at the same time this narrative is a transformative program. There is a plot because there is rivalry between a number of narrative programs, or between a number of ways of reporting on one's life in an infinite tangle of possibilities. Basically, it is time to problematize identity, but the narrative process of identification may retaliate with two answers, with two kinds of identities: there would be an identity same as itself, an *idem* identity, I there would also be a variable identity that would not be 'same as itself,' an *ipse* identity. This last one is the one that matters to Ricoeur:

> To state the identity of an individual or a community to answer the question: "Who did this?" "Who is the agent, the author?" We first answer this question by naming some one, that is, by designating them with a proper name. But what is the basis for permanence of the proper name? ... The

answer has to be narrative. To answer question "Who?," as Hannah Arendt has so forcefully put it, is to tell the story of life. The story told tells about the action of the "who" ... Narrative identity is not a stable or seamless identity ... it is always possible to weave different, even opposed, plots about our lives. ... Narrative identity continues to make and unmake itself.[22]

And in *Soi-même comme un autre* one may say that the overlapping of the studies (about referential or pragmatic semantics, actantial semiotics, narrative identity, ethical aiming, moral rules, practical wisdom, and so on) corresponds to as many answers to the question *who*, as many variations on the subject.

The Circle of Hermeneutics

Let me summarize our itinerary. On the one hand, if we seek the meaning "behind" the text, this meaning is a function of the implicit question to which the text responds. As regards critical distance, our inquiry will be directed toward the analysis of historical and linguistic contexts and will seek to uncover the concrete set of implicit questioning that underlies the text. As regards ontological belonging, our interrogation will bear on the most fundamental, originary question, the question to which all the answers belong, by whatever name we may designate it. On the other hand, if we seek the meaning "in front of" the text, *the question to which the text responds is not the same question as the one the text opens up and to which it refers.* As regards a critical stance concerning the autonomy of the text, meanings are unfolded when exploring the possible worlds proposed by the poetic structure of the text. The reader stands in the gap between these possibilities. But we can also say that, as regards belonging, the text outlines a form of life, we must say an ethics; and the interpreter understands the text that refers to his own existence: he is responsible for it. Ricoeur writes: "Hermeneutics proposes to make subjectivity the final, and not the first, category of theory of understanding. Subjectivity must be lost as radical origin if it is to be recovered in a more modest role according to which, far from beginning, the subject has to respond to the proposals of meaning the text unfolds."[23] That is the reason why imagination makes its way from text to action.

In this way, we have a topology of hermeneutics that divides into four orientations: critical, ontological, poetic, and ethical. There is a circularity to this topology. This infinite circle, however, is a vital, not a vicious, circularity, where we never return to the same point. The reading, interpreting subject is a problematic subject, one that loses its initial naïveté though criticism. It is on that condition that poetics can propose a "naïveté seconde," that of an act of approbation.

NOTES

1. Paul Ricoeur, *A l'école de la phénoménologie* (Paris: Vrin, 1986); for a part of it, see in English, *Husserl. An Analysis of His Phenomenology*, trans. Edward G. Ballard and Lester E. Embree (Evanston: Northwestern University Press, 1967).

2. The great masters of the university of the third Republic have grappled with it, Lachelier, Lagneau, but also Bergson with his attention to the vital and to the immediate givens of consciousness; and for Ricoeur, Dalbiez in Brittany, and, later, in Paris, Léon Robin, Emile Bréhier, Léon Brunschwicg, and Gabriel Marcel, the French master of Christian existentialism, who gathered together a few students each Friday, and with whom Ricoeur found a philosophy of the subject as corporality (before Maurice Merleau-Ponty and Michel Henry were to develop this sort of theme).

3. I would slip into this complex *how* he read Bultmann, for it is perhaps here that the first hermeneutic experience takes place for Ricoeur; the place where it grafts itself upon reflection, that is also a way of answering (or radicalizing) the question of unity of the subject. Indeed, any choice encounters a nonchoice, an unconscious, the accident of birth, of one's corporeal, social, and cultural situation. Critical distance from the considered choice meets with belonging to an horizon: "how to make of chance a destiny accepted through a continuous choice," he says, speaking of his Protestantism. And it is this hermeneutic meaning that immediately tempers the existential radicality of decision, and that reinscribes it in a history, a geography, a context. But Bultmann separates the historical objectivity of the text from existential meaning for us; we will see that Ricoeur wants to show them as inseparable.

4. Paul Ricoeur, *Freedom and Nature: The Voluntary and the Involuntary*, trans. Erazim V. Kohak (Evanston: Northwestern University Press, 1966). But it reappears in the theme of promise, on which Ricoeur has recently done so much work. And the difference is very significant: the promise is no longer the will or the decision before language, but through language, and beyond it.

5. There is no published text on Spinoza, who was, however (notably at the Sorbonne, until 1966), one of his favorite authors. It is this simple and obstinate idea of a perseverance of all things in being that illuminates the theme of *originary affirmation* (taken from the philosopher Jean Nabert): a theme that links Ricoeur to a certain Nietzsche, and also to Albert Camus as opposed to Jean-Paul Sartre.

6. It is the French title of *The Rule of Metaphor: Multi-Disciplinary Studies of the Creation of Meaning in Language*, trans. Robert Czerny (Toronto: University of Toronto Press, 1981). Nowhere does one feel the juncture between these two inquiries so much as in *Fallible Man*, trans. Charles Kelbley (Chicago: Henry Regnery, 1965), the second volume of Philosophy of Will, in which the analyses of temporality unite the Kantian reflection on imagination with the Kierkegaardian feeling of finitude in the theme of the fragility of the subject.

7. Paul Ricoeur, *Oneself as Another*, trans. Kathleen Blarney (Chicago: University of Chicago Press, 1992), p. 96, no. 5. There is also a possible debate with Nietzsche, about his philosophy of will. If the will, be true, is able to destroy everything, veil after veil, to reach its goal, and if it discovers that its goal is in fact nothing but this very destruction, the sole

way out of the impasse is to turn around again and to create: to accept that truth itself is poetic. It seems to me that the project of a "poetics of the will," announced by Ricoeur in 1950, responds to this aporia.

8. Paul Ricoeur, "L'originaire et la question-en-retour dans la Crisis de Husserl," in François Laruelle, ed. *Textes pour Emmanuel Levinas* (Paris: Place, 1980).

9. Paul Ricoeur, *From Text to Action*, trans. John B. Thompson and Kathleen Blamey (Evanston: Northwestern University Press, 1991), p. 251. In Ricoeur, a contemporary, in that matter, of Heidegger as a reader of Kant, transcendental aporia is found when we reach back from speech and action toward imagination, toward the schematization that is their condition of possibility, and which we know is a hidden art or a "blind spot." "The transcendental imagination remains an enigma." The most we can say is that this enigma has to do with temporality. This aporia, in which the aporias of the thought of evil and of time converge in those of the imagination, is probably at the heart of Ricoeur's thinking. It is with this aporia as a point of departure that he turns toward a poetics of the imagination.

10. Paul Ricoeur, "Rhétorique, poétique, herméneutique," in Michel Meyer, ed., *De La métaphysique à la rhétorique. A La mémoire de Chaim Perelman* (Bruxelles: Publications des Facultés Saint Louis, 1987); see also Paul Ricoeur, *Lectures 2* (Paris: Editions du Seuil, 1992), p. 487.

11. Ricoeur, *Oneself as Another*, p. 28.

12. "J'attend la renaissance. Entretien avec Paul Ricoeur," *Autrement* 102 (1988): 177.

13. Ricoeur, *From Text to Action*, p. 266.

14. Ricoeur, *Du texte à l'action*, p. 49.

15. This indeed is what distinguishes Ricoeur from the other French phenomenologists, such as Michel Henry, Emmanuel Levinas, and even Jacques Derrida. Even when Derrida deconstructs the logos speech of Heidegger by the infinite margin of writing, does Derridean writing render criticism possible? This is an uncertain question, and it is probably not exactly his problem.

16. Ricoeur, *The Rule of Metaphor*, p. 321.

17. Here we encounter a difficulty because, for Ricoeur, this fact of a text becoming autonomous depends on the difference between speaking and writing. In this way, question and answer belong to speech, autonomy to writing. The polysemy of words calls for the selective role played by context, where the handling of this context comes down to the interplay between question and answer, which alone is said to be capable of producing univocity relative to a given situation (Ricoeur thus quotes a text in which Husserl shows this selective role of circumstances in the definitions of meanings). Cf. Ricoeur, *From Text to Action*, p. 63. But these conditions are not fulfilled in the written text. So if hermeneutics requires a specific method, this is due to the fact that "interpretation is our reply to that fundamental distance which constitutes man's objectifying himself in his works." In this way, Ricoeur seeks to distance himself from the hermeneutics of Hans-Georg Gadamer that takes the oral dialogue of question and answer, in face-to-face relations, as the act of genuine communication.

18. What Ricoeur wanted to transgress, or traverse, is the absolute separation between a pure philosophy, concentrated on the ineffable singularity of a

subject that neither speaks nor acts, in a word, that does not in any way engage life or history, and, on the other hand, those sciences of language or of history that would limit themselves to the structural inventory of enunciations or actions without subjects. See *Oneself as Another*, Preface.

19. Ricoeur, *From Text to Action*, p. 40, and also: "hermeneutical distanciation is to belonging as, in phenomenology, the *epoche* is to lived experience." Ibid., pp. 40–41.
20. Ibid., p. 40.
21. Ibid., p. 36.
22. Paul Ricoeur, *Time and Narrative* 3, trans. Kathleen Blamey and David Pellauer (Chicago: University of Chicago Press, 1988), pp. 246, 248, 249.
23. Ricoeur, *From Text to Action*, p. 37.

Ricoeur's Critical Theory 11

David M. Kaplan

When it comes to critical theory, Paul Ricoeur is usually left out of the conversation. Hermeneutic philosophers are not considered members of the club of cultural critics. They are seen as belonging to a different area of philosophy, only mentioned by critical theorists as examples of how not to think critically. Yet throughout his entire career, Ricoeur addressed himself to precisely the subjects addressed by critical theory: the relationship of philosophy to psychoanalysis and the social sciences, critique of ideology, literary and legal theory. Ricoeur always sought to establish a connection between philosophical reflection and responsible social action, from his prewar pacifism and contributions to the leftist journal *Esprit* in the 1940s, his postwar articles on violence and socialism in 1950s, his work on the hermeneutics of suspicion in the 1960s, his lectures on ideology and utopia in the 1970s, to his works on ethics, politics, and law in the 1980s and 1990s. Philosophy for Ricoeur is critical in the Kantian sense of identifying the limits of understanding as well as in the Marxist sense of uncovering false consciousness and the material conditions of thought and action.

I want to highlight this latter sense of critique to show how Ricoeur takes the concerns of Western Marxists, like Marcuse and Habermas, seriously. I want to amplify his voice and bring him in the conversation on critical theory in the hope that members of the club of cultural critics will read him, learn from him, and expand the scope of critical theory to include the works of Ricoeur among their philosophical resources. In turn, readers of Ricoeur would benefit if they were to read him as a critical theorist and thereby do their share to tear down an unnecessary disciplinary boundary.

Four themes in Ricoeur's work are particularly relevant to a critical social theory in the Western Marxist tradition: (1) The hermeneutics of suspicion, (2) the mediation of the Habermas-Gadamer debates, (3) the theory of ideology and utopia, (4) the fragility of political language.

These broad, overlapping areas stem from the hermeneutic turn that Ricoeur's philosophy took in the late 1960s. His earlier work, although often more overtly political, was still enmeshed with theological concerns, drawing equally from philosophical and biblical sources. It is better to omit the works from this period in order to show how Ricoeur's work harmonizes with the secular character of critical theory.

THE HERMENEUTICS OF SUSPICION

Ricoeur is, perhaps, best known for the hermeneutics of suspicion. In *Freud and Philosophy* he contrasts Husserlian phenomenology to Freudian psychoanalysis to develop a theory of interpretation geared toward unmasking and decoding hidden meanings.[1] He combines the Husserlian doctrine of intentionality and the methodological techniques of bracketing with the Freudian model of the dynamics of the unconscious and techniques for uncovering the relation of a latent to manifest meanings. Ricoeur argues that phenomenology needs psychoanalytic explanations in the face of the unconscious, which hides and transforms experience. Simply describing phenomena is not good enough; they need to be analyzed as well. Ricoeur uses Freud to overcome this shortcoming in phenomenology by developing a model of language based on the social character of symbolic expressions, and a model for interpretation based psychoanalytic techniques.

There are two advantages to investigating language by investigating psychoanalysis. First, Freud's conception of psychoanalysis is both a theory of the individual and a theory of culture. Individual psychology relates to collective psychology through the interpretation of dreams and neuroses. The corresponding theory of language is meaningful in relation to both individual meaning-conferring acts and social rules of meaning and use. Second, Freudian dream interpretation provides a framework for understanding the relation between desire and language. Dream interpretation is a theory that explains how desire produces distorted consciousness and prevents self-understanding. According to Ricoeur, "if dreams designate the entire region of double-meaning expressions, the problem of interpretation in turn designates all understanding specifically concerned with the meaning of equivocal expressions."[2] The problem of interpreting and deciphering a concealed double meaning defines the hermeneutics of *Freud and Philosophy*. To interpret is to understand a double meaning.

Ricoeur contrasts the hermeneutics of suspicion to the "hermeneutics of belief." The basic hermeneutic situation is that we must already have a prior understanding of what we know in order to know it. Interpretation consists in describing or explicating (*Auslegung*) our experience in terms of our prior understanding. The hermeneutics of belief is geared to recovering and recollecting lost or forgotten meanings embedded in symbols. By contrast, the hermeneutics of suspicion is geared to unmasking and removing the illusions of symbols, which not only reveal but conceal meaning. Ricoeur draws on the "masters of suspicion," Marx, Nietzsche, and Freud, each of whom posit a false consciousness in place of an immediate, self-transparent consciousness, and deception in place of knowledge. The hermeneutics of suspicion deciphers the meanings hidden and distorted by literal and apparent meanings. If the hermeneutics of belief is animated by faith and a willingness to listen, the hermeneutics of suspicion is animated by mistrust and skepticism.

In some ways, despite its notoriety, the hermeneutics of suspicion represents only a transitional concept in Ricoeur's career. It came and went along with the hermeneutics of symbols in the 1960s, never to be mentioned again. Yet in other ways, the hermeneutics of suspicion survived in Ricoeur's subsequent models of language and interpretation in the 1970s. Even though his theory of language as "discourse" and model of the text as paradigm of hermeneutics grew from his response to structuralism (hence from a different set of concerns than the hermeneutics of symbols), Ricoeur's conception of the relationship between interpretation and critique remained intact. To interpret is to describe apparent phenomena and explain hidden meanings. In the 1970s, the text, not the symbol, became Ricoeur's model for both the linguistic mediation of experience and the critique of hidden meanings.[3]

He became particularly interested in the dynamics of textual interpretation—writing and reading—because it highlighted the interpretive character of language more than speaking and hearing. In speech, participants can resolve misunderstandings by asking each other for clarification, or by referring to the shared context for a common point of reference. In writing, the author is absent, the original context is absent, and the audience is an indefinite number of absent readers. Interpretation cannot take recourse to any of these elements that are present in speech. Misunderstandings still occur, but the recourse to resolve them is much more available than in writing. Ricoeur believes that the relationship between reader and author displays the central feature of language and key figure in hermeneutics: the distance between what is communicated and what is understood. This "distanciation" of meaning from both the author/speaker and reader/listener is what Ricoeur sometimes calls the "semantic autonomy of the text" or "matter of the text." It refers to the ability of a text to bear meaning apart from the intentions of the author. The counterpart to distanciation is "appropriation," which is the act of interpretation. The hermeneutical situation is constituted by a play of distanciation and appropriation.

The difference between Ricoeur and Gadamer's version of hermeneutics hinges on the proper balance of distanciation and appropriation. Both maintain that the fundamental hermeneutical act of "making the foreign familiar" is achieved by overcoming an alienating distance to form a new relationship in which the horizon (of experience) of the reader and horizon (of meaning) of the text belong together. Ricoeur, however, contends that Gadamer's version of hermeneutics moves too quickly to overcome the very distance that enables understanding. His conception of distanciation makes it seem as if the kind of objectification that we find in the human sciences is at the same time that which destroys the fundamental relation whereby we belong to and participate in our historical situation. Gadamer unnecessarily forces us to choose between either participation in a tradition or the detached attitude of methodological explanation.[4] Ricoeur's version of hermeneutics affirms a positive and productive character of distanciation that enables communication in and through distance. Distanciation is a vital aspect of belonging, which allows for a critique of ideology to be incorporated, as an objective and explanatory segment, in the process of communication and self-understanding. Distanciation can never be overcome, nor should it be. Ricoeur explains that "distanciation, dialectically opposed to belonging, is the condition of possibility of the critique of ideology, not outside or against hermeneutics, but within hermeneutics."[5]

Ricoeur wants to show that hermeneutics, properly conceived, is also critical and evaluative. By focusing hermeneutics on the problem of understanding (that is) mediated by texts and text analogs, we can see that distanciation belongs to the mediation itself, and the critical instance that is (supposedly) eliminated in Gadamer's hermeneutics is preserved in Ricoeur's. Distanciation opens the possibility of achieving critical distance from oneself and one's tradition because the very medium of understanding itself is distanced from itself. We are never so beholden to our historical perspectives that we cannot detach ourselves from them. To claim that we are misunderstands the distanced character of language. Critique can thus be raised from within Ricoeur's hermeneutic circle because distanciation is never fully overcome. "Distanciation," he argues, "is the soul of every critical philosophy."[6]

The act of appropriating a distanced meaning—or, in ordinary language, the act of reading—serves a potentially critical function by displacing the illusions of subjectivity and by transforming the experience of the reader who encounters new (and possibly better) worlds. Now, for Ricoeur, the act of appropriating the meaning of texts, not just symbols, helps to overcome the illusions of subjectivity. The text in the hermeneutics of the 1970s functions like the symbol does in the hermeneutics of suspicion. Self-understanding is mediated by the text just like for Freud consciousness is mediated by the unconscious.

A critique of the illusions of the subject, in a Marxist or Freudian manner, therefore can and must be incorporated into self-understanding. The consequence for hermeneutics is important: we can no longer oppose hermeneutics and the critique of ideology.[7]

Self-understanding must take a "detour" through the critique of ideology, informed by the matter of the text. Alienating distanciation is the key term for Ricoeur. It is what allows him to show the internal connection between hermeneutic experience and critical consciousness.

HABERMAS–GADAMER DEBATE

Ricoeur took a keen interest in the Habermas–Gadamer debate.[8] He believed that what was at stake in the debate was nothing less than "the fundamental gesture of philosophy."[9] On one side is Gadamer's philosophical hermeneutics, a theory of the operation of understanding in relation to the interpretation of texts. According to Gadamer, experience is always affected by prejudice, authority, and tradition. Everything that can be understood occurs in language; there is no way to transcend the linguistic conditions of understanding. On the other side of the debate is Habermas, who argues that by eliminating the possibility of transcending one's tradition, Gadamerian hermeneutics offers no means to criticize the ideological distortions and injustices that tradition might bear. There must be some perspective we can take that is transcendent to one's historic situation. Critical theory endeavors to uncover the limits, or conditions of the possibility of understanding, and to evaluate the justice and well-being of a society. Habermas achieves this end though a theory of "universal pragmatics," a nonhermeneutical model of language used to establish a genuine consensus free from systematic distortions.

Predictably, Ricoeur believes that the choice between hermeneutic and critical consciousness is false. He attempts to contextualize the transcendental component of Habermasian pragmatics into a hermeneutic philosophy and a theory of practical reason. Yet rather than reconcile hermeneutics and critical theory, Ricoeur claims that he is merely trying to show how each can recognize the universality of the other. He claims not to fuse "a super-system which would encompass both," but instead to let each "recognize the other, not as a position which is foreign and purely hostile, but as one which raises in its own way a legitimate claim."[10] His goal is to eliminate any false antinomies between Gadamer and Habermas and to recognize their different concerns—namely, a rehabilitation of tradition and historical understanding in the case of hermeneutics, and a theory of the intersection of institutions with language, action, and power the case of the critique of ideology. But despite Ricoeur's humble pretensions, he ultimately argues that the critique of ideology is internal to hermeneutics philosophy—creating the very supersystem he tries to avoid.

Ricoeur's proposed reconciliation attempts to recover a transcendental moment of objective reflection and explanation within the hermeneutic circle, thus accounting for the philosophical ends of both hermeneutics and the critique of ideology.[11] He argues that the philosophical aim to recover meaning within a particular context does not necessarily contradict the other philosophical aim to criticize false consciousness and communication on universal grounds. Hermeneutics and the critique of ideology are part of a process of interpretation geared toward "enlarging communication" by eliminating the systematic distortions that prevent understanding. Ricoeur appropriates from Habermas the a priori necessity of a regulative ideal of unconstrained communication that norms actual communication, while insisting that the validation of claims occurs through multiple forms of language, not just rational argumentation. Hermeneutics without the regulative idea of emancipation is blind; the critique of ideology without a concrete content from our practical interest in communication is empty. Ricoeur explains that the "entire question is then whether one can contextualize the universal while keeping it as a regulative idea."[12]

There are several places in Ricoeur's works where he very explicitly incorporates a theory of communicative rationality into a hermeneutic philosophy, creating the very mediation he claims is impossible. Typically, a mediation for Ricoeur is a rapproachment (or juxtaposition) that highlights similarities without assimilating perspectives into a "third term" that would encompass them both. Occasionally, he mediates in a more standard, Hegelian, sense that creates a third term. He does the latter in the 1970s when he described textual interpretation as a movement from guess to validation and from explanation to comprehension.[13] An interpretation consists of a guess based on experiences resulting in explanations that must be validated by others, terminating in comprehension, which is another name for understanding that is informed and enriched by an objective process of validation. Determining which interpretations are more plausible than others requires that we argue for our descriptions and explanations by offering relevant reasons in order to convince another of the superiority of one interpretation over another. Ricoeur echoes Habermas, claiming that "the question of criteria belongs to a certain kind of interpretation itself, that is to say, to a coming to an agreement between arguments. So it presupposes a certain model of rationality where universality, verification, and so on are compelling."[14] Mediating conflicting interpretation in terms of universally acceptable principles is itself a kind of interpretation: a critical interpretation. Hermeneutics and critique are coextensive.

In *Time and Narrative*, Ricoeur again argues that a regulative ideal of communication is operative within communication. He agrees with Habermas that any critique of tradition is mediated by a regulative ideal of unconstrained communication, and he agrees with Gadamer that any judgment is historically situated and must be applied in a particular context. The regulative ideal of unconstrained communication mediates our historically informed understanding. Ricoeur explains that critique and interpretation need one another.

> The transcendence of the idea of truth, inasmuch as it is immediately a dialogical idea, has to been seen as already at work in the practice of communication. When so reinstalled in the horizon of expectation, this dialogical idea cannot fail to rejoin those anticipations buried in tradition per se.... However, at the risk of remaining alien to effective-history, this limit-idea has to become a regulative one, orienting the concrete dialectic between our horizon of expectation and our space of experience.[15]

Any critique of tradition is mediated by an ideal of unconstrained communication, which, in turn, is understood in a particular context. Hermeneutics is to critique as content is to form.

Like Gadamer, Ricoeur believes that tradition makes a claim to truth—but the claim is somewhat more presumptive and tentative than Gadamer would have us believe. The presumption of truth for Ricoeur means

> that confident reception by which we respond, in an initial move preceding all criticism, to any proposition of meaning, any claim to truth, because we are never at the beginning of the process of truth and because we belong, before any critical gesture, to a domain of presumed truth.[16]

What validates the authority of tradition is a process of communication and discursive argumentation as it "makes its plea before the tribunal of reason."[17] Truth for Ricoeur occurs in language as both a disclosure of meaning and rationally-achieved consensus.

In *Oneself as Another* we find the most explicit appropriation of Habermas in Ricoeur's interpretation of communicative ethics. Ricoeur turns to Habermas's communicative ethics for resolving conflicts and reaching consensus regarding moral imperatives. Communicative ethics preserves both the universal validity and impartiality of moral judgments. Above all, it retains the central Kantian notion of autonomy but reinterpreted as "communicative autonomy," which is the ability of speakers to express themselves freely to others. Ricoeur is in full agreement with Habermas that the very process of justifying normative claims presupposes that speakers have a shared understanding of what norms and reasons are and what they expect of us. Valid norms are discursively redeemable, impartial, universal, and rationally justifiable.

His acceptance is, of course, qualified. Rather than contrast argumentation with interpretation, conviction, and convention, Ricoeur argues that argumentation itself is an interpretive practice that leads to a potentially universal practical judgment in a particular situation. As Ricoeur puts it,

> what has to be questioned is the antagonism between argumentation and convention, substituting for it a subtle dialectic between argumentation and conviction, which has no theoretical outcome but only the practical outcome of the arbitration of moral judgment in situation.[18]

Argumentation is a particular, sometimes formalized, practice in which participants clarify their convictions in order to resolve conflicts and reach understanding. Argumentation never stands above our convictions or conventions, but instead is the "critical agency operating *at the heart* of convictions."[19]

The virtue of Ricoeur's version of hermeneutics over Gadamer's is patent. Ricoeur's hermeneutics probes into the workings of communication to show that it is not a matter of choosing between what happens "in language" or "behind the back of language." The act of interpreting critically involves both interpretation and argumentation, which are internally related and yet different. Ricoeur is more attentive than Gadamer to the activity of reaching agreement on potentially universal grounds. He is more attentive to the needs of the social sciences than Gadamer is, as well. As for Habermas, Ricoeur's critical hermeneutics gives a better account of the relationship between communication and the meaning-giving contexts of language and action. He is attuned to the way that written works—particularly creative works—bear meaning. Of course, the relationship between the self and communication is far more developed by Ricoeur, since selfhood is the focus of his work in a way that it is in neither Habermas nor Gadamer. Most important, the virtue of Ricoeur's mediation of the Habermas–Gadamer debate is the way that he demonstrates the intimate relationship between critical theory and hermeneutics.

IDEOLOGY AND UTOPIA

Another of Ricoeur's contributions to critical theory is found in his 1975 *Lectures on Ideology and Utopia*.[20] This overlooked collection of essays forms a link between Ricoeur's theories of metaphor and narrative with a novel interpretation of ideology and utopia. His thesis is that ideology and utopia form two poles of a single "cultural imagination" (a concept borrowed from Cornelius Castoriadis). The cultural imagination is made up of ideas, stories, and images a society has about itself that integrate human action through interpretive schemas. What distinguishes ideology and utopia from other ideas and images are the way they function. Ideology acts to consolidate, integrate, and order a society according to the interests of a dominant group; utopia calls a society into question, and seeks to shatter a social order for the sake of liberation.[20] Both are ultimately about power: ideology attempts to legitimate power, while utopia attempts to replace power with something else. Ideology and utopia are opposing images a society has about itself.

According to Ricoeur, they each have both positive and negative senses. The positive, constructive function of ideology is to constitute and preserve social relations; the negative, destructive function is to resist the transformation of an order that has frozen social relations in such a way that sustains domination. Ideology is always conservative yet constitutive of a society. Ricoeur claims that there is "no social integration without social subversion."[21] The pathological function of ideology is a condition of community, as such. As for utopia, its positive function is to call a society into question from an imagined vantage point; the negative function is to provide flight from social reality. A utopia is a view from nowhere in terms of which we might examine—or flee from—our social reality. "Utopia is the mode in which we radically rethink the nature of family, consumption, government, religion, and so on. From 'nowhere' emerges the most formidable challenge to what-is."[22]

Ricoeur describes ideology and utopia as forms of "noncongruence" with social reality. They represent imaginary, false perspectives that are nonetheless vital for members of a community. From a Marxist perspective, the noncongruence of ideology and utopia with reality is the problem: ideology is false-consciousness, utopia is naïve escapism. From the perspective of the cultural imagination, both ideology and utopia are simply imaginative interpretations of what a society is and what it could be. They are among the creative ways that members of society affirm and question their history and their collective identity.

There are two important ways that Ricoeur's theories of ideology and utopia are tied to his theories of metaphor and narrative. One is through the "split reference" of metaphoric reference. All creative language refers to the world in a way that literal, descriptive language does not. It refers to a world "as if" it were actually like that. The reference is "divided" or "split," meaning that such writing points to some aspect of the world that cannot be described but only suggested at and referred to indirectly. The referent in such creative discourse is "discontinuous" with that of ordinary language, although it refers to "another level" that is "more fundamental" than that attained by descriptive language.[23] All discourse is distanced from the everyday world. But by pointing beyond the everyday world by projecting new possibilities, the creative language points back to the everyday world and presents new ways to see the world and, potentially, new ways be in the world. Metaphors, fiction, depictions—and even history—project an absent world. Therein lies the critical dimension of poetic and fictional discourse, including ideology and utopia. The imaginary, noncongruent character of creative discourse is its virtue, not its failure. It is precisely because it is unreal that imaginative discourse can present perspectives that do not actually exist but might be preferable alternatives. Fiction can act as a regulative ideal that allows us to step back and reflect on our world in light of a different, possibly better world. The unreal acts as a vantage point for criticism of the real.

Another point of connection between creative discourse and ideology and utopia is the symbolic mediation of action. Creative interpretations (narratives, in particular) share a common form with human action. We can narrate actions because they are already articulated by the kinds of things that narrating picks out and organizes. Ricoeur adopts Geertz's notion that actions are symbolically mediated by the signs, rules, and norms of a culture.[24] Culture is public because meaning is public. The symbolic mediation of action refers to systems of symbols and patterns of meanings that provide the background and context for describing, interpreting, and judging actions. We must have a preunderstanding of what is a relevant feature in human action before we interpret it in speech or writing. As Ricoeur says, "unless social life has a symbolic structure, there is no way to understand how we live, do things, and project these activities in ideas, no way to understand how reality can become an idea or how real life can produce illusions."[25] This symbolic structure is what Ricoeur elsewhere calls the cultural imagination. The same symbolic level of action that is prefigured in narratives is operative in the constitution of social life through the cultural imagination. Ideology and utopia are but two among many variations of this "social imaginary"—interesting because they are polar opposites in terms of how they construe and contend with social power. The reason they are able to have such a strong purchase on social life because they operate at the most basic level of intelligibility.

The contribution of Ricoeur's theory of ideology and utopia to critical theory is the way that he deepens the scope of the cultural imagination down to the core of human thought and action, and shows how creative uses of language can be used to interpret the world critically. He affirms that our being-in-the-world is constituted by language, and thus no social life exists apart from the underlying symbolic structure of action. We think *from* the cultural imagination, not *about* it. That means we think from ideology and utopia as well. Ricoeur claims that "a nonideological discourse on ideology" can never reach "a social reality prior to symbolization."[26] It is impossible to exercise a critique that would be absolutely radical "because a radically critical consciousness would require a total reflection."[27]

In the absence of total reflection, Ricoeur gives two answers to the problem of finding a perspective for a critique distorted consciousness and communication. First, ideology and utopia can be identified and criticized by a hermeneutic philosophy, if properly conceived to preserve a critical moment of distanciation. Hermeneutics and critique are internal to one another, as he affirms in his mediation of Habermas and Gadamer. Second, ideology can be identified and criticized on the basis of utopia, and utopia on the basis of ideology. They form a circle. We can criticize the negative dimensions of ideology in terms of the positive dimensions of utopia, and the negative dimensions of utopia by the positive dimensions of ideology. In other words, we criticize conservative social relations in terms of an imaginative possibility, and utopian escapism by what is "wholesome" in ideology, namely, the social bonds that hold a society together. The only way out is to try "to make the circle a spiral" through the practical activity of interpretation and critique.[28]

POLITICAL FRAGILITY

A theme that reappears throughout Ricoeur's career is his notion of the "political paradox." On one hand, political authority is legitimate if it comes from the rational consent of the governed; on the other hand, political practice is often so violent and coercive that it is something to which individuals, in principle, cannot consent. The paradox of authority is permanent. Any attempt to eliminate it is mistaken. The political sphere is a fragile balance of authority and domination, reason and tradition. Both (authoritarian) defenders of state power and (libertarian) critics of state power fail to recognize power's fragile nature. Power can never be entirely legitimate because it is potentially too violent to be entirely just. The fragility of politics stems from fragility of political language, situated in what Ricoeur calls a "vulnerable zone" between rational argumentation and rhetoric. It is vulnerable because ideology and utopia are permanent features of our social life, always present in politics, frustrating any attempt to purify our language into a vehicle for transparent political representation. So, instead of pure democracy, Ricoeur advocates an impure democracy—one that is always tied to particular situations, specific institutions and practices, and, above all, ineliminable conflicts. A political theory should read political power in light of the fragility of politics to correct its claims to legitimacy. Neither too much nor too little legitimacy is desirable. Instead, the conversation about political power is interminable because so are its conflicts.

Ricoeur identifies three kinds of conflicts in democratic political institutions.[29] There is a different kind of political rhetoric for each realm of conflict. First is the relationship between consensus and conflict in political deliberation. Open discussion is the hallmark of consensus making, yet political language is "a language that is conflictual and consensual at the same time."[30] That is why it is so vulnerable. Nothing in political discussion is ever fully decidable: neither the rules of discourse, the subject matter, the participants, nor the conclusions. The first level of political rhetoric is about consensus itself. The second level of political rhetoric is over the ends of government. Terms like "security," "prosperity," "freedom," and "justice," are necessary yet problematic. Necessary because they are essential for political deliberation in the liberal tradition about the ends of government; problematic because these terms are ambiguous, open to interpretation, and subject to ideological appropriation. Ricoeur reminds us that each term is characterized by a plurality of senses given the plurality of ends of government. Government may not be able to fulfill every end. Instead, we should treat the idea of a "good government" as a loosely defined goal that our civic life should aim at.

The third and most problematic level of political discourse has to do with conflicts over what counts as the good life. At issue is the unspoken ambivalence many feel about modernity itself. Its silence about ends forces people to find meaning and a sense of identity in some place other than civic life. It is what Habermas calls a "legitimation crisis": a government is unable to promote the general welfare when citizens have conflicting interpretations about what the pursuit of happiness means in the first place. Ricoeur explains that "from such conflict, such a plurality of ends, and such a fundamental ambivalence come the fragility of political language."[31]

The dual task of political philosophy (or critical theory, really) is to expose how the conditions of modernity systematically undermine its own legitimacy, and to diagnose advanced industrial societies by comparing them to ideals of the past. Ricoeur believes we need not only Enlightenment ideal but the ideals of our premodern heritage that extend back to biblical teachings. He agrees with Habermas that the Enlightenment project has not yet been achieved, but believes we need to take a longer look at our history and relearn the lessons from the countless failures, revolutions, and successes of the past. "It is by calling to mind all the beginnings and all the rebeginnings, and all the traditions that have been sedimented upon them, that "good counsel" can take up the challenge of the legitimation crisis."[32] Although we can never be sure when our political discourse is perverted by ideology or rhetorical language in the bad sense, Ricoeur is confident that we can use political rhetoric in the good sense to complete the Enlightenment project and recover the unfulfilled promises of the past. He implores us

> not to flee the field of political confrontation, but to enter it with a sense of measure that leads to great respect for the extreme fragility of the 'good life' a life for which 'good' government serves as the most proximate figure open to us as political animals.[33]

We can steer our way through the thickets of rhetoric and argument and aim at the good life by continually interpreting and criticizing our traditions. That is the best we can do, given the fragility of politics.

This method of mediation—interpreting in light of the past, criticizing in light of the ideal, both imaginary and universal—is one of Ricoeur's most important contributions to critical theory. He left us with several examples of how this to-and-fro from universal to particular spirals forward. For example, his 1961 article "Universal Civilization and National Cultures" very clearly expresses the balance he sought between universalism and particularism.[34] He adds complexity to the opposition by noting that each side has its good and bad forms. The good form of universalism is political liberalism with its attending Enlightenment political institutions, scientific and technological advances, aiming at universal recognition; the bad form of universalism is a dehumanizing homogenous global economic-political order based on a reductivist scientism and technocracy. The good form of particularism (or nationalism, in this case) is membership in community and transmission of tradition that promotes the creative renewal of the past, leading to genuine dialogue and exchange with other cultures; the bad form of nationalism is reactionary traditionalism that perpetuates injustices and prevents alternative interpretations of one's heritage. The aim is, of course, to foster the good senses of universal civilization and national cultures and expose and correct the effects of the bad senses. The great challenge facing nations and cultures is to communicate with each other to establish mutual understanding and recognition so that we may all rethink and renew the traditions that shape who we are. The method and the outcome attempt to strike a balance between universalism and particularism.[35]

Ricoeur returns to this theme in his 1995 article, "Reflections on a New Ethos for Europe," here adding a hermeneutically informed and chastened critique of ideology into the balance of universalism and particularism.[36] The aim in this article is to conceive of new, legitimate institutions to bring together nations and cultures. Ricoeur proposes three models to help to create international understanding, respect, and reconciliation. The first model is an "ethics of linguistic hospitality" designed to translate beliefs and traditions from one culture to another to prevent people from retreating into their own linguistic traditions. The second model is the "exchange of memories" designed to help groups to understand the experiences of others, thereby helping people understand themselves differently. The danger of the way groups interpret and recount themselves—especially their "founding events"—is that these accounts tend to become oversimplifications, expressed in slogans and caricature, sedimented into tradition and resistant to reinterpretion. An exchange of memories opens up communication, by revisiting the past and challenging conventional versions of history.

> In this exchange of memories it is a matter not only of subjecting the founding events of both cultures to a crossed reading, but of helping one another to set free that part of life and of renewal which is found captive in rigid, embalmed and dead traditions.[37]

We have to clear away the ideological formations within our traditions that prevent new interpretations of the past.

Third, is the "model of forgiveness." An exchange of memories opens the possibility of forgiveness, which is a specific act of reinterpreting the past concerned with understanding the suffering of others for the sake of coping with the present. "Forgiveness," explains Ricoeur, consists in

> shattering the law of the irreversibility of time by changing the past, not as a record of all that has happened but in terms of its meaning for us today. It does this by lifting the burden of guilt which paralyzes the relations between individuals who are acting out and suffering their own history. It does not abolish the debt insofar as we are and remain the inheritors of the past, but it lifts the pain of the debt.[38]

Forgiveness is the best way of "shattering the debt" and removing the impediments to social justice and recognition. Nations and groups who have been in conflict must be able to recount events differently in order to understand and overcome their differences, and perhaps even to reconcile and forgive. Conflicts are a part of human experience; Ricoeur maintains that understanding one another, exchanging memories, and forgiving are the best way to cope with conflicts and to move forward.[39]

IN CONCLUSION

The aims of a critical social theory and a general theory of interpretation are clearly inseparable for Ricoeur, yet his longtime readers fail to pay sufficient attention to the critical dimension of his works. They treat him as if he's simply another hermeneut or narrative theorist when, in fact, there's a critical spirit in his work that distinguishes him from the typically apolitical philosopher. The burden of bringing Ricoeur into broader conversations falls on his longtime readers who wish to engage the world of critical theory. Rather than wait for the world of critical theory to discover him, we should take the lead and continue conversations that Ricoeur is now no longer able to have for himself.

NOTES

1. Paul Ricoeur, *Freud and Philosophy: An Essay on Interpretation*, trans. Dennis Savage (New Haven: Yale University Press, 1970).
2. Ibid., p. 8.
3. For the response to structuralism, see Paul Ricoeur, *The Conflict of Interpretation: Essays in Hermeneutics*, trans. Willis Domingo et al. Ed. Don Ihde (Evanston: Northwestern University Press, 1974). For the theory of discourse and hermeneutics of texts, see Paul Ricoeur, *Interpretation Theory: Discourse and the Surplus of Meaning* (Fort Worth: Texas Christian University Press, 1976).
4. Hans-Georg Gadamer, *Truth and Method*, 2nd ed., trans. Joel Weinsheimer (New York: Continuum, 1975).
5. Paul Ricoeur, *From Text to Action: Essays in Hermeneutics, II*, trans. Kathleen Blamey and John B. Thompson (Evanston: Northwestern University Press, 1991), p. 268.
6. Paul Ricoeur, *Political and Social Essays*, ed. David Stewart and Joseph Bien (Athens: Ohio University Press, 1974), p. 249.
7. Ricoeur, *From Text to Action*, p. 88.
8. For Habermas's critique of Gadamerian hermeneutics, see Jürgen Habermas, *On the Logic of the Social Sciences*, trans. Shierry Weber Nicholson and Jerry A. Stark (Cambridge: MIT Press, 1988), pp. 143–75. Habermas, "The Hermeneutic Claim to Universality," trans. Josef Bleicher in Bleicher, *Contemporary Hermeneutics* (London: Routledge, 1980), pp. 181–211. For Gadamer's response, see Hans-Georg Gadamer, "The Universality of the Hermeneutical Problem," *Philosophical Hermeneutics*, trans. and ed. David E. Linge (Berkeley: University of California Press, 1976), pp. 3–17. Gadamer, "The Scope and Function of Reflection," in *Philosophical Hermeneutics*, pp. 18–43.
9. Ricoeur, *From Text to Action*, p. 270.
10. Ibid., p. 271.
11. For a detailed discussion of Ricoeur's mediation of the Habermas–Gadamer debate, see David M. Kaplan, *Ricoeur's Critical Theory* (Albany: SUNY Press, 2003), pp. 3–61.
12. Paul Ricoeur, *Critique and Conviction* (New York: Columbia University Press, 1998), p. 61.
13. Ricoeur, *Interpretation Theory*, pp. 71–88.
14. Paul Ricoeur, "Interview with Charles Reagan," in *Paul Ricoeur: His Life and His Work* (Chicago: University of Chicago Press, 1996), pp. 104–105.
15. Paul Ricoeur, *Time and Narrative*, vol. 3, trans. Kathleen McLaughlin and David Pellauer (Chicago: University of Chicago Press, 1988), p. 226.
16. Ibid., p. 227.

17. Ibid., p. 228.
18. Paul Ricoeur, *Oneself as Another* (Chicago: University of Chicago Press, 1992), p. 287.
19. Ibid., p. 288
20. Paul Ricoeur, *Lectures on Ideology and Utopia*, ed. George H. Taylor (New York: Columbia University Press, 1986).
21. Ibid., p. 16.
22. Ricoeur, *From Text to Action*, p. 184.
23. For the theory of the split reference, see Paul Ricoeur, *The Rule of Metaphor. Multi-Disciplinary Studies of the Creation of Meaning in Language*, trans. Robert Czerny, Kathleen McLaughlin, and John Costello (Toronto: University of Toronto Press, 1977).
24. Clifford Geertz, *The Interpretation of Cultures* (New York: Basic Books, 1973).
25. Ricoeur, *Lectures on Ideology and Utopia*, p. 8.
26. Ricoeur, *From Text to Action*, p. 261.
27. Ibid.
28. Ricoeur, *Lectures on Ideology and Utopia*, p. 312.
29. Paul Ricoeur, "The Fragility of Political Language," *Philosophy Today* (Spring 1987): 35–44.
30. Ibid., p. 39.
31. Ibid., p. 43.
32. Ricoeur, *Oneself as Another*, p. 261.
33. Ricoeur, "The Fragility of Political Language," p. 41.
34. Paul Ricoeur, "Universal Civilization and National Cultures," in *History and Truth*, trans. Charles A. Kelbley (Evanston: Northwestern University Press, 1965).
35. Ricoeur returns to the balance between universalism and particularism in *Oneself as Another*, where the third term is "practical wisdom," geared toward coping with difficult, even tragic, situations. He later develops the political dimensions of this theory of practical wisdom taking political liberalism and communitarianism to be the exemplars of universalism and particularism. He agrees with the claims of communitarian philosophers that our political identities are formed in relation to our cultural heritage, shared experiences, and membership in communities. But the primacy of particular, historical ideals of the good life need not challenge the liberal requirement of social justice that universal rights and liberties be protected. The right and the good in politics, as in ethics, stand in a dialectical relationship. Democracy is a fragile, imperfect attempt to balance social justice and our desire to live well together. See Paul Ricoeur, *The Just*, trans. David Pellauer (Chicago: University of Chicago Press, 2000).
36. Ricoeur, "Reflections on a New Ethos for Europe," in *Philosophy and Social Criticism* 21 (5/6) (1995): 12–16.
37. Ibid., p. 8.
38. Ibid., p. 10.
39. Ricoeur develops these themes at length in *Memory, History, Forgetting*, trans. Kathleen Blamey and David Pellaeur (Chicago: University of Chicago Press, 2004). In this work, ideology critique also plays a crucial role in how we might remember events differently.

Justice and Interpretation 12

David M. Rasmussen

Allow me to begin by expressing the profound effect that the work of Paul Ricoeur has had on my own thought. From my early book on his work through my latest reflections on public reason, I remain deeply indebted to his original insights regarding the dilemmas of interpretation. On this occasion I would like to reflect on issues regarding public reason that can be developed through Ricoeur's *Oneself as Another* and *The Just*. When one turns to public and global justice two problems emerge: given the vast differences between cultures, nations, and peoples it is impossible to reduce one political entity to the perspective of another. Given the diversity of cultures, it is an oversimplification to call this a clash of civilizations, but there is a certain truth in Stanley Hoffman's phrase, "the clash of globalizations."[1] An appropriately interpretative perspective would attempt to avoid an avowedly ethnocentric perspective that superimposes Western values on non-Western cultures. At the same time, from the perspective of universal human rights, it is necessary to avoid consideration of the rights of one political group as superior to another. Consequently, global justice contains a paradox that can be posed in the following question: how is it possible to acknowledge the distinctiveness of other political cultures while at the same time granting both legitimacy and validity to individual claims for rights? It would seem that the first perspective would cancel the second while the second would overshadow the first. A consideration of Ricoeur's recent work will help us think through this dilemma.

THE ASYMMETRY OF INTERPRETATION

The position I wish to develop with the help of Ricoeur's reflections on political philosophy deals with his interpretation of the work of John Rawls. Ricoeur through his interpretation of Rawls makes two very important points. He characterizes Rawls's *A Theory of Justice* as seeing justice as the first virtue of social institutions that, when understood appropriately, incorporates a certain "pre-understanding" involving "considered convictions." On the basis of this pre-understanding, Ricoeur is able to link Rawls's deontological approach with a teleological presupposition, implying that Rawls links ethics with politics.[2] I think that there is a certain truth in Ricoeur's claim that can be highlighted by reference to Rawls's early concern with having a 'sense of justice'[3] that takes him beyond a purely procedural perspective. When Ricoeur distinguishes the later from the earlier Rawls the term "wager," well known to Ricoeur scholars, occurs. The wager is simply that the political can be separated from the metaphysical in such a way that the political, no longer dependent on a theory of institutions, can receive its own justification.[4] Although Ricoeur does not dwell on these points, he might have noted that it is because of this, the wager in his terms, that public reason and reasonability emerge as the handmaidens of political justification. What Ricoeur does not do, but what he could have done given his own hermeneutic position, is to characterize the move from the earlier to the later Rawls as a move from a constructivist to an interpretative position. My own point of departure will be first to show how the move to reasonability and public reason requires an interpretative[5] as opposed to a purely constructivist framework, then to show how that framework can be enhanced by reference to the position laid out in *Oneself as Another.*

In *Political Liberalism*, Rawls begins his argument by making a distinction between a comprehensive and a political form of justification on the basis of an essentially intrepretative claim, namely, that philosophy must apply the principle of toleration to itself. This means that reasoning about politics is informed by principles not given by philosophy itself but by the political culture that informs that reasoning process. There are constructivist elements within the position; however, it is my view that the ultimate claim of public reason is both a constructive and an interpretative one. I don't want to underestimate the constructivist character of Rawls's argument in *Political Liberalism,* yet the move from *A Theory of Justice* to *Political Liberalism* opens up a much broader role for interpretation. The decision to subordinate reason to reasonability, which occurs in Rawls's writings in 1979 and 1980, makes it possible to take account of "the other" in terms of a judgment about what is reasonable.[6] Public reason under the aegis of reasonability makes it possible to articulate social interaction in a political context. Whether or not overlapping consensus occurs depends on the reasonable judgment of others within the political community. Because justification is contextualized by toleration, public reason becomes the forum through which self and other are mutually acknowledged within a political context. Reasonable judgment governs both agreement or consensus as well as disagreement, which can be expected given the historical context in which that judgment is exercised.

Rawls's later position is rather carefully specified as political constructivism that, in contrast to moral constructivism of a Kantian variety, is not regulative for all of existence but is restricted to the context of the political. The model for political constructivism, justice as fairness, specifies the content of a political conception of justice with associated conceptions of person and society in accord with practical reason. If we were to test the validity of the politically constructed, it would appear that there are no objective criteria apart from reasonable judgment and interpretation, with the consequence that reflection on politics occurs within the circle of interpretation. Rawls says as much:

> Political convictions (which are also, of course, moral convictions) are objective—actually founded on an order of reasons—if reasonable and rational persons . . . would eventually endorse those convictions, or significantly narrow their differences about them, provided that these persons know the relevant facts and have sufficiently surveyed the grounds that bear on the matter under conditions favorable to reflection.[7]

This would mean that the ultimate criterion for "objective reasons," what others might call validity, would be the appropriate judgments of others so interpreted. One might conclude that the procedural element in the Rawls of *Political Liberalism* is governed by judgment and interpretation given by the political context in which it occurs. By his own admission, then, Rawls is not taking a purely procedural position that can be objectively evaluated solely in terms of procedures. In his "Reply to Habermas," when accused of conceiving justice as fairness as substantive and not procedural, Rawls responds: "I see my reply as a defense of liberalism since any liberal view must be substantive, and it is correct in being so."[8]

So Rawls's political constructivism not only involves judgment and interpretation in the abstract but also characterizes judgment and interpretation as an obligation, that is, as the "duty of civility" that commits citizens to "be able to explain to one another on those fundamental questions how the principles and policies they advocate and vote for can be supported by the political values of public reason."[9] Hence, citizens are obligated to be involved in a hermeneutics of translation in which certain values implicit in one comprehensive framework can be sorted out and translated into the framework of another.[10]

The argument for higher law further contextualizes Rawls position on public reason basing it on an even more interpretative framework. At the beginning of the chapter on public reason in *Political Liberalism,* Rawls refers to "constitutional essentials." He waits until the end of that chapter to tell us what he has in mind. His now familiar thesis is that the Supreme Court is the exemplar of public reason. In other words, public reason is reasoning about the Constitution, a form of reasoning that is informed by the history of interpretation. Following the distinction between higher law and ordinary law originally made by Locke, Rawls endorses a branch of American constitutional interpretation that specifies higher law as taking precedence over ordinary law, the principled expression of higher law being the Constitution. Rawls adds to this interpretation the idea that the articulation of constitutional essentials is the task of public reason. Clearly, the constructivist task of public reason is limited and constrained by the interpretative task, namely, to interpret the Constitution. Hence, the exemplar of public reason will be the Supreme Court, which need not be viewed as an elitist organization that through judicial review constrains democratic lawmaking. Rather, it can be conceived as a representive of "we the people" whose role is to preserve and protect democratic freedoms against possible encroachment by the tyranny of the majority.[11]

If it is true that the later Rawls no longer endorses a pure proceduralism and that his subordination of reason to reasonability opens the way to an interpretative framework (I think that was Rawls's true wager), then it is possible to turn to Ricoeur's framework proposed in *Oneself as Another* to develop in terms of a friendly interaction between Rawls and Ricoeur an asymmetric model of self and other that can be used not only for individual self-understanding in politics but also for constructing a global framework. Ricoeur's negative thesis in that work is that the philosophy of language has only been able to conceive of the self as sameness, which is to say, the construction of an identity in terms of linguistic reference. This is thought to be the great achievement of the philosophy of language when seen in relationship to prior philosophy, namely, to overcome the dilemmas of subjectivity. Ricoeur's argument is that the self is both the same and other in the sense that the self has an identity that changes over time. While the philosophy of language through "identifying reference" can designate the self in terms of its identical character, it cannot account for its temporality. Ricoeur's wager is to construct an alternative epistemological hypothesis while remaining within the philosophy of language that will account for the self both in its sameness and in terms of its manifestation in time, its temporality. Hence the positive thesis: that the self can be accounted for over time not only in terms of its identity but also in terms of its transformations. Ricoeur, using the distinction between "the Latin *ipse* or *idem*," makes the claim that not only can the self be its sameness over time, its *idem* identity, but also that the self can be conceived in terms of its *ipse* identity. According to Ricoeur, this latter identity "implies no assertion concerning some unchanging core of personality."[12] In another context,[13] I summarized Ricoeur's position in the following manner: Ricoeur's argument, conceived as a critique of analytic theories of reference and reflexivity, would incorporate the following claims: (l) semantics is only able to capture the self in terms of *idem* or sameness, (2) pragmatics of language attempts to get beyond semantics by positing a theory of interlocution. The important breakthrough of pragmatics was to be able to transform the semantic analysis by postulating an inter-subjectivist hypothesis in terms of the claims of speech-acts. In Ricoeur's terms, the great advance of pragmatics was to move from identity to self-identity. (3) However, and this is the significant point of Ricoeur's critique, even though pragmatics was able to move from identity to self-identity, it was only able to do so through positing a concept of the self that was characterized as sameness (*idem*) and not otherness (*ipsété*). Stated positively, the theory of interlocution is that it moves beyond the problem of "identifying reference" by considering actual utterances by speakers who refer in different ways. By concentrating on the notion of utterance, illuctionary acts are joined by acts of predication that concentrate on the reflexive implications of this notion. Significantly, the theory of interlocution moves the problem of self-identity to intersubjective identity. But, according to Ricoeur's argument, the achievement of inter-subjectivity is based on a notion of identity in accord with sameness. Speech-acts are intersubjective only to the extent that utterance "is mirrored" in the act of another. To the extent that this is the case, the promise of speech-act theory is inhibited by a Cartesian bias, unable to preserve the asymmetry between self and other.

Ricoeur claims that the way one preserves the nonidentical relation between self and self and between self and other is through the construction of narrative identity. Through the construction of the narrative with its relationship of character and emplotment, discordance and concordance, synthesis of the heterogeneous and imaginative variation the distance between self and other is preserved. In this sense, the model of narrative identity as a model for interpretation can be effectively used as a model for political understanding.[14] When one tries to get beyond the ethnocentricity implied in mirroring the other it is necessary to enable the other, to manifest itself in the context of its difference, its nonidentity. Hence, the critique of interlocution authored by Ricoeur as well as the concept of narrative identity proposed by him would fill out the interpretative dimensions of the associated notions of reasonability and public reason.[15]

THE SUBJECT OF RIGHTS

How does one move from an interpretative position that preserves the uniqueness of political culture to a global conception of human rights?

In the first instance, that is, in the case of narrative identity, it is necessary to postulate the uniqueness as well as the distinctive character of the political other. In the second instance, it is necessary to grant legitimacy on the level of equality to individuals who are entitled to have rights. Ricoeur approaches the latter by raising the question "Who is the subject of rights?"[16] Beginning with the idea of "the capable subject," Ricoeur's strategy already developed in *Oneself as Another* addresses the subject of speech and action by focusing on the question "who?," who is speaking, who is acting, and finally advancing to the narrative component of personal and collective identity. As noted earlier, narrative identity incorporates change and in our terms conveys the distinctness of both personal and cultural identity.[17] The final stage in the development of the capable subject is, for Ricoeur, the moral or ethical stage in which the subject assumes responsibility for herself through the introduction of "ethical or moral predicates." The subject advances to her "highest level" capability, the level of self-esteem and self-respect, meaning that she is the subject of "ethico-juridical imputation." As such, the subject is capable both of assuming responsibility for herself and of being able to fulfill obligations to others. For Ricoeur it is here that the claim of justice enters. The capable subject is not simply responsible to another as in the case of friendship or family obligation; instead here one transcends the face-to-face relation.[18] Here the relationship between the I and the you becomes a relationship in which the *you* is conceived under the conditions of international law; the you becomes *everyone*. For Ricoeur, this is the level of politics proper because justice stands not simply in relationship to the you, but to everyone in the sense that with justice one introduces a standard, a *third-person* perspective. This is not simply a subjective claim, but both a linguistic and an institutional claim in the sense that justice can only be realized in what Hegel thought of as a state, but which can perhaps be more appropriately said to be a people.

Clearly, there is no parallel between Ricoeur and Rawls in terms of the development of Rawls's position from *Theory* to *Political Liberalism* and the later works.[19] However, Rawls's move to a form of justification that requires reasonability and public reason does present us with a model that can be illuminated by the move from narrative identity to justice. Ricoeur's claim that there is a certain pre-understanding in *Theory* that goes beyond the realm of deontology is correct. In his 1963 article, "The Sense of Justice," Rawls makes the following statement: "The capacity for a sense of justice is, then, necessary and sufficient for the duty of justice to be owed to a person—that is, for a person to be regarded as holding an initial position of equal liberty."[20] To be sure, Rawls goes on to distinguish this view from utilitarianism, which holds that "a capacity for pleasure and pain, for joy and sorrow is sufficient for a full subject of rights."[21] Also, he distinguishes his position from what he takes to be Aristotle's, which, in his view, does not sustain a commitment to equality. This statement supports the claim that a certain pre-understanding makes Rawls's orientation to justice possible. It is my view that, when one turns to the work of the later post-1980 Rawls with the development of a much more nuanced notion of justification, the notion of obligation plays a more central role. The duty of civility means that it is one's political obligation to be able to reconstruct one's political view in terms that another political subject can understand and reconstruct in terms of her own comprehensive position. The notion of reasonability implies both a capacity and a duty. The capacity is based on the assumption that it is possible to translate the view of one person into that of another. The obligation, an obligation of public reason, is that one, within the context of democratic culture, is required to be able to translate one's views into terms that are politically acceptable. In the later work of Rawls, the terms that emerge to designate the complex task of justification are the *conjecture*[22] and the *proviso*.[23] The conjecture means that there can be a mutual exchange on a political level when different comprehensive views are being appropriated. The proviso suggests that the translation from the comprehensive will occur in terms appropriate to public reason.

What Ricoeur construes as ethical obligation I would, along with Rawls, categorize as political obligation. However, Ricoeur's reflections on rights help to clarify what is involved in the process of justification. Using Ricoeur's framework, I would claim that the very act of justification raises the question "Who is the subject of rights?" Indeed, it is in this concrete hermeneutic way that the question of universality is presented because the subject of rights is "everyone." As one tries to envision how justification would work, particularly in the context of the confrontation of liberal with nonliberal points of view, the question of rights would not be overlooked because the very act of justification requires the postulation of a universal subject. This Ricoeurian insight helps explain the ambiguity of the later Rawls on the issue of rights as expressed in *The Law of Peoples*. Some would interpret his view regarding nonliberal societies to be that it is sufficient that these societies endorse or have endorsed the 1948 Declaration on Human Rights. The problem with that view is that it overlooks the question of the actual enactment of human rights. If we see the very act of justification as an affirmation of the other as the subject of rights, one's view of Rawls's later work takes on a more positive perspective.

Now it is possible to return to the seeming paradox with which this reflection began. As one attempts to understand other nonliberal, non-Western political cultures, it is necessary that we avoid a kind of ethnocentrism that finds in the image of the other the mirror image of ourselves. That is the preoccupation of the Rawls of the *Law of Peoples*.

Ricoeur's more recent work provides an epistemological model for understanding the other, both as the other self and as the other political culture through his conception of narrative identity. When we turn to the problem of justification in terms of reasonability, we encounter the subject of rights, the you that is everyone. Hence, the move from narrative identity to justification resolves the seeming paradox that effects one's encounter with global justice. In this sense, Ricoeur's recent work provides a distinctive way to develop the notions of reasonability and public reason.

NOTES

1. Globalization is a dangerous if necessary term and Hoffman is concerned to endorse neither the Hunnington's clash of civilizations thesis nor the "end of history" position. His approach is both more modest and more rational. His question is the following: "How can one make the global house more livable? The answer presupposes a political philosophy that we are both just and acceptable even to those whose values have other foundations. As the late philosopher Judith Shklar did, we can take as a point of departure and as a guiding thread the fate of the victims of violence, oppression, and misery; as a goal we should seek material and moral emancipation. While taking into account the formidable constraints of the world as it is, it is possible to loosen them." Stanley Hoffman, "The Clash of Globalizations," *Foreign Affairs* 18, 4 (2002): 115.

2. In the essay, "Is a Purely Procedural Theory of Justice Possible?" regarding the working out of the two principles of justice in Rawls's *A Theory of Justice,* Ricoeur states: "But if we look closer at the decisive argument directed against utilitarianism, namely, that it must be ready to sacrifice some unfavored individuals or groups if that is required by the greatest number, I cannot help thinking that we have here an ethical argument disguised as a technical argument borrowed from decision theory in its most elementary form, game theory, where there are winners and losers divested of any ethical concern." Paul Ricoeur, *The Just* (Chicago: University of Chicago Press, 2000), p. 52.

3. I will show later in the argument where Rawls specifically turns to the issue; significantly, he sees this issue in the tradition of Rousseau.

4. Ricoeur states: "Where does the motivation and, if we may put it this way, the instruction in such a moral capacity come from? It is here that the idea of an overlapping consensus intervenes. Short of this point, the theory of justice rests only on the strategy of *avoiding* controversies, along the lines of the idea of tolerance that ended the wars of religion in the Christian West. Now it is necessary to take a step in the direction of a *wager,* namely, that rival "metaphysical" conceptions that have fed and continue to nourish the strong convictions of citizens belonging to Western democracies can motivate, justify, and found the same minimal body of beliefs likely to contribute to the reflective equilibrium required by *A Theory of Justice.*" Ibid., p. 72.

5. In terms of political philosophy Ricoeur's position is outlined in his essay entitled "Interpretation and/or Argumentation" (ibid., pp. 109–26). Contrasting the work of Robert Alexy and Ronald Dworkin, Ricoeur

argues that argumentation requires interpretation, which in turn involves judgment. I understand the move to *Political Liberalism* in Rawls as one that represents a turn from an argumentative constructivism to an interpretative constructivism that gives a much larger role to judgment in the context of justification. Rawls's idea of "Overlapping Consensus" requires a notion of reasonability on the part of the participating parties who in turn must make the appropriate judgment regarding their shared political world. Significantly, for Ricoeur, the model for judgment in a judicial context goes beyond the Kantian model of determinate judgment to include reflective judgment. Unfortunately, Rawls made no such specification. However, it is evident that his pragmatic approach opens the way for something like the model of reflective judgment.

6. In "Kantian Constructivism and Moral Theory," when giving an account of rational and full autonomy, Rawls states the following: "the Reasonable presupposes and subordinates the Rational. It defines the fair terms of cooperation acceptable to all within some group of separately identifiable persons, each of whom possesses and can exercise the two moral powers. All have a conception of their good which defines their rational advantage, and everyone has a normally effective sense of justice: a capacity to honor the fair terms of cooperation. The Reasonable subordinates the Rational, because, without conceptions of the good that move members of the group, there is no point to social cooperation nor to notions of right and justice, even though such cooperation realizes values that go beyond what conceptions of the good specify taken alone. The Reasonable subordinates the Rational because its principles limit, and in a Kantian doctrine limit absolutely, the final ends that can be pursued." John Rawls, *Collected Papers* (Cambridge: Harvard University Press, 1999), p. 317. Similar statements can be found elsewhere in Rawls's work dating from this period.

7. John Rawls, *Political Liberalism* (New York: Columbia University Press, 1996), p. 119.

8. Ibid., p. 421.

9. Ibid., p. 214.

10. See Jim Josephson and Jonathan Bach, "A Critique of Rawls's Hermeneutics as Translation," *Philosophy and Social Criticism* 23, 1 (1997): 99–124.

11. Rawls effectively follows a branch of American constitutional legal interpretation that argues that the function of the Supreme Court with its procedure of judicial review is democratic procedure enacted in such a way to protect democratic freedoms from being eroded by majorities.

12. Paul Ricoeur, *Oneself as Another* (Chicago: University of Chicago Press, 1992), p. 2.

13. David M. Rasmussen, "Rethinking Subjectivity: Narrative Identity and the Self," in *Ricoeur as Another*. ed. Richard A. Cohen and James I. Marsh (Albany: SUNY Press, 2002), pp. 57–70.

14. Seyla Benhabib adds to this understanding of narrative when she writes: "Culture presents itself through narratively contested accounts for two principle reasons. First, human actions and relations are formed through a double hermeneutic: We identify *what* we do through an *account* of what we do; words and deeds are equiprimordial, in the sense that almost all socially significant human action beyond scratching one's nose is identified as a certain *type of doing* through the accounts the agents and others give of doing. This is so even when, and especially when, there is disagreement between doer and observer. The second reason why culture presents itself

through contested accounts is that not only are human actions and interactions constituted through narratives that are together a "web of
narratives," but they are also constituted through the actors' evaluative
stances toward their doings." Seyla Benhabib, *The Claims of Culture:
Equality and Diversity in the Global Era* (Princeton: Princeton University
Press, 2002), pp. 6–7.

15. I think the ideas of reasonability and public reason as they appear in
    Rawls require further development. It is apparent that reasonability in the
    context of public reason requires a certain constraint on the part of the
    person making and offering judgments for the interpretation of another.
    Hence, different narratives would be akin to different comprehensive views
    that world require an interpretative stance in terms of reasonability. It
    would be necessary to find what is reasonable within a narrative in the
    sense of finding out what could be acceptable from the point of view of
    public reason, and this would be a matter of judgment. Rawls tries to
    clarify this view of reasonability in relationship to comprehensive
    doctrines in the following way: "I assume, then, that a reasonable compre-
    hensive doctrine accepts some form of political argument for toleration.
    Of course, citizens may think that the grounding reasons for toleration
    and for other elements of a constitutional democratic society are not polit-
    ical but rather are to be found in their religious or non-religious doctrines.
    And these reasons, they may well say, are the true or the right reasons: and
    they may see the political reasons as superficial, the grounding ones as
    deep. Yet there is no conflict here, but simply concordant judgments made
    within political conceptions of justice on the one hand, and within
    comprehensive doctrines on the other." John Rawls, *The Law of Peoples
    with The Idea of Public Reason Revisited* (Cambridge: Harvard University
    Press, 1999), p. 176.

16. *The Just*, pp. 1–11.

17. Ricoeur states, "This notion of narrative identity is of the greatest impor-
    tance in inquiry into the identity of peoples and nations, for it bears the
    same dramatic and narrative character we all too often confuse with the
    identity of a substance or a structure. At the level of the history of
    different peoples, as at that of individuals, the contingency of turning
    points in the story contributes to the overall significance of the story that
    is told as well as of the protagonists. To recognize this is to free ourselves
    of a prejudice concerning the identity claimed by different peoples under
    the heading of arrogance, fear or hate." Ibid., pp. 3–4.

18. Ricoeur states: "The first other, if I may put [it] this way, offers himself
    through his face, in his voice, with which he addresses me, designating me
    as the second person singular. This is the other of interpersonal relations.
    Friendship, opposed in this context to justice, is the emblematic virtue of
    this immediate relationship that accomplishes the miracle of an exchange
    of roles between beings that cannot be substituted for each other. You are
    the you that says 'you' to me and to whom I respond, as Emmanuel
    Levinas loved to repeat, 'here I am'—me, in the accusative case. But
    however wonderful the virtue of friendship may be, it is not capable of
    fulfilling the task of justice, nor even of engendering it as a distinctive
    virtue. The virtue of justice is based on a relation of distance from the
    other, just as originary as the relation of proximity to the other person
    offered through his face and voice. This relation to the other is, if I may so
    put it, immediately mediated by the *institution*. The other for friendship is

the 'you'; the other for justice is 'anyone,' as is indicated by the Latin adage *sum cuique tribuere* (to each his own)." Ibid., p. xiii.

19. My argument is that the work of the later Rawls constitutes a pragmatic turn that involves an openness to arguments made by Ricoeur. Contrary to Dauenhauer, I find Ricoeur to be much closer to Rawls and potentially much more open to the work of the later Rawls. With regard to Ricoeur's account of constitutions, Dauenhauer states, "Ricoeur's account, by contrast, gives us a better way to understand both the impetus to establish constitutions containing universal norms, and the need for an interminable process of interpreting and modifying them." *Ricoeur as Another*, p. 219. On the contrary, Rawls follows Ackerman's position on the Constitution which is essentially an interpretative one, open to the change through constitutional amendment and political transformation and continuously reinterpreted. Also, to the extent that Rawls has moved from his earlier "comprehensive" position, his work has accommodated some of the earlier criticisms of Ricoeur.

20. Rawls, *Collected Papers*, pp. 115–16.

21. Ibid.

22. *Conjecture* is defined by Rawls as follows: "We argue from what we believe, or conjecture are other people's basic doctrines, religious or secular, and try to show them that, despite what they may think, they can still endorse a reasonable political conception that can provide a basis for public reason. The ideal of public reason is therefore strengthened. However it is important that conjecture be sincere and not manipulative. We must openly explain our intentions and state that we do not assert the premises from which we argue, but that we proceed as we do to clear up what we take to be a misunderstanding on others' part, and perhaps equally on ours." Rawls, *Law of Peoples with The Idea of Public Reason Revisited*, pp. 155–56.

23. With regard to what Rawls calls "the wide view of political culture," the first requirement has to do with the proviso. The proviso amounts to a requirement that "reasonable comprehensive doctrines, religious and non religious, may be introduced in public political discussion at any time, provided that in due course proper political reasons—and not reasons given solely by comprehensive doctrines—are presented that are sufficient to support whatever the comprehensive doctrines introduced are said to support. This injunction to present proper political reasons I refer to as *the proviso,* and it specifies political culture as distinct from the background culture." Ibid., p. 152.

Rethinking Ricoeur: The Unity of His Work and the Paradigm of Translation 13

Domenico Jervolino

Ricoeur's long march is over. Now that he is behind us, yet continues to guide our journey with his example and his teachings, I wish to dedicate to him this chapter. This homage, a gift of thoughts in response to his gift: his work, which provokes and stimulates our questioning.

Paul Ricoeur had in the utmost degree this gift for giving a sign of faithfulness to his vocation as philosopher, which he manifested already as a teenager, at the school of Dalbiez, his high school philosophy professor in Rennes. In the light of the richness of his thinking, from which we have all benefited, we honor this steadfastness, which marked his entire existence, selecting as its pacific realm the dominion of the philosophic word. A discipline cultivated, mediated, and transmitted through the simple joy of teaching: "The word is my realm," "I have been a happy teacher" — we all remember these statements by Ricoeur. His adherence to his philosophical vocation is visible also in his concern, as a believer, "not to mix genres," that is, to safeguard the autonomy of philosophical thinking and the shadows in which it necessarily walks even from the blinding light of the revealed Word (which indeed creates yet other forms of obscurity in the life of believers).

The question of the unity of Ricoeur's work has long been the object of what I have called a "loving struggle," following Jaspers, between the author and his interpreters, who have sought to identify a common thread in his vast and variegated production, while Ricoeur seemed more interested in his moments of discontinuity, in the breaks in his thinking, in the question that engendered each work, and the unsolved residue left by each work, prompting a continuation of the journey.

While interpreters focused on the problem of identifying the question of questions, the question underlying all others, the guiding question in the long journey of the philosopher, Ricoeur avoided the problem and delegated it to his interpreters, defending the freedom to follow his own path (I do not cite examples of this "loving struggle" because I have already done that elsewhere[1]).

However, Ricoeur's interest in the activity of reading made a third option possible: the author becoming his own reader. We know that this possibility materialized in recent years and that Ricoeur himself indicated the notion of the "*homme capable*" as a "thin but continuous" common thread of all his work. This thread kept together the variety of his approaches and developments, starting from his early phenomenology of the will, from the "I can" that constitutes us as willing subjectivity, always correlated to the involuntariness of nature, to the summarizing of the many ways in which the self conquers itself in the constant dialectics between immediacy and reflection, between the sameness that belongs to the way of being of things and the being oneself that belongs to people, between the self and the other, or, rather, the multiple forms of alterity.

This self that is not the jealous property of the first person I, but the omnipersonal reflexive pronoun *self* that ultimately coincides with the condition of humans who act and suffer, addressed in the at once simple and yet regal gesture of philosophical thought.

In my view, this framework provides the conditions for a conclusion to the loving struggle between author and interpreters. The conflict is followed by peace, a *pax philosophica* that bears in itself the solved conflict, consisting in the reciprocal extraneousness of the author and his readers and interpreters.

Like the conflict that preceded it, and with more reason, this *pax philosophica* entails love and *reconaissance* for both author and readers, *reconaissance* in the dual sense of gratitude and recognition—the recognition of the "thing of thought" that guides the sequence, in a sense infinite, of interrogations, all revolving around what for Kant is the fundamental question of philosophy: "What is man?" a question that Augustine posed in more dramatic terms: "*Quaestio mihi factus sum,*" "I have become a question for myself."

Recognition and gratitude for the answer: "It is the man capable of ... ," an answer which, in turn, can give rise to an infinite series of answers: "The man capable of ... speaking, acting, narrating and narrating himself, taking responsibility for his actions ... , but also remembering and forgetting, making history and writing it, judging and being judged, understanding his human condition, through the painstaking work of interpretation and translation, which is a way to say something again but differently. And capable also, at the end of a long lifetime journey, of realizing, through the difficult experience of forgiving, that humans are worth more than their actions and their faults and that the climax of wisdom is the capacity to be amazed by the splendor of the simple fact of being alive as human beings ... as we are taught by those simple masters, the lilies of the fields and the birds in the sky.[2]

Recognition and gratitude, as I was saying at the beginning, for the gift of thought he gave us, which invites us to philosophize in turn. The relationship between author and readers is neither one of fusion nor of extraneousness, but becomes one of reciprocal recognition and an appeal to the liberty of philosophizing.

This perhaps allows us to better understand why the last word of *La mémoire, l'histoire, l'oubli* is "Inachèvement" (Incompletion) and why the image with which Ricoeur distinguishes his hermeneutics from Gadamer's "fusion of horizons" is that of the "receding of horizons."[3]

Developing the common thread offered by Ricoeur himself, I have elsewhere suggested that his entire work can be described as a spiral, in which the same themes are taken up again years later in different terms: the early philosophical anthropology of Ricoeur's philosophy of the will resurfaces in the works of 1990–2000, after a long detour through the universe of language, out of which, in all truth, an hermeneutic philosophy never emerges, not because everything is language, but because everything must be said through language, with the unsayable as the ultimate borderline.[4]

I also suggested the existence of a progression in Ricoeur's hermeneutic journey through language, going through three paradigmatic stages: symbol, text, translation. The paradigm of translation is less explicit than the first two, which were explicitly theorized by the author in two different moments, but is, I feel, secretly at work as a sort of third stage in Ricoeur's hermeneutics. In saying this, I am exercising my rights as reader, with no pretense of juxtaposing my perspective to that of the author, but rather of developing the stimuli received from him. The exemplary value of translation as paradigm appears to me to agree with the attention shown by Ricoeur, in the most recent phase of his hermeneutics, to the plurality of humankind in all its forms (diversity of languages, culture, religion, beliefs, schools of thought, and ethical solutions).

In the spiral movement extending from the beginning to the end, the meaning of Ricoeur's work does not remain the same, but is gradually enriched, in the transition, simplifying, from the anthropology of the *homme faillible* to that of the *homme capable*. Yet, while the work grows (*crescit cum legente*, in Gregorius Magnus's splendid statement, but also grows also in itself and with the awareness that the author is his own first reader), in this growth something is also lost: what is lost is, for the author, the obsession with guilt. This means that the philosophy of guilt and the obsessive search for responsibilities is followed by a philosophy of compassion, a universal attitude of *pietas erga homines*.

The answer to the question "What is a man?" is therefore the *homme capable*. In other words, a plural ensemble of powers that belong to us and constitute us as human beings, which are not the object of *episteme* (scientific demonstration) but are rather *attested* by conscience, which is a form of belief, of being ourselves, of being the person who is capable of.... To this attestation one can oppose suspicion, which, however, can be confirmed or defeated only on the base of the most credible attestations.

In Ricoeur's latest philosophy, attestation takes the place of the Cogito but preserves from the Cartesian cogito the problematic of the truthfulness of God, and comes closer to what I like to call the Cogito of Pascal, the thinking reed that can be destroyed by a single drop of water and is aware of dying.

In any case, Ricoeur's philosophy is much more than a rigorous description of these powers, attested by the moral certainty of our being the agents of our actions and the patients of our affections. It implies certainly a descriptive moment—which starts from the *what*, from what we are capable of, and goes through the *how* of each human "capability—but finally arrives at the source of these capacities, *the act of . . .* : powers that are plural, but ultimately unified as the multiple expression of the capacity to act, along with its inescapable correlative, *suffering*, and its necessary interweaving with speaking in all its forms. All of Ricoeur's philosophy remains basically a "practical" philosophy. For Ricoeur, *l'homme capable* and *l'homme agissant* are synonyms.

But *l'homme capable* or *agissant* must express himself. The act of speaking is a form of action, but what really counts is that in this action in itself expresses itself, it inserts itself into a symbolic order—shared with others and ultimately with all humanity—and at the same time returns to itself, it *reflects*. This return to oneself is the only constitution of the Self that our finite and contingent condition allows us. And philosophy is also necessarily reflexive: there is an inescapable reflexive node provided by the immanent reflexivity of language, even if any philosophy of conscience or the subject were to be exhausted or excluded.

The return to the self, the appropriation of this act that is most intimately ours, is accompanied in Ricoeur by a critique of immediacy. The return to the self is always a deviation, a detour; it is never a pure, self-transparent and self-creative act. It is an affirmation of oneself, *embodied*, against the background of a being in which we are incorporated but with which we only partially coincide, for it is structurally plural and open to others and the world. I am a human being, a living body, within the community of humans and in the framework of nature. I am the effort and the desire to exist, *conatus, appetitus, energheia-dynamis, essentia actuosa*: we therefore need to reread Ricoeur's pages on initiative as the capacity to make present, which mediates between the space of experience and the wait for the future, and prevents both the closure of the past and the escape toward tomorrow, on the body as a living combination of passivity and activity. Pages that outline Ricoeur's cautious effort to grasp the ontological significance of the self on the basis of a reinterpretation of the metaphysical tradition, start from the primacy of the act more than from substance.

This is the *homme capable*, the agent of history, the subject of praxis and practices, the custodian of memory, the person who lives in time and space. Living for one's contemporaries means "growing old together," using a dazzling expression of Schutz's quoted by Ricoeur.[5] The *homme capable* is the person to whom life is donated and, ultimately, the addressee of religion, because, as in Kant the final question on humanity comes at the end, after others ("what can I know?," "what should I do?," "what can I hope for?"), so religion is what finally offers us a global perspective on people and on the possibility of recovering or curing their constitutive powers, beyond individual actions: recovering an original goodness beyond radical evil. Evil, in the Judaic-Christian view of humanity, is radical, not original. Humans are worth more than their actions, though the latter are corrupted by their tendency to go against moral laws.

Ricoeur's hermeneutics culminates therefore in a great practical philosophy whose main tenets are found in the hermeneutics of the human condition articulated in *La mémoire, l'histoire, l'oubli* and in the "petite éthique" as reformulated in Ricoeur's more recent essays and especially in *Le Juste 2* (2001).

But in Ricoeur's last works we perceive also an effort to rethink the relation between metaphysics and morals, through a meditation on the Plato of the "great kinds" and on the Aristotle of the polisemy of Being (*to on leghetai pollachos, ens dicitur multipliciter*), but also through the French tradition of the *Revue de Métaphysique et de Morale*, founded by Ravaisson in 1893. For the centenary of the journal, Ricoeur wrote "De la métaphysique à la morale." Next to this work, mention can be made of "Multiple étrangété," a paper presented at Halle, at the European Congress of Hermeneutics in 1994, and "Justice et vérité," a talk given in Paris for the centenary of the Faculty of Philosophy of the Institut Catholique (now in *Le Juste 2*, of which the ample introduction is also important).[6]

Though this last phase of his thinking is an unusual or exploratory meditation, as Ricoeur states, it still revolves around the *homme capable*. A subject who encounters the metafunction of metaphysics and acknowledges that both practical and theoretical philosophy are second philosophies in relation to a first philosophy, which is first only in reference to the human condition.

Thus, in the relation among the multiple forms of alterity we find inside and outside ourselves, and in our relating to the supreme categories that the ancients saw as transcendental—the Truth, the Good, the Beautiful—we always to return to a question on humankind. The culmination of moral life is, in a certain sense, taking full responsibility for one's actions. But beyond personal existence there is the possible relation with all other existences. They are equally important in principle, yet this ethical principle clashes with the reality of a self-divided humanity. How then can one reconcile universalism and contextualism? How can one unify justice and truth? Without having the titanic pretense of going beyond the finite state of our human condition, we may state that this formulation, in some way ultimate, of the Kantian question about man, coincides with the *epimeleia tes psiches* (cure of the soul), which for Patočka represents the heritage of the Platonic-Christian humanistic tradition.[7] And it can be addressed only as a problem of *translation*, in a speculative sense, as the resumption of the ancient problem of the convertibility of transcendentals, in a practical-existential sense, as an unending search for the co-possibility of the multiple forms of what is human, guided by practical wisdom.

In the introduction to *Le Juste 2,* Ricoeur, defending his choice to place his 1999 essay on the paradigm of translation[8] at the end of the *Études*, which are the first part of the book, returns to that theme, showing its ethical implications (or even, I would risk saying, its metaphysical implications) in that journey "from metaphysics to morals" that marks the last phase of Ricoeur's thought.

To speak of translation in relation to Ricoeur does not mean discussing the typical topics of translation studies, though evidently interdisciplinary research in that field should be taken into account. It means reflecting on what is the model for the act of translating, what is the paradigmatic meaning of this act, precisely.

This transition from a linguistic or literary problematic to a philosophical level is helped by the broadening of the notion of translation to include that of translation within the same language. For this reason, Ricoeur speaks of two types of translation (to these two types, interlinguistic and infralinguistic translation, Jakobson would add intersemiotic translation, i.e., translation from one semiotic system into another).

When considered in the full extension of its meaning, translation tells us two things: on the one hand, the difficulty of translating, which can reach the point of untranslatability, on the other, the existence of an incessant work of translation, which remains an inescapable commitment of humanity in its millenarian history. In any case, we must renounce the utopian aspiration to a perfect translation.

The difficulty of translating is a sign of the negativity that affects our capability for saying and, as a consequence, all our constitutive capabilities. *Humans are capable of* . . . , but to every capability corresponds a specific form of vulnerability: *humans cannot.* . . . The diversity of languages reveals a specific form of vulnerability, reminding us that we are a single fragment of humanity, that the other outside us is the stranger who can become, and historically has become, the enemy. But the labor of translation tells us that this situation of extraneousness must not necessarily lead to incommunicability and hostility toward the other.

The diversity of languages is paradigmatic, a sign of the fragmentary and plural nature of humanity. The labor of translation is also paradigmatic, necessary, I would add, already located in the context of conflict and war. Establishing a relation with the other, and his or her language, means searching for an equivalent meaning in our language. The desire to translate, which can originate also from a desire to dominate and appropriate the other, necessarily requires some kind of acceptance of the other and ultimately turns into linguistic hospitality, a desire and pleasure to accept the other in his or her diversity.

Livius Andronicus, the first great translator of the Odyssey into Latin, was a slave, a prisoner of war, but for all those who, through him, entered the fantastic world of Homer, the slave became, perhaps unawares, a host, and hostility was turned into hospitality.

This is the almost Hegelian movement (in a phenomenological sense) we find in Ricoeur. But if this is Hegelianism, it is a Hegelianism of finitude, since the conversion from hostility to hospitality can only occur through the acceptance of the limit and thanks to the concrete, finite, and necessarily imperfect labor of translating, in which the theoretical alternative between translatability and untraslatability—irresolvable in terms of pure theory—is changed into the practical alternative, always to be negotiated, between faithfulness and unfaithfulness.

It is impossible not to perceive at work here two structural aspects of philosophy, of human philosophizing, as evidenced by Ricoeur. Not simply aspects of Ricoeur's thought, but of the great classics, especially Kant, though perhaps one could add two masters of the twentieth century, Nabert and Jaspers: namely, the philosophy of reflection and the philosophy of existence. Two aspects, that is: the productive nature of aporia and its dissolution in practical-existential terms, on the one hand, and, on the other hand, the sequence affirmation-negation-limitation. To this sequence corresponds a second triad: capacity, vulnerability, the practice of translation.

I summarize: affirming the human capacity of reasonably speaking and acting; frankly acknowledging human vulnerability as something more than a limitation, as a true negativity, the impossibility of speaking, of acting (nonsense *versus* sense); struggle against adversity to practically change it into finite possibility through labor, in this case, the labor of translation, which, I wish to restate, is paradigmatic of the human condition, of its need to constantly and patiently transform adversity in practical work. Here comes into play the limit as acceptance of the limited nature of practical synthesis or, in other words, as the acceptance of the conditioned nature of humanity. Translating always entails also the possibility of retranslating, of offering a better translation or at least a different one.

The paradigmatic character of interlinguistic translation can be exalted by the extension of the notion of translation to include intralinguistic translation, the possibility of saying the same thing in the same language in another way, the capacity to exploit the self-interpreting resources that belong to every language. Saying in another way, resaying, therefore saying imperfectly (or, in Umberto Eco's words, saying *almost the same thing*[9]): otherwise there would be no need to resay.

After all, the power of translating does not belong solely to individual speakers, but to languages as languages and to language in regards to itself. In one way or the other, translation forces us to confront extraneousness, the other outside ourselves, but even more the other inside ourselves.

This is where the theme of translation encounters that of language as verbal body, a theme discussed by Merleau-Ponty and Thévenaz.[10] The analogy between language and body is rich in resonances and paves the way to a specific problematic. It can go so far as to unilaterally emphasize the mother tongue,[11] thus emphasizing the difficulty of translation, which would almost entail a sort of exit from one's body. For this reason, it is important to correct this one-sidedness by observing that the body, in Ricoeur's terms, already represents an early form of alterity, which we necessarily encounter in our search for identity.

Be that as it may, we are once again faced with the dialectic between extraneousness and hospitality, extraneousness and acceptance, acceptance of ourselves and of others, of other cultures, languages, and religions. This is a dialectic that belongs to the order of interhuman praxis and is not aimed at unlikely theoretical syntheses, which could easily turn into questionable forms of eclecticism, but is subject to the rule of of justice.

In fact, Ricoeur, in his introduction to *Le Juste* 2, after having extended the concept of translation to culture, religion, the spirit of the various historical ages, writes:

> One might ask, at the end of these great excusions, well beyond the torment of translation, what is justice? But, one did not cease speaking about it! To translate is to return justice to a foreign intelligence, it is to establish the proper distance from one linguistic whole to another. Your language is as important as mine. It is the formula of the fairness-equality—the formula of a well-know heterogeneity. Moreover, the bond with the idea of justice is perhaps the most concealed, but most

pronounced, in renouncing the dream of perfect translation which I evoked at the end of my essay. There I spoke about mourning the idea of a perfection translation. This mourning is the most rigorous existential condition to which the desire to translate is invited to subject itself. The work of translation, like the work of memory, does not go without the work of mourning. It makes the idea acceptable of equivalence without identity which is the formula even of justice in the field of the translation.[12]

I would like to relate these words by Ricoeur to the extraordinary reflections contained in the final pages of his last book *Parcours de la reconnaissance,* in regard to the notion of mutual acknowledgment, the final dialectic between the asymmetry between the self and the other and the mutual character of their relation. If translation counts as a paradigm of the relation with the other in all its forms, under the sign of finitude and the rule of justice, then what Ricoeur writes in regards to the "*entre*" of the protagonists of the exchange of gifts applies also to translation and the "*entre*" of his protagonists.

It is in the "between" of the expression "between the protagonists of the exchange" that is concentrated the dialectic of disymmetry between me and others and the mutuality of our relations. And it is to the full meaning of this "between" that the integration of this dissymmetry into mutuality in the exchange of gift contributes. Admitting the threat that lies in forgetting this dissymmetry first calls attention to the irreplaceable character of each of the partners in the exchange. The one is not the other. We exchange gifts, but not places. The second benefit of this admission is that it protects mutuality against the pitfalls of a fusional union, whether in love, friendship, or fraternity on a communal or a cosmopolitan scale. A just distance is maintained at the heart of mutuality, a just distance that integrates respect into intimacy. Finally, gratitude, the last form of recognition considered in this work, receives from the dialectic between dissymmetry and mutuality a surplus of meaning. We have considered reception as the pivotal term between giving and giving in return. In receiving, the place of gratitude, the dissymmetry between the giver and the receiver is affirmed twice over: other is the one who gives and the one who receives; other is the one who receives and the one who gives in return. This twofold alterity is preserved in the act of receiving and in the gratitude it gives rise to.[13]

Translation as a labor of memory and the mourning it requires, being always faced with the challenge of the untranslatable, helps us maintain the appropriate distance from the other, the appropriate distance that reconciles respect with intimacy. The human nature of humans is dual, and so is the alterity of the other. This is the valuable lesson that Ricoeur left for us. In receiving it and reflecting on it may our gratitude to him be voiced.

NOTES

1. See Domenico Jervolino, "The Depth and Breadth of Paul Ricoeur's Philosophy," in *The Philosophy of Paul Ricoeur*, ed. Lewis Edwin Hahn (Chicago and La Salle: Open Court, 1995), pp. 533 ff.
2. Cf. Paul Ricoeur, *La mémoire, l'histoire, l'oubli* (Paris: Edition du Seuil, 2000) pp. 656–57; *Memory, History, Forgetting*, trans. Kathleen Blamey and David Pellauer (Chicago: University of Chicago Press, 2004), pp. 505–506. Ricoeur quotes here Kierkegaard's *Upbuilding Discourses in Various Spirits*, trans. Howard V. Hong and Edna H. Hong (Princeton: Princeton University Press, 1993), p. 155–212: "What we learn from the Lilies in the Field and from the Birds of the Air."
3. Ibid., p. 537 (Engl. trans., p. 413): "Horizon does not mean only the fusion of horizons, in the Gadamerian sense I am assuming, but also the receding of horizons, incompletion. This admission is not unexpected in an enterprise placed fron the start under the banner of merciless critique directed against the *hubris* of total reflection." The last words of *La memoire . . .* are: " Under History, memory and forgetting. Under memory and forgetting, life. But writing a life is another story. Incompletion," p. 657 (Engl. trans., p. 586).
4. See especially my book Ricoeur, *Une herméneutique de la condition humaine* (Paris: Ellipses, 2002), pp. 47 ff. and my article "La question de l'unité de l'oeuvre de Ricoeur à la lumière de ses derniers développements. Le paradigme de la traduction," in *Archives de Philosophie* 4 (hiver 2004): 659–68.
5. Cf. Paul Ricoeur, *La mémoire, l'histoire, l'oubli*, op. cit., p. 160; Engl. trans., p. 130.
6. The essay "De la métaphysique à la morale" is now found as an appendix to Paul Ricoeur, *Réflexion faite. Autobiographie intellectuelle*, (Paris: Éd. Esprit, 1995), pp. 83–115; "Multiple étrangété" was published very late in *Fremdheit und Vertrautheit*, *Hermeneutik im europäischen Kontext*, ed. E. Enskat (Leuven: Peeters, 2000), pp. 11–23. See also Paul Ricoeur, *Le Juste* 2 (Paris: Éd. Esprit, 2001), especially the introduction, pp. 7–51, and "Justice et Vérité," pp. 69–83. Another important text by Ricoeur on the homme capable is "Le destinataire de la religion: l'homme capable," in *Archivio di Filosofia* 1–3 (1996): 19–34.
7. Cf. Jan Patočka, *Platon et l'Europe*, French trans. Erika Abrams (Lagrasse: Verdier, 1983). See also Jan Patočka, *Philosophy and Selected Writings*, ed. Erazim Kohák (Chicago and London: University of Chicago Press, 1989).
8. *Le paradigme de la traduction*, now in *Le Juste* 2, op. cit., pp. 125–40. Ricoeur's three main works on translation, which were also presented in Naples at philosophy conferences I organized between 1998 and 2002, are now in Ricoeur, *Sur la traduction* (Paris: Bayard, 2004).
9. Cf. Umberto Eco, *Dire quasi la stessa cosa* (Milan: Bompiani, 2003).
10. Cf. Yves Thierry, *Du corps parlant. Le langage chez Merleau-Ponty* (Brux-

elles: Ousia, 1987). On language as verbal body in Thévenaz I refer the reader to my book *Pierre Thévenaz e la filosofia senza assoluto* (Rome: Studium, 2003), pp. 91–102. On the relationship between Thévenaz and Ricoeur see my essay *"Entre Thévenaz et Ricoeur: la "philosophie sans absolu,"* in *Le souci du passage. Mélanges offerts à Jean Greisch,* ed. Philippe Capelle, Geneviève Hébert, and Marie-Dominique Popelard (Paris: Beauchesne, 2004), pp. 180–190.

11. The mother tongue is the place where consciousness is born; it is no mere set of instrumental signs. In the mother tongue, words embody reality itself; through it the world is born into our conscience. Nevertheless, we cannot stop here. In fact, we *are and we are not* our body, we conform to our mother tongue, but at the same time it has its own relative autonomy. Language is placed between the world and us, with everything that this implies, i.e. to say and not to say, the possibility of equivocation and deception, a world of implicit or hidden meanings that need to be reactivated and rediscovered. This *ambiguity* of language, which has its roots in our mother tongue, makes it possible for us who are born to the world thanks to it, to also take stand back from it. We always can and have to distance ourselves. The mother tongue, which is my verbal body, does not shut me in. Rather, it opens me to other languages, to humanity and to history.

12. *Le Juste* 2, op. cit., p. 40.

13. Paul Ricoeur, *Parcours de la reconnaissance* (Paris: Stock, 2004), pp. 376–77. *The Course of Recognition*, trans. David Pellauer (Cambridge: Harvard University Press, 2005), pp. 262–63.

Binding and Loosing: Promising and Forgiving, Amnesty and Amnesia 14

Charles Reagan

And I tell you, you are Peter, and on this rock I will build my church, and the powers of death shall not prevail against it. I will give you the keys of the kingdom of heaven, and whatever you bind on earth shall be bound in heaven, and whatever you loose on earth shall be loosed in heaven.

—Matthew 16:18

What does it mean to bind or to loose? There are many forms of binding, such as making a promise, signing a contract, adopting a child, making a will, indicting someone, sentencing a convicted person, committing a person to a mental hospital, just to name a few examples. Wherever there is a form of binding, there is a form of loosing. One can be released from a promise, pay off a mortgage, change a will, pardon a prisoner, annul a marriage. Binding and unbinding is the focus of this chapter and our analysis will take many hermeneutic detours. I begin with an account of promising in Paul Ricoeur's *Oneself as Another*,[1] his masterpiece on personal identity. For him, promising is an essential element in narrative identity, representing one form of sameness through time. Forgiveness is far more complicated. I use as my text Ricoeur's *Memory, History, Forgetting*,[2] especially the Epilogue, "Difficult Forgiveness." I finish with a discussion of the relation between forgiveness, particularly in its political form, amnesty, and the role of forgetting or amnesia.

PROMISING

In his book on personal identity, Ricoeur claims that promising plays a central role in narrative identity. He begins chapter 5 with the question of the meaning of "identical." He says there are two meanings of identical, sameness and selfhood. What is at issue is the identification and reidentification of someone or something as identical through time. In

237

taking sameness first, he gives a list of kinds of identity, beginning with numerical identity. Here we say that "he is the same man I saw there yesterday." The contrary is plurality. He is one and the same. The second example is qualitative identity: "They are wearing the same suit." Here resemblance is the identifying characteristic. A third form of identity-sameness is continuity through time. We recognize a person as the same person even though the photo album shows him at different stages of his life. Progressive changes in appearance do not prevent us from identifying him as the same person.

Other forms of identity-sameness are biological identity, now usually based on DNA coding. This is an especially powerful identification tool where identity by resemblance is not possible (she did not see the attacker) or unreliable (I can't remember what he looked like). Fingerprints are a physiological form of identification, while passports, names, addresses, social security numbers, and so on are social forms of identification of a person as the same.

Ricoeur says, "When we speak of ourselves, we in fact have available to us two models of permanence in time which can be summed up in two expressions that are at once descriptive and emblematic: *character* and *keeping one's word*."[3] By "character," he means the whole set of identifying marks that allow us to identify an individual through time, including numerical identify, qualitative identity, and uninterrupted continuity. He says that character "designates the set of lasting dispositions by which a person is recognized."[4]

But there is another sense of personal identity that Ricoeur calls "selfhood" or "keeping one's word." Promising is a way of establishing a permanence through time. In fact, the very purpose of a promise is to defeat the changes wrought by time: even if I change my mind, even if my desires are different, even if the circumstances change, I will do what I promised to do. If we look at the normal occasions of making a promise, it is made precisely when we know from experience, ours or mankind's as a whole, that we are likely to change our minds. Our most solemn promises are made when the stakes are the highest: marriage vows, swearing an oath to tell the truth in court, or the promise to keep a secret, for example. We know that in all of these cases there will be temptations to break the promise and we may suffer regrets for having made it. Our social institutions depend on promise-making and promise-keeping, as does language itself. Promises bind us to be or to do, to be a husband or to do something someone else wants done.

REMEMBERING AND FORGETTING

If promising binds us to a future act, forgiving unbinds us from a past act. To understand all of the ramifications of forgiving, we must take a detour through the labyrinth of remembering and forgetting. In his Preface to *Memory, History, Forgetting*, Ricoeur says that the book is composed of a phenomenology of memory, an epistemology of the historical sciences, and a hermeneutics of forgetting. The first thing to notice is that we all know what memory is, and forgetting is an experience in everyday life. History, in the common view, is the true account of what has happened in the past, usually supported with references to documents, testimony of witnesses, or artifacts and monuments.

With memory, we are all familiar with remembering a person, or a place, or an event in our own past. Similarly, we are all used to the experience of forgetting, such as a proper name, or the name of the restaurant we went to years ago. We all learned history in school, the history of our country, our state, Europe in the Middle Ages, and so forth. Most of all, we enjoy reading history and historical novels.

The history of philosophy teaches us that while we take for granted the experiences of memory and forgetting, there are profound philosophical problems, which date from the earliest days of philosophy. Questions such as "where is the memory when we are not thinking about it?" It is not lost because we can remember it with effort, or sometimes it just comes to us without even trying. How does memory work that we can recall something? How can something that we experienced in the past be brought back into the present? These questions have baffled philosophers and psychologists from Plato to the present. When we forget, where do the memories or images go? And why do some vanish and not others? Where do repressed memories come from when they are reconstituted by psychoanalysis?

With respect to history, what is its relationship to memory? And what is the difference between history and fiction, a history book and a novel? How do historians establish the truth and accuracy of their narratives? Is there an objective historical truth, or is all history a construct from a particular point of view, expressing the interests of those who have the power to write it? From these few questions, it is clear that each one is worthy of a separate study, but that none of them can be completely understood without reference to the other two. Memory needs to be analyzed in conjunction with its opposite, forgetting. And history is always in tension between memory and forgetting; it depends on the first and is an antidote to the second.

Ricoeur begins his investigation with a phenomenology of memory, in the Husserlian sense of the term. It is centered on two questions: memories of what? And whose memory is it? The first question raises the problematic of "representation" in the present of something from the past. The object of the representation no longer exists, but the representation is in the present. This is one of the very original problems of memory and the first Western philosophers in Greece struggled with it.

For Plato, for example, the problem of the *eikon* begins with the image as an imprint in a piece of wax. But where is this wax? How can we recover the image? And how can we distinguish a true image from a false one, a *phantasma*? This is the origin of the idea of a "trace," one of the main connections between memory and history. What is missing is an indepth analysis of the relation between the image and temporality.

In claiming that "memory is of the past," Aristotle draws attention to the temporal aspect of the phenomena of memory. It is not simply a matter that the image-memories are related to people and things and places, but they have a before and an after in their order. Aristotle also adds to the discussion the distinction between *mnēnē* and *anamnēsis*, between a memory that just arises and a memory that is the result of the effort of remembering. Unfortunately, neither Plato nor Aristotle were able to resolve the aporias of memory.

Ricoeur continues his phenomenology of memory by cautioning us against the temptation of beginning the phenomenological study of memory with the failures or disfunctioning or mistakes of memory. The pathologies of memory and the phenomenon of forgetting presuppose a description of memory. "What, in the final analysis, will justify taking this position in favor of 'good' memory is my conviction, which the remainder of this study will seek to establish, that we have no other resource, concerning our reference to the past, except memory itself."[5] In the final analysis, it is testimony that justifies true memories in the face of false memories. Testimony that is more credible, more trustworthy justifies memories when confronted with false memories backed by testimony fraught with suspicion. Most important, it is testimony, in all of its forms, that is the link between memory and history.

At the end of a long and detailed historical review of the problems of memory, Ricoeur raises again the issue of the truthfulness of our memories and the distinction between an image and a memory. "Let us call this search for truth, faithfulness. From now on we will speak of the faithfulness of memories, of memories being true to ... in order to express this search, this demand, this claim, which constitutes the veridical-epistemic dimension of the *orthos logos* of memory."[6]

Ricoeur puts the abuses of memory under three general headings: *impeded* memory, *manipulated* memory, and *abusively commanded* memory. Impeded memory recalls all of the forms of wounded or sick memory. It is by means of a psychoanalytic "working through" that we can recover lost or blocked memories. And because collective memory suffers from the same ailments, there are similar problems on the social level. Ricoeur says, "More precisely, what, in historical experience, takes the form of paradox—namely, *too much* memory here, *not enough* memory there—can be reinterpreted in terms of the categories of resistance and compulsion to repeat, and, finally, can be found to undergo the ordeal of the difficult work of remembering."[7] Blocked memory and compulsive repetition are manifested on the social level as well as the individual level. Repetitions of national anthems and the rituals of everyday life such as marriage and funeral ceremonies, for example. Of course, all social groups block memories of their more shameful past acts and events. The transition of individual memory to collective memory is one of the links between memory and history. If history is a form of collective memory, it is subjected to the same abuses as individual memory.

A second form of abused memory is manipulated memory. Here, Ricoeur has in mind ideology as a form of manipulated memory. Ideology is, above all, an attempt to legitimize a government or a power, founded on an original event, founding documents, and common memories. It is through a narrative that the identity of a country, a people, or an individual is constructed. For Ricoeur, "It is, more precisely, the selective function of the narrative that opens to manipulation the opportunity and the means of a clever strategy, consisting from the outset in a strategy of forgetting as much as in a strategy of remembering.... However, it is on the level where ideology operates as a discourse justifying power, domination, that the resources of manipulation provided by narrative are mobilized."[8]

The third form of abuse is commanded memory. This is what is happening when schoolchildren recite official histories or when national anthems are played before sporting events or official commemorations such as parades on national holidays.

Obviously, Ricoeur's analysis of memory is far more complex and detailed that this brief summary. His main points are that we have no other resource to the past than memory and false memories can only be corrected by true memories, just as false testimony can be corrected only by true testimony. The importance of this is that history is founded on the archive that itself is based on testimony, especially written testimony. We are going to bypass Ricoeur's analysis of history and the historical condition to go directly to forgetting.

Ricoeur begins this section by saying, "Forgetting and forgiveness, separately and together, designate the horizon of our entire investigation."[9] Forgetting represents a danger and a challenge to memory and to history. The archive is the first line of defense against forgetting and the obliteration of traces. The phenomenon of forgetfulness is seen in ordinary forgetting, the analogue of ordinary memory but also in the cases of clinical amnesia. Ricoeur takes up the idea of a "blocked memory" as the first type of forgetting. He cites Freud saying that once something has been experienced, the memory is permanent, even if it is not always accessible. Another type of abuse of memory is manipulated forgetting of which the counterpart is manipulated memory. If there is an official, authorized, commemorated history, there is also an official forgetting of those forbidden things about which one does not have the right to remember. "In all of this, the pathological structure, the ideological conjuncture, and the staging in the media have, on a regular basis, compounded their perverse effects, while the passivity of excuses has joined forces with the active ruses of omission, blindness, and negligence."[10] All social groups block memories of their more shameful past acts and events.

To pathological forgetting and to manipulated forgetting is added commanded forgetting, or amnesty. Here, forgetting and forgiving are intercrossed by a judicial act of the state. Amnesty, institutional forgetting, aims to put an end to civil disorder such as those in periods of civil war. A clear example is the Edict of Nantes of Henry IV in 1598. Amnesty does not seek historical truth. To the contrary, it sacrifices truth on the altar of state rationalization. There are events in the past that must not be remembered. The question of amnesty opens the whole field of forgiveness.

FORGIVENESS

In the Epilogue of *Memory, History, Forgetting*, entitled, "Difficult Forgiveness," Ricoeur begins by saying, "Forgiveness—if it has a sense, and if it exists—constitutes the horizon common to memory, history, and forgetting. . . . If forgiveness is difficult to give and to receive, it is just as difficult to conceive of. The trajectory of forgiveness has its origin in the disproportion that exists between the poles of fault and forgiveness."[11] What is at stake here are the relations among forgiving, forgetting, promising, and pardoning. Ricoeur claims that there is an asymmetrical relation between promising and forgiving and his evidence is that there is no genuine political institution of forgiving. This will lead us to a discussion of amnesty.

But what do we forgive? The fault. Ricoeur devoted almost a whole book, *Fallible* Man,[12] to the notion of the fault and how evil enters the world of human action. His answer, in the briefest terms is that there is a disproportion between our possibilities and our limitations, represented most clearly by the perpetual anxieties from what he calls, "*avoir, pouvoir, valoir.*" When will I possess (*avoir*) enough? When will my possessions be secure? Am I living a life of continual acquisition? Power (*pouvoir*). When will my power and position be secure? When will I have enough power? And finally, when will I be recognized (*valoir*), appreciated, esteemed? When will my worth be affirmed by others? Avarice, cruelty, and arrogance are always lurking in the background because our possessions, our power, and our worth are perpetually at risk.

Ricoeur says that "fault in its essence is unforgivable."[13] He joins his friend, Jacques Derrida, in saying that "forgiveness is directed to the unforgivable or it does not exist. It is unconditional, it is without exception and without restriction."[14]

But there are many kinds of guilt, such as criminal, political, moral, and individual guilt. In the case of criminal guilt, we have several kinds of "forgiveness," such as the statute of limitations that prevents us from pursuing a criminal charge against someone after a certain period of time because of the difficulties of evidence and witnesses. Another form would be a pardon. People are pardoned only after they have been tried and found guilty and sentenced to a particular punishment. A pardon wipes out the conviction while a commutation reduces or eliminates the punishment. But, of course, the most serious crimes, murder, or even worse, genocide, crimes against humanity, war crimes have no time limit, no possibility of pardon, and no proportional punishment. Ricoeur says, "Pardon cannot be substituted for justice. To forgive would be to ratify impunity, which would be a grave injustice committed at the expense of the law and, even more so, of the victims."[15] These crimes are precisely unforgivable. The guilt here is that of the individuals who commit the crimes or the leaders of a state that commits such abominable crimes.

Political guilt is that of the citizen of such a country "in the name of which the crimes were committed."[16] This kind of guilt results from simply being a citizen, and it is completely independent of whether or not a person committed any acts or was merely acquiescent while others committed them.

Moral guilt is attributable to all those persons and those individual acts that make up the crimes of the state. After all, it takes many politicians, police, soldiers, intelligence agents, and so forth to actually commit the crimes against humanity such as genocide, death squads, and terrorist bombings.

Ricoeur mentions metaphysical guilt that arises "from the fact of being a human being, in a transhistoric tradition of evil."[17] However, he does not elaborate on this tradition. I assume he is thinking of the doctrine of original sin, or his underlying thesis that evil creeps into the world because of the dispropostion between our possibilities and our limitations.

Thus far, we have been considering fault as a legal phenomenon, a crime, and with it the question of punishment or pardon. We can move to the next step in the analysis by looking at the question of "exchange," that is, the asking for pardon or forgiveness and the granting of it. Vladimir Jankélévitch raises the question, "Has anyone asked us for forgiveness?" Has the wrongdoer asked us for forgiveness and should we forgive him? But, says Ricoeur, "this very assumption is directly opposed to the primary characteristic of forgiveness, its unconditionality."[18] How can forgiveness be unconditional if it requires that someone ask for it? On the practical level of everyday life as well as in the courts, there is a kind of exchange between forgiveness requested and forgiveness granted. Yet this raises another question: can only another forgive? Can only the victim or the wronged person forgive? If so, what can we make of the notion of "forgiving oneself"?

But what is forgiveness on the social and political level? To answer this question, Ricoeur looks at the Truth and Reconciliation Commission in South Africa that met from January 1996 to July 1998. Its goal was to "collect testimony, console the injured, indemnify the victims, and amnesty those who confessed to committing political crimes."[19] This form of reparative justice was quite different from the war crimes trials in Nuremberg and Tokyo after the Second World War. The goal was not justice, but reconciliation. It was a utilitarian move to put firmly in the past the ugly history of apartheid and to make possible a new country with a very different future.

FORGIVING AND PROMISING

In our dialectic of binding and loosing, we need to consider, once again, the relation between promising and forgiving. In her book, *The Human Condition*,[20] Hannah Arendt pairs them and relates them to the uncertainty that comes from the irreversibility of the consequences of our actions and unpredictability in expected courses of action. Promising instills predictability and only forgiveness can restore what is irreversible. On the political level, there are reliable ways of institutionalizing promising, such as contracts, oaths, vows, wills, and so forth. Amnesty is the institutional form of forgiveness. Ricoeur claims that amnesty is a "caricature" of forgiveness because it is conditional and it defies justice for utilitarian ends. He says, "It seems to me that Hannah Arendt remained at the threshold of the enigma by situating the gesture of forgiveness at the point of intersection of the act and its consequences and not of the agent and the act."[21] For Ricoeur, forgiveness should unbind the agent from his act. He concludes, there is a "monstrous failure of all efforts to institutionalize forgiveness."[22]

Ricoeur wants to know how we can bridge the gap between "the unforgivable fault and the impossible forgiveness."[23] The symmetry between promising and forgiving is broken on several fronts. First, a person can choose to bind himself by making a promise, but we cannot forgive ourselves. The exchange between asking someone to promise something and promising them is not the same as asking for forgiveness and receiving it. The reason is, once again, that forgiveness must be unconditional.

I have difficulty with Ricoeur's claim that forgiveness must be unconditional. He does not mention in his discussion of guilt and forgiveness the ideas of sorrow, repentance, absolution, and penance that play such an important role in traditional Christian theology. Here, forgiveness depends on sorrow, one being sorry for one's evil act. Repentance means the resolve to not do the act in the future. Absolution is the theological concept that God's forgiveness is requested and granted. And penance is the punishment one must pay as retribution recompense to make up for the consequences of the evil act. One may suppose that he does not go down this path because of his devout Protestantism in which forgiveness is an absolute and unconditional gift of God and nothing we can do can merit it.

Our legal system seems to be more in tune with the traditional view of guilt and forgiveness. For example, in the granting of amnesty, there is a requirement that all of the evil acts must be acknowledged by those who did them. There is also an understanding that if justice were meted out, there would be no proportional punishment for those "unforgivable" crimes. Finally, it is recognized that amnesty is the only way to break the circle of violence and begin anew. Thus, amnesty is a form of absolution, a forgiveness that always acknowledges the crime and requires the regrets and sorrow of the criminal.

In our everyday lives, we say, "forgive and forget." The paradox is that forgiving requires memory, not amnesia. In fact, amnesty and amnesia are incompatible. Thus, Ricoeur claims that there is "asymmetry between forgetting and memory with respect to forgiveness."[24] There is no art of forgetting as there is the art of memory. Ricoeur concludes with these poetic words:

A subtle work of unbinding and binding is to be pursued at the very heart of debt: on one hand, being released from the fault, on the other binding a debtor who is forever insolvent. Debt without fault. Debt stripped bare. Where one finds the debt to the dead and history is the sepulcher.[25]

EPILOGUE

This chapter was being composed during Paul Ricoeur's last year. At the end of February 2005, I went to Paris to see Paul for his 92nd birthday and visited him four afternoons that week at Châtenay-Malabry. He would be seated on the sofa in his living room and he was weak, but totally lucid. We would converse for a while, and then he would doze off. While he slept, I read and when he awakened ten or fifteen minutes later, we continued our conversation. One of the topics we discussed on two occasions was the possibility of forgiving oneself. He was struggling with regret and self-forgiveness. We spoke of memory and forgetting. I reminded him that he had dedicated his book, *Memory, History, Forgetting*, "dans la mémoire de Simone Ricoeur." The usual formulation is "à la mémoire." He was writing this book during Simone's last days and it was his work of mourning after she died. He told me she was there on every page and that is why he used the less common dedication. When I was checking the translation for the University of Chicago Press, I called him and asked him how it should be translated. His answer was to leave it in French since there was no adequate way of conveying the difference in English. Our conversations that week ranged from current events, such as the Iraq War, to philosophical questions. He had been reading an article on authority in *Esprit* and we discussed sovereignty and how sovereignty is constituted and legitimized.

On Friday of that week, there was an unusual and heavy snow in Paris and neither Pastor Kabongo nor Catherine were able to come. So Paul and I were alone for the afternoon until the Czech student came at 7:00 P.M. He was very weak and I knew that this time I would never see him again. Before leaving, I told him what an enormous influence he had had on my personal and my professional life. He took my hand and put it to his face. That was our farewell.

Early in the morning of Friday, May 20, 2005, Paul Ricoeur died. I was notified that afternoon and left for Paris the following Sunday. After arriving on Monday, May 23, I went to Châtenay-Malabry to visit the family and pay my respects. It had been forty-three years ago that we first met when I was his student in Paris. I spoke with his sons, Jean-Paul—whom I had not seen in twenty-five years—and Mark, whom I had seen frequently when he was working in Paris and I was staying in the house at Les Murs Blancs. Etienne was there as was Paul's daughter, Noëlle. When we lived in Paul's house the first time, Etienne was invited with Olivier to dinner on many occasions. Noëlle had been at Préfailles one summer when I was visiting, so I got to know her as well. Several of the grandchildren were also there. I was invited by the family to the private interment the next morning before the memorial service at the Reformed (Protestant) church in Châtenay-Malabry.

It was a warm, sunny day and those invited assembled at the entrance of the cemetery of Châtenay-Malabry. The hearse and the cars with the immediate family arrived. The casket was taken out of the hearse and set on a stand. Father Franz Vansina, a Franciscan monk and a longtime friend of Paul's read some prayers. He was followed by the Protestant pastor, Philippe Kabongo, who also said some prayers. Then, the casket was borne by four men who worked for the funeral home to the gravesite. Once again, Father Vansina and Pastor Kabongo said some prayers. The casket was lowered into the grave and we filed by, each of us tossing a rose onto the casket. We slowly left in silence and went to the Protestant Church in Châtenay-Malabry.

There we were joined by several hundred friends and parishioners for a memorial service. In addition to Father Vansina and Pastor Kabongo, Etienne, the youngest son, was chosen to speak for the family, and Geneviève Fraisse, the daughter of Paul and Simone Fraisse (who also had lived at Les Murs Blancs—the estate established by Emmanuel Mounier) spoke of life in the Christian socialist community of Les Murs Blancs. She was followed by Olivier Abel, a professor of philosophy at the Institute of Protestant Theology in Paris. Olivier has been a long-time friend of Paul's and Olivier's father had been the pastor at the Protestant church in Châtenay-Malabry. The final speaker was Antoine Garipon, a jurist, and the person who got Paul to give lectures and participate in the discussions at the Advanced School for Judges in Paris. Paul's articles in his book, *The Just*[26] were, for the most part, papers he had given at this school.

After more prayers and some singing, the service was ended and the mourners were invited to the Ricoeur house for a light buffet. I returned to Paris and sat in a café and contemplated my personal loss. I knew I would come back to Paris, but for the first time in over forty years, it would not be to see Paul Ricoeur.

Paul Ricoeur's last book, *Parcours de la reconnaissance*,[27] was published in 2004 and the English translation, *The Course of Recognition*, was published in 2005 by Harvard University Press.

This chapter has been written "*dans la mémoire de Paul Ricoeur*" and is my personal work of mourning.

Note on Catherine Goldenstein

Paul and Simone Ricoeur were very fortunate to have many friends all over the world and to the very end, Paul's friends visited him in Paris. But, above all his friends was his special angel, Catherine Goldenstein. She was a friend of the Ricoeurs from the Protestant temple of Châtenay-Malabry and, beginning in the early 1990s, she would come in the afternoon to take tea. She was a devoted companion to Simone and aided Paul immensly during the period of Simone's decline and death. She was an extraordinary friend who encouraged Paul during his bereavement. She helped him with his correspondence, making appointments for his friends' visits, and managing the household. In the last few years of his life, Catherine supervised his medical appointments and treatments and visited him daily. I know from Paul himself that without Catherine Goldenstein and her husband Jean-Pierre, he would have died many years sooner. All of us who were friends of Paul's and loved and admired him owe her a debt of gratitude.

NOTES

1. Paul Ricoeur, *Oneself as Another*, trans. Kathleen Blamey (Chicago: University of Chicago Press, 1992).
2. Paul Ricoeur, *Memory, History, Forgetting*, trans. Kathleen Blamey and David Pellauer (Chicago: University of Chicago Press, 2004).
3. Ricoeur, *Oneself as Another*, p. 118.
4. Ibid., p. 121.
5. Ricoeur, *Memory, History, Forgetting*, p. 21.
6. Ibid., p. 55.
7. Ibid., p. 79.
8. Ibid., p. 85.
9. Ibid., p. 412.
10. Ibid., p. 452.
11. Ibid., p. 457.
12. Paul Ricoeur, *Fallible Man*, trans. Charles Kelbley (Chicago: Henry Regnery, 1965).
13. Ricoeur, *Memory, History, Forgetting*, p. 466.
14. Ibid., p. 468.
15. Ibid., p. 473.
16. Ibid., p. 474.
17. Ibid., p. 471.
18. Ibid., p. 478.
19. Ibid., p. 483.
20. Hannah Arendt, *The Human Condition* (Chicago: University of Chicago Press, 1958).
21. Ricoeur, *Memory, History, Forgetting*, p. 489.
22. Ibid., p. 488.
23. Ibid., p. 490.
24. Ibid., p. 503.
25. Ibid., p. 503.
26. Paul Ricoeur, *The Just*, trans. David Pellauer (Chicago: University of Chicago Press, 2000).
27. Paul Ricoeur, *Parcours de la reconnaissance* (Paris: Stock, 2004). *The Course of Recognition*, trans. David Pellauer (Cambridge: Harvard University Press, 2005).

Contributors

OLIVIER ABEL is Professor of Philosophy, Faculté de Philosophy, L'institut Protestante de Théologie de Paris. He is author of *Le Pardon* (Seuil, 1998), *Paul Ricoeur: la promesse et la règle* (Michalon: Paris, 1997) and numerous articles on Ricoeur in the French journals *Autres Temps, Autrement,* and *Esprit.* He is the director of the *Fonds Ricoeur* (Ricoeur Collection) at IPT, Paris.

PATRICK L. BOURGEOIS is William and Audrey Hutchinson Distinguished Professor of Philosophy at Loyola University, New Orleans. He is author of *Philosophy at the Boundary of Reason: Ethics and Postmodernity* (SUNY Press, 2001), *Traces of Understanding: Profiles of Heidegger's and Ricoeur's Hermeneutics* (Kluwer, 1990), and *Extention of Ricoeur's Hermeneutic* (Kluwer, 1975), and numerous articles on Ricoeur.

BERNARD P. DAUENHAUER is Professor Emeritus at the University of Georgia. He is author of *Paul Ricoeur: The Promise and Risk of Politics* (Rowman & Littlefield, 1999), *Citizenship in a Fragile World* (Rowman & Littlefield, 1996), *The Politics of Hope* (Routledge, 1986), the *Stanford Encyclopedia of Philosophy* entry on Paul Ricoeur, and numerous articles on Ricoeur.

DOMENICO JERVOLINO is Professor of Philosophy, Dipartemento di Filosofia, Università di Napoli. He is the author of *Paul Ricoeur: Une herméneutique de la condition humaine* (Ellipses, 2002), *Ricoeur: L'amore difficile* (Stadium, 1995), *The Cogito and Hermeneutics: The Question of the Subject in Ricoeur* (Kluwer, 1990), and dozens of articles on Ricoeur in Italian and French.

DAVID M. KAPLAN is Assistant Professor of Philosophy at the University of North Texas. He is author of *Ricoeur's Critical Theory* (SUNY Press, 2003), and several articles on Ricoeur including, "Ricoeur's Theory of Truth," "Ricoeur and the Philosophy of Technology," "Ricoeur and Development Ethics," and "Paul Ricoeur and the Nazis." He is the author of the *Encyclopedia of Philosophy*, 2nd edition, entry on Paul Ricoeur.

RICHARD KEARNEY is Professor of Philosophy at University College, Dublin. He is the author of *Paul Ricoeur: The Owl of Minerva* (Ashgate, 2004), *The God Who May Be: The Hermeneutics of Religion* (Indiana University Press, 2001), *The Wake of Imagination* (Routledge, 1998), *Poetics of Imagining* (Fordham University Press, 1998), and editor of *Paul Ricoeur: The Hermeneutics of Action* (Sage Press, 1996). He organized, with Jean Greisch, "Décade de Paul Ricoeur," an international conference held in honor of Ricoeur in Cérisy-la-Salle in 1988.

DAVID E. KLEMM is Professor of Religious Studies at the University of Iowa. He is the editor (with William Schweiker) of *Meanings in Texts and Actions: Questioning Paul* Ricoeur (University of Virginia, 1993) author of *Hermeneutical Inquiry: Interpretation of Existence* (Oxford University 1987), and *The Hermeneutic Theory of Paul Ricoeur* (Associated University Press, 1983), and other articles on Ricoeur in English and German.

ANDRÉ LACOCQUE is Professor Emeritus of Old Testament at Chicago Theological Seminary. He is coauthor with Paul Ricoeur of *Thinking Biblically: Exegetical and Hermeneutical Studies* (University of Chicago Press, 2003), *Ruth* (Fortress Press, 2004), *The Book of Daniel* (Knox Press, 1979).

JAMES L. MARSH is Professor of Philosophy at Fordham University. He is editor (with Richard Cohen) of *Ricoeur as Another: The Ethics of Subjectivity* (SUNY Press, 2002), author of *Process, Praxis, and Transcendence* (SUNY Press, 1999), *Critique Action and Liberation* (SUNY Press, 1995), *Post-Cartesian Meditations: An Essay in Dialectical Phenomenology* (Fordham University Press, 1988).

DAVID M. RASMUSSEN is Professor of Philosophy at Boston College. He is founder and editor-in-chief of the journal *Philosophy and Social Criticism*, and editor (with Peter Kemp) of *The Narrative Path: The Later Works of Paul Ricoeur* (MIT Press, 1989). He is author of *Symbol and Interpretation* (Kluwer, 2002), and *Mythic-Symbolic Language and Philosophical Anthropology: A Constructive Interpretation of the Thought of Paul Ricoeur* (Martinus Nijhoff, 1971).

CHARLES REAGAN is Executive Assistant to the President of the Kansas State University. He is author of *Paul Ricoeur: His Life and His Work* (University of Chicago Press, 1996), editor of *Studies in the Philosophy of*

Paul Ricoeur (Ohio University Press, 1979), and author of numerous articles on Ricoeur. He is responsible for the *Paul Ricoeur Collection* at the University of Ohio.

WILLIAM SCHWEIKER is Professor of Theological Ethics in the Divinity School of the University of Chicago. He is the editor (with John Wall and David Hall) of *Paul Ricoeur and Contemporary Moral Thought* (Routledge, 2002), editor (with David Klemm) of *Meanings in Texts and Actions: Questioning Paul Ricoeur* (University of Virginia Press, 1993), author of *Mimetic Reflections: A Study in Hermeneutics, Religion, and Ethics* (Fordham University Press, 1990).

POL VANDEVELDE is Associate Professor of Philosophy at Marquette University. He is the translator and editor of *Paul Ricoeur: A Key to Husserl's Ideas I* (Marquette University Press, 1996), "L'interprétation comme acte de conscience et comme événement," *Les processus de la création de littéraire*, ed. Laurent van Eynde (Bruxelles: Editions Saint Louis), "Ontologie et recit selon Ricoeur," *Etudes de lettres*, n. 3–4 (1996), "Phénoménologie et Existentialisme," *Histoire des poétiques*, ed. J. Bessier, Ed Kushner, et al. (Presses Universitaire de France, 1997).

MEROLD WESTPHAL is Distinguished Professor of Philosophy at Fordham University. He is the general editor of the Indiana University Series in Philosophy of Religion, and author of *Transcendence and Self-Transcendence: On God and the Soul* (Indiana University Press, 2004) *Overcoming Onto-Theology: Toward a Postmodern Christian Faith* (Fordham University Press, 2001), *Suspicion and Faith: Religious Uses of Modern Atheism* (Fordham University Press, 1998), *God, Death, Guilt: An Existential Phenomenology of Religion* (Indiana University Press, 1984).

Index